BTR/ANN

Mary Gladstone

In 1879 Pre-Raphaelite artist Burne-Jones was a guest of the Gladstones
at Hawarden Castle. While family and friends were listening to a reading
from Jane Austen's *Emma* he made this drawing of Mary Gladstone.
Reproduced by kind permission of Sir William Gladstone.
Photograph by Barry Hamilton.

Mary Gladstone

A Gentle Rebel

Sheila Gooddie

WILEY

Copyright © 2003 Sheila Gooddie

Published in 2003 by John Wiley & Sons Ltd, The Atrium, Southern Gate, Chichester,
West Sussex PO19 8SQ, England

Telephone   (+44) 1243 779777

Email (for orders and customer service enquiries): cs-books@wiley.co.uk
Visit our Home Page on www.wileyeurope.com or www.wiley.com

Other Wiley Editorial Offices

John Wiley & Sons Inc., 111 River Street, Hoboken, NJ 07030, USA

Jossey-Bass, 989 Market Street, San Francisco, CA 94103-1741, USA

Wiley-VCH Verlag GmbH, Boschstr. 12, D-69469 Weinheim, Germany

John Wiley & Sons Australia Ltd, 33 Park Road, Milton, Queensland 4064, Australia

John Wiley & Sons (Asia) Pte Ltd, 2 Clementi Loop #02-01, Jin Xing Distripark, Singapore
129809

John Wiley & Sons Canada Ltd, 22 Worcester Road, Etobicoke, Ontario, Canada M9W 1L1

Wiley also publishes its books in a variety of electronic formats. Some content that appears
in print may not be available in electronic books.

British Library Cataloguing in Publication Data

A catalogue record for this book is available from the British Library

ISBN 0-470-85423-5

Typeset in 11/13pt Photina by Mathematical Composition Setters Ltd, Salisbury, Wiltshire
Printed and bound in Great Britain by Biddles Ltd, Guildford and King's Lynn
This book is printed on acid-free paper responsibly manufactured from sustainable forestry
in which at least two trees are planted for each one used for paper production.

Contents

CONTENTS

Acknowledgements

I began my research into the Gladstone family 12 years ago, unaware of the vast archival treasure trove that awaited my endeavours. My greatest debt of gratitude goes to the staff of the Flintshire Record Office (in the early years of my work the Clwyd Record Office); Christopher Williams and Paul Mason were among the first to guide me into the Glynne – Gladstone manuscripts and in recent time Elizabeth Pettitt and Fiona Skett have always been most helpful.

I am indebted to Sir William Gladstone who has made me most welcome at Hawarden Castle, given me permission to reproduce pictures in his possession and allowed me to absorb the atmosphere of his home, especially the Temple of Peace. I should like to thank Miss Penny Gladstone who invited me to her home to talk about her great aunt Mary Gladstone and who has always given me enouragement and friendship.

I should like to thank Lord Cobham for allowing me to visit Hagley Hall and giving me access to the Lyttelton archives; I was able to experience the tranquillity and beauty that Mary felt was special to Hagley as well as to her own home of Hawarden Castle.

I remember with gratitude my visit to Haygrass House, Taunton in 1995 where the late Lady Paget, Mary's granddaughter, made me most welcome and gave me access to her private library. I have happy memories of helping her gather up apple windfalls that would be made into Devon cider.

I should like to thank the late Rt Hon Lord Jenkins whose biography of William Gladstone has been my constant guide and who gave me much needed encouragement when my determination faltered. Thanks to Anne Thwaite whose biography of Emily Tennyson brought us into correspondence and who has given me help and encouragement.

The Revd Peter Francis, warden of St Deiniol's Library, Hawarden has helped and encouraged; he introduced me to Dr Anne Isba who was kind enough to read my manuscript in its earlier draft. I should like to thank the rector of St Deiniol's Church, Hawarden and the vicar of Buckley parish church for talking to me about life at Hawarden and Mr T. P. Pritchard for his work on Stephen Gladstone, published in the Flintshire Historical Society Journal volume 35 in 1999 which gave me useful insights into Stephen's relationship with Mary and Harry Drew.

My work would never have progressed beyond its manuscript stage without the help of my agent Charlotte Howard who has worked so successfully on my behalf and I should like to thank Sally M. Smith, senior publishing editor and her assistant Jill Jeffries for their friendly help. It has been a joy to work with them.

Finally I would like to thank all the tutors of the Arvon Foundation courses and Ty Newydd Writing Centre who have given me encouragement over the years and strengthened my determination to hold on to my ideas until they could stand the light. Any mistakes and misapprehensions are entirely my own.

The Gladstone Family

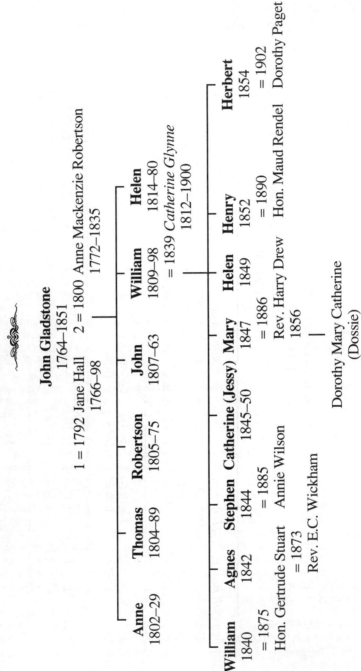

John Gladstone
1764–1851

1 = 1792 Jane Hall   2 = 1800 Anne Mackenzie Robertson
1766–98   1772–1835

Anne
1802–29

Thomas
1804–89

Robertson
1805–75

John
1807–63

William
1809–98
= 1839 *Catherine Glynne*
            1812–1900

Helen
1814–80

William
1840
= 1875
Hon. Gertrude Stuart
= 1873
Rev. E.C. Wickham

Agnes
1842
= 1885
Annie Wilson

Stephen
1844

Catherine (Jessy)
1845–50

Mary
1847
= 1886
Rev. Harry Drew
1856

Helen
1849

Henry
1852
= 1890
Hon. Maud Rendel

Herbert
1854
= 1902
Dorothy Paget

Dorothy Mary Catherine
(Dossie)
1890

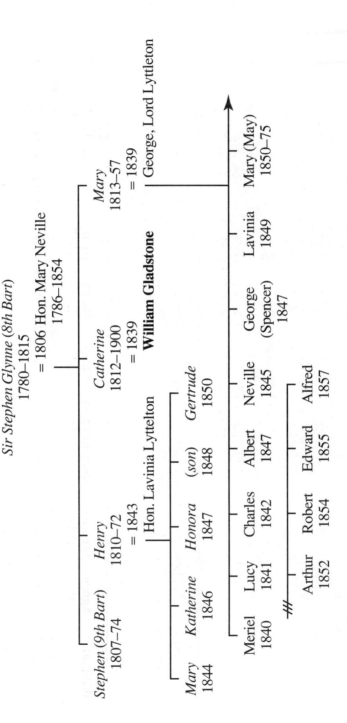

The Glynne Family and the Lyttelton Family

Sir Stephen Glynne (8th Bart)
1780–1815
= 1806 Hon. Mary Neville
1786–1854

Stephen (9th Bart)
1807–74

Henry
1810–72
= 1843
Hon. Lavinia Lyttelton

Catherine
1812–1900
= 1839
William Gladstone

Mary
1813–57
= 1839
George, Lord Lyttelton

Mary
1844

Katherine
1846

Meriel
1840

Lucy
1841

Honora
1847

Charles
1842

(son)
1848

Gertrude
1850

Albert
1847

Neville
1845

George
(Spencer)
1847

Lavinia
1849

Mary (May)
1850–75

Arthur
1852

Robert
1854

Edward
1855

Alfred
1857

Births

LYTTELTONS		GLADSTONES	
Meriel	17 June 1840	William	3 June 1840
Lucy	5 September 1841		
Charles	27 October 1842	Agnes	18 October 1842
Albert	29 June 1844	Stephen	4 April 1844
Neville	28 October 1845	Jessy	27 July 1845
Spencer	12 June 1847	Mary	23 November 1847
Lavinia	4 January 1849	Helen	28 August 1849
Mary (May)	26 May 1850		
Arthur	7 January 1852	Henry (Harry)	2 April 1852
Robert	18 January 1854	Herbert	7 January 1854
Edward	23 July 1855		
Alfred	7 February 1857		

Preface

Many people have asked, Why Mary Gladstone? I discovered her deep within a mountain of family papers in the Glynne – Gladstone manuscripts at Clwyd Record Office (now Flintshire R.O. since the counties were reorganised once again) that had once been Hawarden Rectory. A few steps away is St Deiniol's Library that was built to house William Gladstone's library and as a place of scholarship for students. I had spent many happy hours and days here on my first research work on the Summers family and their family business, Shotton Steel Works. I had worked in the Search Room under the gaze of Gladstone portraits.

Of course I knew the name of Gladstone. I had grown up only ten miles away on the Welsh side of Hawarden and William Gladstone was to me a man of near mythical stature. His dignified, austere face had decorated plates and jugs on Welsh dressers in my home village.

As I explored the family relationships, I learnt that William Gladstone and Catherine Glynne had married at Hawarden parish church, sharing the wedding service with Catherine's younger sister Mary who married Lord George Lyttelton of Hagley Hall in Worcestershire. I also learnt that Catherine's brother Henry later married Sir George's sister Lavinia and they lived at the Rectory. And at Hawarden Castle, a short walk from the Rectory, lived Catherine's bachelor brother Stephen. I was caught up in a vast net of relations.

There were babies and children galore, so what was it about Mary Gladstone that appealed to me? She was the third daughter and fifth child, born in 1847 to William and Catherine, and three more would follow. It seemed to me that she had a privileged, secure childhood at a time when one-fifth of all who were born died before their first birthday from diseases such as tuberculosis, scarlet fever, diarrhoea, smallpox,

measles or gastroenteritis. Mary's sister Jessy died at the age
of four from meningitis, and two-and-a-half-year-old Mary
scolded her parents for taking her darling 'Detty' away from
her.

Her mother and father were often absent from home following their busy adult lives but her little world was crowded
with brothers and sisters, cousins, aunts and uncles, nurses,
nannies and governesses. She learnt to take her turn in her
parents' attention and she found her place within the family.
She was a shy, eager-to-please girl with low self-esteem, happiest when she was serving others. When her brothers and
Lyttelton cousins went off to Eton and Oxbridge she was the
one to write to them, sharing their confidences and always
available with loving support. Their friends became her friends
and she shared their passionate love of music, their serious
pursuit of cricket and tennis, their deep commitment to religious matters. She was the stay-at-home daughter while her
elder sister married and set up her own home and her younger
sister became a Cambridge student and academic.

I was curious to learn more. How did she emerge into a
strong and confident woman, the mainspring of her family
and 'all sufficing' to her father? She was a talented pianist and
in the world of music she found a release for her emotions from
the rigid demands of Victorian society and met people who
took her seriously. In her twenties she fell in love with Arthur
Balfour who used her generous affection to satisfy his selfish
vanity. Hallam Tennyson fell in love with her and would have
married her, but she did not love him and would not compromise. She faced the realities of life and gained strength through
loss and tragedy. She enjoyed safe friendships with older married men and became indispensable to her father.

Her chance to find a purpose to her days came during his
second term as Prime Minister in the 1880s. For five years she
organised his life and mediated between him and his younger,
ambitious, restive colleagues. Her family pet-name was 'von
Moltke', identifying her with Bismarck's young aide-de-camp.
She had her own tiny office on the political floor of 10 Downing
Street, which was cause for concern and gossip among some

members of her family. Wives and daughters of Victorian politicians had useful social roles as hostesses, supporters of charities, confidantes, organisers, positions of quiet influence. Households were large with many servants and it was the women who dealt with these domestic arrangements. Mary's role in Victorian politics took her into male territory far beyond the domestic.

Many of the Prime Minister's contemporaries and ambitious politicians like Lords Acton and Rosebery regarded her as a useful means of gaining her father's ear and a sympathetic friend for their own troubles. Her warm and generous nature attracted Ruskin and Burne-Jones, of an older generation than herself. They came to Hawarden for her sake, admired and sometimes suffered her famous father. Henry Scott Holland, tutor of Christ College Oxford, later canon of St Paul's and founder of the Christian Social Union, was a friend for over forty years.

Her absence from Downing Street during her father's fourth term of office, when he was eighty-two, was a loss. When criticism was levelled at family interference, she would have been the perfect foil, persuading, pursuing, obstructing where necessary and advising those who sought the attention of the P.M. who was then living in a perpetual fog.

She did not marry until she was thirty-eight. When twenty-eight-year-old Harry Drew, curate to her brother in Hawarden parish, fell in love with her, and she realised that she loved him in return, she agonised over her decision to marry him and give up the independence she had won for herself. She was terrified of losing her identity in marriage, but her husband gave her the space and freedom to continue her old life. She remained as much her father's daughter as the Reverend Drew's wife.

Her father died in 1898, just when Mary had begun to live for the first time in a home of her own. My portrait concentrates on the fifty years of her life up to this time. The events are true. The characters are real, of their time and moulded by society's morals and expectations, yet they experience the same desires and heartaches that we struggle with today. Mary's parents were conventional parents but unconventional people which made Mary a typical and, at the same time, unique woman of her time. She had her father's bursting energy and her mother's impulsiveness. A contemporary once called her 'definitely not commonplace'. She once told Lord Rosebery that unusualness and distinctiveness were necessary qualities for a subject of biography. Perhaps it was for just those qualities that I chose her.

Setting the scene

'History is not what happened, but what people felt about it when it was happening.'

G. M. Young, *Portrait of an Age*, 1936 (Young was born in 1882)

*I*n 1851 the Great Exhibition in London in the Crystal Palace in Hyde Park brought together every aspect of the nation's manufacture, art and invention as well as raw materials from every far-flung corner of the British Empire. It was a display that engendered a new mood of confidence and optimism in the country and spearheaded innovations in industry, art and design. Fourteen thousand exhibits were housed in a vast, fantastic glass creation that had been devised by Joseph Paxton, gardener to the Duke of Devonshire. Ruskin scornfully dismissed it as 'a cucumber frame between two chimneys' and the Astronomer Royal predicted that the building would collapse in the first strong gale. Yet its doors stood open for five months and, in that time, six million people poured in from all corners of the British Isles, taking advantage of the new railways and the first package tours introduced by Thomas Cook.

The crowds were so huge that the die-hard conservatives forecast the spread of disease and petty crime. One peppery colonel advised those who lived in the vicinity of Hyde Park to lock up their spoons and their daughters; but the mood of the people was good-natured and law-abiding. A newly-awakened confidence was spreading across the country, taking root in the mushrooming towns and cities linked by the growing network of railways. This was the year that the word 'Victorian' was coined to reflect this awakening of the people.

On the first day of May 1851, in fitful sunshine, Queen Victoria drove with Prince Albert and their eldest daughter Princess Victoria through the cheering crowds to declare the exhibition open. Her Majesty wandered down the aisles with ever-increasing delight, her thoughts on her 'dearest Country, which has shown itself so great today' and on her dear husband who had stage-managed this event. When the couple returned to Buckingham Palace they went out on to the balcony that looked down on the Mall to acknowledge the cheers of the crowds. This was the beginning of the balcony tradition that has marked a relationship of affectionate loyalty between monarch and people.

In 1865, seventeen-year-old Mary Gladstone was certainly aware of the national mood when the July general election gave the Liberal party an increased majority and brought back Lord Palmerston as Prime Minister. It was a rollercoaster time for the Gladstones as William Gladstone was ousted from his Oxford constituency and three days later secured a seat for South Lancashire. The Cabinet met only once and then was off on holiday for seven months, by which time Lord Palmerston, aged eighty-one, had died. In the new government Mary's father, who was Chancellor of the Exchequer and Leader of the House of Commons (Prime Minister Lord Russell being in the House of Lords), became the most important figure in the land. The political stage would now resound to the heroic clash of ideologies between Benjamin Disraeli and William Gladstone. At the next election in 1868 the Liberals swept to power and Gladstone, now almost sixty, became Prime Minister, an office he would hold three more times.

Our modern, freely elected government was said to be a model for all the world but there was still plenty of bribery and corruption. The people were not yet ready for a secret ballot, or so the aristocracy and landed gentry thought; they declared that voting in public was a dignified affair and why did any honest man need to skulk in a private corner? Underlying this declaration was their need to know how their workers and tenants were voting, and on election day the beer flowed freely to encourage the electors to vote for the right man.

William Gladstone was the first politician to use the modern means of communication to his advantage; his speeches were published in pamphlets which sold by the thousands, and also reported in the national newspapers. Each time, his rallying call was freedom for individuals and for nations, especially after his conversion to the cause of Irish Home Rule. He pursued his policies with evangelical zeal as he stormed around the country, preaching his message from the platforms of railway carriages at every halt and station.

The Victorian age was one of stability, peace, certainty, increasing wealth and materialism. The great moral institutions of Church, State and Family reigned over all, forming the people's conscience. A father's occupation, trade or profession defined the place of the family, gave it status; man had his appointed place, woman her destined role which lay unquestionably within the home where she was the undisputed authority. Every woman was the prospective wife of someone, and if she had the misfortune not to fulfil her destiny, she could only hope to be a companion, governess or domestic servant, unpaid within the family or meagrely paid without. It was unthinkable that she should wish to raise her eyes above the domestic horizon.

In 1861 Prince Albert died after a tragically brief illness and the Queen entered upon a lifetime of widowhood; her modest widow's weeds became her symbol of monarchy. Prince Albert's state funeral displayed all the pomp and circumstance of a proud nation. Confidence in science and industry spilled over into religious faith; England had a Bible-reading, church-going society whose virtues were respectability, thrift, duty and hard work, but where discipline could harden into rigidity and esteem into hypocrisy.

It was an age of great contrasts. As Charles Dickens wrote in 1854, 'it was the best of times, it was the worst of times'. Life for the poor was a struggle for survival and only the fittest and the luckiest won through. In the same year Mrs Gaskell, novelist and wife of a Unitarian minister in Manchester, pointed out the contrasts of the lives of the poor and the middle class in *North and South*. The poor were huddled together in tenement slums with no hope of any space or privacy day or night; here they were born, here they would stay and in God's good time here they would die.

How different were the lives of the upper middle-classes and aristocracy whose lives followed a migratory pattern of a London season, a home in the country, a mini-season at Brighton for healthy sea breezes, a move to Scotland for hunting and shooting, and an escape to the continent from England's damp and foggy winters. How fortunate for Mary Gladstone that she was born into those few privileged families. Her first experience of continental travel was at the age of three when she was taken by her parents to spend the winter in Naples. Such journeys were not for the faint-hearted; bumping over the Alps in a full diligence left stiff and aching bones and overnight stops meant sleepless nights fighting fleas. This was at a time when most families thought themselves lucky if they could take a day's outing to the sea-side by charabanc or on one of the new excursion trains.

Victorian society erected a rigid set of rules to separate the classes, to control the large numbers of adults and children thrown together. Their answers lay in religion; their actions in this world would be called to account in the next. Personal behaviour was controlled by an appeal to moral goodness, purity, standards of hygiene, responsibility and punctuality.

As the middle classes grew in affluence and influence they built museums, libraries, churches and town halls to reflect their new status. The newly rich built huge mansions up and down the country in the style of castles, Renaissance palaces or French chateaux. The Gladstone home Hawarden Castle, set in beautiful parkland above the sands of the Dee estuary with the Welsh mountains at its back, had been turreted, crenellated and enlarged by Mary's great-grandfather Sir Stephen Glynne at the beginning of the nine-teenth century.

There was a blossoming of art and literature as the newly aware reading public, avid for self-improvement, seized and devoured the new novels. *Vanity Fair, Jane Eyre, Wuthering Heights* and *Dombey & Son* were all published in 1847, the year of Mary's birth, and two years later, *David Copperfield* was published. New works by Charles Dickens and Anthony Trollope tumbled out in monthly installments and the stars of the artistic and cultural firmament were Ruskin, Carlyle, Browning, Leighton, Millais and the Pre-Raephaelite Brotherhood. In 1859 came Darwin's *On the Origin of Species*, Samuel Smiles' *Self-Help* and John Stuart Mills' essay *On Liberty*.

In 1869 Matthew Arnold's *Culture and Anarchy* was published. In his prose and poetry he writes of the complacency that can bring about reaction and revolt. His poem *Dover Beach* warns that a world offering so much peace and plenty can be dark and joyless:

'Swept with confused alarms of struggle and flight,
Where ignorant armies clash by night.'

Every decade of Mary Gladstone's life brought its tragedies of war and famine. In the 1840s the Irish potato famine sent boatloads of exiles over the sea to America with bitterness and hatred in their hearts. In the 1850s, Britain's involvement in the Crimean War took some 25 000 British lives. In the 1860s the American Civil War brought poverty and famine to Lancashire homes, because the cotton trade in England could not function without the cotton that was imported from the Southern states of America, and a Northern blockade of Southern ports meant a halt in cotton exports, causing Lancashire factories to shut down. In the 1870s came the Franco-German war and the Bulgarian atrocities. In the 1880s there were more Irish troubles, and in the 1890s the Boer struggles. These wars were fought on foreign shores and, in Britain, others' struggles for liberty could be praised or condemned, manipulated, misunderstood or ignored.

The Suez Canal was opened in 1869, bringing shorter routes to India and encouraging Disraeli's imperialism, which reached its climax in 1877 with Queen Victoria's assumption of the title of Empress of India, an act described by Gladstone as 'theatrical bombast and folly'. It was a time when patriotism overflowed into jingoism and the popular music-hall refrain was

'We don't want to fight, but by jingo if we do, We've got the ships, we've got the men, we've got the money too!'

The Victorian scene is vast, crowded, swiftly changing and complex so that each shake of the kaleidoscope reveals a different picture. If we are to enter this 'foreign country', we must remember that the worlds of men and women are different and separate. Even the most enlightened believed that women's brains and bodies were biologically and psychologically different from men's and that irreparable harm to the individual and to society would ensue if these differences were not observed and honoured. The Education Act of 1870 brought schools for everyone but they were not compulsory until 1880 and not free until 1891. Higher education for women was fought for and slowly won as exclusively male bastions were gradually breached. Pioneers like Octavia Hill and Josephine Butler sought to alleviate the suffering of women but not to change the structure of society. The only safety lay within the home and this is where Mary and her sisters were educated by governesses who placed more value on obedience and humility than on reading and arithmetic, while their brothers were sent to boarding school, Eton and university. In 1871, when Mary was twenty-three, George Eliot's *Middlemarch* appeared in which she describes girls' education as 'comparable to the nibblings and judgements of a discursive mouse' and reminds her readers that 'women were expected to have weak opinions', their social life being but 'a labyrinth of petty courses, a walled-in maze of small paths that led no whither'.

This is the world that we must enter to find Mary Gladstone, who could have remained one of George Eliot's domestic mice but did not. She struggled to find her identity and, through heartache and loss, she grew into a confident woman with opinions valued by her father and his colleagues in Westminster. She held a special place in Downing Street during her father's second term of office as Prime Minister in the 1880s and was invaluable to him in his declining years. Her personal story is told against a backdrop of public achievements and world events.

CHAPTER ONE

Prime time (1879)

It was 24 November 1879 and quite dark by the time they reached Edinburgh. The journey had begun nine hours earlier at Edgehill Station, Liverpool; the hubbub began at Carlisle where the train made a brief stop. Mary and her mother were hurried behind father through a great crowd of working men, cheering and waving their hats. They had gathered on the platforms and even crowded the rails to catch a glimpse of their hero, William Gladstone. The lucky ones were close enough to hear him speak. Then the small family group climbed back on board, waved farewell and the train steamed on. The same performance was repeated at Hawick and Galashiels, the crowds growing ever greater and the cheering ever more enthusiastic.

Mary had to admit that they were travelling in style, in a saloon carriage with a luxury luncheon provided, but she had shaken so many hands that she felt that her own had been pulled through a wringer. At Galashiels she was given a nosegay of flowers, the first of many on this triumphant Midlothian tour.

Yesterday had been Mary's thirty-second birthday and not a happy one. She described it as 'most grim-looking'. The whole day had been spent indoors at her Gladstone cousins' Liverpool home, everyone's minds on the coming journey. They were all so nice but oh so boring. 'It is stagnation', she wrote in her diary, 'and calls out for some fascinating spirited being to put life and soul into them'. As the unmarried, stay-at-home daughter, she had become the family organiser and was well suited to the role. Her father increasingly depended on her to deal with his correspondence, to make travel arrangements for continental holidays, and to invite the right mix of important and congenial house guests for weekends at their home, Hawarden Castle, set in the beautiful countryside of the North Welsh Marches.

During one typical mid-summer party weekend of 1879, among guests that included the Crown Prince of Sweden, the Duke of Newcastle, his brother and tutor and an assortment of Gladstone cousins, Sir Edward Burne-Jones had made a drawing of Mary as they sat listening to a reading of Jane Austen's *Emma*. Her face has a thoughtful, faraway expression. Her thick, wavy brown hair is drawn back to the nape of her head in a coiled plait but with wisps of soft hair gently framing large, wide-apart dark eyes, a sensible nose and a generous mouth. When she showed it to sixty-year-old Ruskin, another family friend who came to Hawarden as much to enjoy Mary's company as her famous father's, his opinion was that the 'pale and subtle hints' give 'nobleness of expression' and 'a serene depth', but her hand to her forehead suggests troubled inner depths rather than serenity.

The train steamed through the Scottish lowlands, the sun setting with a luminous golden light as though adding a blessing on their journey. Lord Rosebery was awaiting their arrival at Edinburgh and guided them through the noisy, densely packed crowds to his open four-horse carriage. Away they galloped through the welcoming roars, many outriders keeping pace alongside and hundreds running dangerously close to the side of the carriage. Fireworks were exploding and cascading, bonfires shooting sparks up into the night sky; the whole way to Dalmeny was lit by flaming torches. Mary was overwhelmed by the theatricality of it all.

Lord Rosebery had organised this campaign as a means of attracting national attention to Gladstone's pre-eminence in Liberal politics, ready for the general election whenever it should be called. William Gladstone had been adopted as Liberal candidate for Midlothian, its present Conservative sitting member being Lord Dalkeith, son and heir of the Duke of Buccleuch. Gladstone was close to his seventieth birthday, no longer leader of the Liberal party and officially retired from the political scene. He had been assured that the Midlothian seat was his for the taking.

Dalmeny, Lord Rosebery's Scottish home, was a Victorian Gothic castle with numerous tall chimneys looming over the turrets and battlements. It stood in parkland that rolled down to the Firth of Forth and the open sea. After a good night's rest, Mary was delighted to find at breakfast her Lyttelton cousin Alfred. They took a brisk walk together along the sea path as far as the ruins of the original castle on the estate. There were sleet and snow flurries in the keen wind. She was glad of the fresh air to clear away the cobwebs of travel before the campaign began in earnest. That afternoon there were speeches in Edinburgh and a dinner with the city dignitaries.

Next day a special train was laid on to carry them to Dalkeith, 'the heart of the enemy's country' Mary called it, by which she meant a Tory stronghold. The enemy must have gone to ground, for everywhere were cheering supporters. She was quite frightened by the people's enthusiasm; they recklessly pressed up against the carriage as it came to a stop at the platform. They even hung on the wheels and came close to being crushed to death.

The hall was packed and crowds, unable to get in, were waiting outside. Nearly fifty thousand people had applied for six thousand seats. People had travelled from all parts of Scotland – weavers, farmers, villagers, ordinary working people – to see and hear their hero who wore 'an ancient, short-cut, much-frayed cape'. Henry Lucy, a young journalist covering the campaign, described it as,

> ... of the kind Shem, Ham, and Japhet might have worn when they took their walks abroad before the Flood necessitated the ark. It was compact, of a cheap, shoddy material called, I believe, vicuna. It was in vogue, among other monstrosities of fashion, in early Victorian days. This was probably the only specimen left in the last quarter of the nineteenth century.[1]

Mary sat with her mother on the platform and looked down at the crowded hall. She could not help but be moved by the 'pinched, haggard, eager faces'. Her father did not talk down to them but addressed them as if he were in the House of Commons. It was an appeal to reason, responsibility, to the conscience of a great and free people and the hall responded with a 'perfect storm of applause'. She thought the speech, lasting over an hour and a half, was 'wonderfully moving and inspiring'.

Tea with the Provost followed and then another meeting, that went on well into the evening. Everywhere it was the same story: overspilling halls, cheering crowds in the streets, triumphal arches, lanterns and torches lighting their way. The London newspapers carried every word as Gladstone denounced Disraeli's foreign policy as pursuing 'false phantoms of glory' and dared to criticise the Queen's assumption of the Empress role. The rallying cry was freedom for all peoples; he warned his audiences not to be blind to the wrongs and injustices being committed in the name of national pride. Mary wrote to her cousin Lavinia that it was all astonishing 'as you will have gathered from the papers, but even they can give you no real idea of the spontaneous burst of feeling; we are told the Queen has never had anything approaching to it'. In fact, the Queen was exceedingly alarmed and annoyed, and her private opinion was that nothing would induce her to accept Mr Gladstone as Prime Minister. Disraeli, Earl of Beaconsfield since 1876, pretended to be bored by the whole business, dismissing the Gladstonian rhetoric as 'wearisome'. But to the people of Scotland it was a passionate appeal to their honour and they were lifted out of their everyday selves by the brilliant oratory.

After a week at Dalmeny the family moved on to Perthshire. At Taymouth Castle, Mary was at last able to draw breath and enjoy the parties that were laid on by their host. There was a good selection of young men in kilts and they all enjoyed the skating, although Mary noticed that curling was far more popular. Dinner was celebrated in Scottish fashion with five bagpipers solemnly marching round and round the table as they dined. It was, she told Lavinia, 'a regular regal Highland Castle'. She had given her all the details of their triumphant entry into Edinburgh, which had been stage-managed by Lord Rosebery who stood to gain a firm hold in Scottish politics. He was Mary's age, proud and handsome, married to the very wealthy Hannah Rothschild. He and Mary became great friends and she was able to smooth what was often a prickly path between him and her father.

She thought that she had grown used to the crowds of cheering people, the mounting tension as her father held his audiences like the most gifted actor, but the day that he was installed as Rector of Glasgow University was 'the fullest, most exciting and altogether greatest day of all'. The students, Conservative in blue cap and gown, Liberal in red, sat in spellbound silence. She believed that she would never forget 'the solemn earnest tone of voice with which he ended his appeal to the youths. So noble, so strong, and so high was this appeal that no one could listen without being moved, and the shout that burst from every corner of the building when he ended could never be forgotten'.[2] She looked around at the eager young faces, many with tears blinding their eyes. How could she be anything but a devotee, giving her unquestioning allegiance, her talents and energies in his service? Those who scorned and disparaged him would become her enemies. As she explained to Lavinia, her father was much too great to mind the horrid things that were said about him, especially by those who 'profess and call themselves Christians'. She minded so much more for him than for herself. She would make it her job to protect him from the daily frustrations, to smooth his path and take upon herself whatever responsibilities might further the Liberal cause towards freedom and justice for all.

Mary was about to step from the pale, passive world that Victorian middle- and upper-class women were supposed to enjoy into the robust male world of politics, assurance and authority. A general election would soon be called and she would be right in the midst of the hurly-burly. To understand how she came to be a part of this world, we must look at the interweaving of family relationships in the earlier generation.

CHAPTER TWO

Glynnes, Gladstones and Lytteltons (1833—49)

In February 1833, William Gladstone entered Parliament as Tory member for Newark, taking his seat alongside his brother Tom, Tory member for Portarlington. His maiden speech (if we ignore a couple of minor petitions) was in opposition to the Slavery Abolition Bill, defending his father's West Indian interests in sugar plantations. The Bill was passed, settling the questions of compensation to landowners, the length of apprenticeship and working hours on the plantations in most British colonies.

His political career can be said to have taken off the next year with a summons from the Prime Minister, Sir Robert Peel, offering a Junior Lordship at the Treasury. In 1835 he was Under-Secretary for War and the Colonies at a time when interest was awakening in commercial trade with China and India. Britain was becoming increasingly embroiled in skirmishes in China; the Chinese government was unwilling to open the country to the full impact of Western commerce and strongly resisted the import of Indian opium by the British. Gladstone had spoken out strongly against the war being waged by Foreign Secretary Lord Palmerston, 'a war more unjust in its origin, a war more calculated in its progress to cover this country with disgrace, I do not know and I have not read of.'[1]

In 1837 Queen Victoria succeeded to the throne after William IV. Three years later, the country celebrated her marriage to Prince Albert.

On 25 July 1839, the villagers of Hawarden were buzzing with excitement; there was to be a double wedding at the parish church. The two Glynne sisters from the castle, known to everyone and inseparable since birth, were getting married. The bridegrooms, William Gladstone and Lord George Lyttelton, had been at the castle for some days and been spied in the village street. A passer-by had remarked, as he gave Mr Gladstone an admiring glance, that it was easy to see which was the lord.

Twelve carriages bore the bridal party from the castle through the parkland past the ruins of the old castle through the gates and into the village street. The narrow road that led to the church was decorated with floral arches. Bands led a procession, in which walked people from all the local societies, and children ran ahead to scatter flowers along the way. Every house carried a floral arch and every doorway was filled with excited faces.

'Oh, what a scene' wrote William Gladstone in his diary later, 'such an outpouring of pure human affection on these beloved girls, combined with so solemn a mystery'. He was marrying Catherine Glynne and Catherine's younger sister Mary was giving her hand to Lord George Lyttelton of Hagley Hall in Worcestershire.

St Deiniol's Church stands on high ground above the sands of Dee, the Cheshire Plain on one side and the Wirral Peninsula at its back. It looks towards the Welsh hills, the spiritual home of its founder Deiniol who, in the sixth century, planted his preaching cross on this hill. Castle and church had been intimately connected through the years and all the rectors since 1770 were related to the Glynne family. It was Catherine and Mary's uncle, Rector George Neville Grenville, who conducted their marriage ceremony. When he was promoted to be Dean of Windsor, their brother Henry would become the new rector. The living was the richest and most influential in the land, known as an ecclesiastical peculiar with the rights to grant marriage licences, prove wills and hold its own court.

The Glynne sisters had lived with their widowed mother Lady Glynne and brothers Stephen and Henry at Hawarden

Castle which had been in the family for nearly two hundred years. Stephen, the elder brother, was the ninth baronet and owner of castle and estate. The old castle, probably a mix of stone and timber, had been destroyed in 1647 on Parliamentary orders following the seizure of Chester by Cromwell's men. Slowly it mellowed into a picturesque ruin. A hundred years passed before the sixth baronet built a three-storeyed brick hall in the shadow of the ruins. In the early part of the nineteenth century, it was given a Gothic stone dressing; turrets and crenellations were added as well as more practical items: bedrooms and library.

Pigot's Commercial Directory of 1835 describes Hawarden as 'a respectable thriving little market township in the parish of its name, hundred of Mold and county of Flint, 195 miles N.W. of London.' A visitor to the Glynne home in the 1830s described the house as 'having no pretension inside to anything but comfort' and 'just the sort of place one would like to have'. William Gladstone once described the estate as 'not in the first class but quite at the top of the second class'. However, with this double marriage, Gladstone wealth and Glynne social status, honeyed over with Lyttelton connections, made the families formidable players on the Victorian scene.

Part of the marriage settlement between the families had been that the two bridegrooms would take a tenth share in the Glynne iron works in Staffordshire. Stephen Glynne was heavily involved and in need of capital. He had no head for business and gratefully handed over the responsibility of running the works to an agent while William's father, John Gladstone, advised on financial matters. What seemed a promising venture would quickly turn into wild and worrisome speculation, but that lay in the future and did not mar the happiest of wedding days.

The marriage service over, the sisters changed their bridal clothes and set off on their honeymoons, the Lytteltons to Hagley and the Gladstones to Norton Priory in Cheshire which had been offered to them by close friends. But separation was short for they were all back at Hawarden Castle in August for the servants' ball. Then the two couples set off by sea from

Liverpool to Greenock and on by road, sometimes walking, sometimes driving, staying at wayside inns at night, across the Scottish hills and glens to Fasque, the Gladstone family home that lay on the east coast. A traveller whose path crossed theirs as they walked through the wild passes described the sisters 'mounted on Highland ponies, each one attended by her most faithful and attentive squire, holding her bridle over the gullies and burns', adding that 'a prettier, happier party never crossed the heather'.

The Lytteltons moved on to Chatsworth, home of the Duke of Devonshire who was a distant relative. Daily letters must replace daily meetings. On 23 September, Catherine wrote to share the news that she was pregnant with Mary, imagining her 'dressed very smart and sitting in a fine dressing-room, unless in one of the grand rooms below. Poor little thing, you will feel shy, I know.' Catherine was still at Fasque when she heard from Mary that she too was pregnant, and she wrote to her in great delight. She herself was suffering from morning sickness but a little boiled bread and milk, taken at bedtime, had helped. She gave Mary details of her health cares: 'I go into a cold hip bath, just bob in and out to strengthen my back, it sometimes aches a little ... I also spunge my chest and arms and throat in the cold water regularly – you ought to do this'.[2] William also wrote, to share in their glad news. He hoped that Mary night escape morning sickness, 'that in this instance, you will be content to differ from Catherine'. A new dynasty of Gladstones and Lytteltons was about to begin.

In 1841 Gladstone was offered the position of Vice-President of the Board of Trade and was urged to accept by Peel who saw it as valuable experience for his future career. He accepted reluctantly as he could not support the government stance on China which culminated in the Treaty of Nanking where Hong Kong was ceded to Britain. Two years later, as colonial expansion reached Canada and New Zealand, Gladstone was promoted to President of the Board of Trade; the right man to master details of commercial treaties, customs regulations and duties, and to oversee the legislative framework for the mushrooming railway system. He gained valuable experience in political compromise as agitation against the Corn Laws increased and he had to balance his free trade against duties on corn.

The first child born to Catherine and William was a son, named after his father and always called Willy in the family. A fortnight later Mary Lyttelton's first daughter was born and William went along to introduce himself to the new baby in the evening. He reported that she was large and healthy with a gentle expression. Both confinements were in London, considered the safest place, with Dr Locock, the Queen's favoured obstetrician, in attendance.

Two years later, Catherine gave birth to her first daughter and ten days later Mary followed with her first son, having given birth to a daughter the year before. There was then a brief respite of eighteen months. In April 1844 a second son was born to the Gladstones and two months later the Lytteltons caught up with their second son. The next year in July another daughter arrived for the Gladstones and in October there was another son for the Lytteltons.

In 1845 Gladstone became Colonial Secretary which meant that he had to vacate his Newark seat. He was without a seat for twenty months, mainly due to his stance on the Repeal of the Corn Laws which was carried in June 1846. The government fell on an Irish Coercion Bill and Peel resigned, one of his last actions being to offer Gladstone's father a baronetcy for his years of tremendous support, both financial and political. The Tory party was out of power for twenty years. In 1847 Gladstone was elected as junior member for Oxford University, a seat he clung to for eighteen years.

When Mary Gladstone was born on 24 November 1847, she already had two brothers, two sisters and nine cousins, six Lyttelton and three Glynne. (Henry Glynne had married Lavinia Lyttelton in 1842, thus weaving another strand into the family tapestry.) William wrote in his diary that baby Mary was a very plump and pretty little girl. Unlike most Victorian husbands, who stayed well away from the scene of childbirth, he was a most loving and attentive husband, attending to Catherine's needs in every way he could. He stayed by her side through the hours of labour. This time the pains were more severe and trying than usual and his diary records that Catherine 'had gruel with a little brandy which seemed entirely to restore her'. As he watched her endure far more than he had ever experienced in his life, he could only marvel at the religious significance of woman's suffering. He believed that she gained a special and privileged relationship with God and he turned for assurance to the Bible. 'In sorrow shalt thou bring forth children' (1 Genesis 111.16) is the woman's peculiar curse and the note of Divine judgement upon her in Adam: 'so shall she be saved in childbearing' (2 Timothy 11.15) is her peculiar promise in Christ – How many thoughts does this agony excite?'.[3] After each birth their love and happiness spilled over into a prayer of thankfulness for God's mercy.

There had been difficult months for both parents before this birth in 1847. They had spent the summer months at Fasque and there had been more than the usual share of trouble with Helen Gladstone. William's sister was thirty-three, unmarried, and living at home under the rule of a dominant father and with little to fill her days. After her mother's death when she was twenty-one, she had sunk into depression and had turned to drugs. Struggling against dependency, she had turned for solace to the Roman Catholic faith, much to her family's consternation and brother William's horror. She did not enjoy these visits with babies and small children, nurses and nannies. This time she was in a depressed and drugged state and, in the early hours of one morning, William was awakened by her maid, who came to say that her mistress was having a fit. Adding to their worries, four-year-old Agnes was ill with a fever and erisypelas was diagnosed, the illness that had killed William's mother. The worry and lack of rest brought Catherine close to a miscarriage.

William's days had been taken up with his elderly father's demands, with his political preoccupations and with his struggles to keep the Oak Farm iron works from bankruptcy. The great speculative boom in the railways had collapsed and a bank crisis was looming. When they reached London to await Mary's birth he had plunged into mountains of accounts, trade agreements and legal entanglements. He wrote wearily to his sister-in-law at Hagley that he feared they were all involved in 'a most wild and extravagant and in my view almost immoral speculation, namely in conducting an ironwork without either the knowledge or the means for doing this with safety'.[4] On the day of Mary's birth he wrote in his diary that it had been a day of sad and strange distractions. He could not dispel the thought that the Oak Farm struggles 'involve true dishonour. Here is their sting. But it is surely a trial meant to work out good alone though also in the nature of a chastisement'. It was a burden that he would bear for the next two years and he came close to removing himself from political and public life in order to deal with the family's financial mess.

It was a time of family discussions: how should the money be found to meet the mounting debts? Would they be forced to sell the Glynne family home? Catherine's uncle Lord Braybrooke wrote sternly to Stephen Glynne: 'Without mincing matters I must say you are mainly in fault and that most of these grievances arise from your apathy and want of firmness in not managing your own affairs as other persons do. And I must say that large estates were not given us to be wasted'.[5] William determined that the Hawarden estate must be saved at all costs and he discussed future plans with Catherine, as she nursed their new baby. Once Mary had been baptised and her mother had attended the churching service, a public offering of thanks for her safe delivery, they headed home to the fresh air and peace of Hawarden away from London's 'turmoil, its clack, its fog, its cold', as Catherine described it.

At the end of 1847, William Gladstone reported in his diary on his growing family that two-month-old Mary 'shows a very placid, and I hope sweet (for it is not a dull) temper: and a very great susceptibility to musical sounds in the most unequivocal way.' Two-year-old Jessy has 'a strong will which has yet to be broken' whereas six-year-old Agnes is easily ruled which he fears 'may partake of slightness in the texture of character'. Four-year-old Stephen is 'the slowest in development' and difficult to understand but his doting father felt that when he is understood, it is well worth the effort. He only has praise for his eldest son, 'a noble boy; generous, ingenuous, modest, tender, energetic, reflective and conscientious in a very high degree' and he is particularly impressed by his Sunday discussions with him on his sins, omissions, advances in the week, and by his Christian progress, 'I mean in practical Christianity, the discipline of the will, not in notions and pretensions'.

For only the briefest time Mary was the new baby. Just before Christmas, a Glynne son and heir was born at the rectory. On the heels of the glad tidings came the dreadful news that the baby had died that same day. The shock was very great, for his death in his mother's bed was not immediately discovered, but only an hour or so after. William Gladstone was exceedingly concerned that the baby had not been baptised but Catherine's concerns were of a more practical nature, for a week later, another Glynne child, Honora, not yet one year old, was having convulsions. She took herself and two-month-old Mary to the rectory where they stayed for over a fortnight.

These shared experiences strengthened the family bonds and in 1849, it was to the rectory at Hawarden that Catherine Gladstone journeyed nine days before her next confinement. The baby was overdue, Dr Locock had gone on holiday, and it was considered safer to escape the August heat and risk of cholera in London. There was another reason for moving to Hawarden for the birth. Their London home at 13 Carlton House Terrace had been sold to Lord Grey. It was, William wrote in his diary, a weight off his mind 'tho' at what wd. be called a wretched price'. He saw his wife safely on to the express train to Chester while he took a later train for the five-hour journey. There had been a scare three months into the pregnancy when Catherine had fallen downstairs with Mary in her arms. Her old slippers had been blamed for the accident, but the worst that befell her were bruises and a cut to her forehead while Mary was unharmed and may even have protected the unborn child.

Baby Helen arrived safely in August 1849. By this time the Oak Farm works had been declared bankrupt; William Gladstone, Lord Lyttelton and Sir Stephen Glynne had bought out the liquidators and paid £1000 for the company's assets. Some Hawarden land had to be sold and the proceeds used to support the company; everyone had to economise and the burden on

William Gladstone was so great that he even thought of withdrawing from public life so that he could give all his energies to family demands.

Until now, Gladstones and Lytteltons had followed each other's pattern of childbearing, with the Lytteltons only one child in the lead. They were all fortunate that they could seek the best medical advice available and employ enough domestic servants to ease their burdens despite the financial sacrifices they had had to make since the collapse of Oak Farm iron works. Pregnancy among the privileged classes was considered the joyous outcome of marriage. Confinements were a part of the natural rhythm of family life. There would be more pregnancies; but it is time now to move away from births and babies and to follow two-year-old Mary to Scotland.

CHAPTER THREE

A visit to Scotland (1847–1850)

It was 2 October 1849 and Mary, now almost two years old, was paying her first visit to Scotland. The purpose of the trip was to introduce baby Helen to her aunt and namesake, and to visit her grandfather. It was no easy journey for the family with six children, from nine-year-old Willy to baby Helen, who was less than two months old. They journeyed north by sea from Liverpool to Greenock and on by train across Scotland to Forfar. At long weary last, after nine hours of travelling, they reached the north-east coast and Sir John Gladstone's home at Fasque.

It was the Victorian custom to take along personal servants with the luggage and along went three from Hawarden; one for Papa, one for Mama and one for the children. Surely there were enough servants to cater for every need at Fasque with the cook-housekeeper, butler, laird's valet, lady's maid, plus an assortment of footmen, housemaids, kitchen and scullery maids, laundry and dairy maids, not forgetting coachmen and grooms in the stables?

John Gladstone had been made a baronet in 1846 and he had used some of his wealth to add to his estate and home in ways that befitted a man in his position. When he was twenty-two he had left Leith on Scotland's north-east coast to seek his fortune in England, in the expanding port of Liverpool. He had joined a partnership trading in corn, sugar, cotton and timber and had prospered. He bought his own ships and moved into property development and West Indian plantations, owning by 1816 one of the largest and most productive properties in Demerara and master of 330 slaves. As chairman of the Liverpool West India

Association he played an active part in the development of the docks and the construction of the Customs House. He acquired an interest in the *Liverpool Echo* which was a useful public voice for his opinions. He brought four of his brothers to join him in Liverpool and helped them to set up businesses. Within a generation his assets had climbed to more than £502 500 which today would make him a multimillionaire.

He had moved into politics when George Canning entered his life and became his hero. In the 1812 election John Gladstone was party manager for Canning and on his victory gained a prominent place in Liverpool politics. Two years later he was appointed a magistrate and was regarded as a confidante of the Prime Minister, Lord Liverpool. In 1818 he was elected MP for Lancaster, moving on to Woodstock in the 1820 election to a seat controlled by the Duke of Marlborough, but he remained the driving force in every aspect of Liverpool progress, all of which promoted his own interests. Six years later he found another seat at Berwick-in-Tweed but, before he could become its representative, he was accused of bribery and corruption, found guilty and unseated; so ended his political career.

His first marriage to Jane Hall of Liverpool had ended, childless, after six years, with her death in 1798. Two years later he had married Anne Mackenzie Robertson at St Peter's Parish Church, Liverpool. Their first child, named after her mother, had been born two years later on Christmas Eve. Four sons followed, Thomas in 1804, Robertson sixteen months later, John Neilson in January 1807, and William Ewart on 29 December 1809. Five years later, their last child Helen Jane was born.

His first home had been newly built in Rodney Street, Liverpool and John Gladstone went on to acquire enough frontage to build and own numbers 1–10. Here he installed Gladstones and Robertsons but by 1813 he was looking to move his family out of the city centre to the fresh sea breezes blowing around Seaforth House with its own church, farm and cottages on the Litherland estate. He acquired the habits of the English landed gentry, adopting their code of honour, duty and philanthropy, mixing his evangelism with a large dose of materialism. He built and endowed first St Andrew's Church and School in Liverpool and then Seaforth Church and School. Everything was done on a business footing so that he could balance his expenditure by the rental of pews and sale of burial plots, allow five per cent interest on his investments and end the year in profit.

In 1830, forty-two years after leaving Scotland, he brought wife and daughter Helen Jane (Anne having died in February 1829) to the estate of Fasque and Balfour for which he paid just under £80 000. When wife and daughter complained of the long, cold winters and the distance from civilised society, he bought an Edinburgh house. He already had a rented base in London and within a few years had bought a family house at 6 Carlton Gardens. He always intended his four sons to move in the highest circles, and with this purpose he sent them to Eton College; the eldest, Thomas, and the youngest, William, to Christ Church, Oxford, Robertson to Glasgow College and John Neilson into the Navy.

As a young man, William Ewart Gladstone travelled a privileged path, making friendships that would underpin his later career and life. His acquaintance with the Glynne family was a direct result of his father's ambitions; he and Stephen Glynne were students together at Oxford. During a continental tour of 1838 they met up in Ems where William was escorting his sister Helen. The privileged paths of the Victorians crossed just as easily in Paris, Rome or Naples as they did in London. Whether by accident or design, the two families met again in Naples and agreed to meet in Rome. Catherine Glynne was a beautiful, vivacious twenty-six-year-old. She was impetuous, completely unself-conscious and openly confident. William, two years older, was tall, dark and handsome as any romantic hero with his closely cropped hair framing a pale face that added soulful depths to his dark eyes. He was painfully shy with women and had already suffered two rejections from beautiful aristocratic young ladies whom he had wooed and lost. As soon as the Glynnes were back in London at their Berkeley Square home, William pressed his attentions. Within two months he was writing to his father at Fasque to say that he could no longer conceal his feelings. He proposed and was accepted. Catherine said that she fell in love with his noble intellect and righteous earnestness. He had confided in her that his early ambition had been to take Holy Orders but that now he was resolved to serve God through the State.

He had entered politics in 1832 as Conservative MP for Newark and when he looked back in 1897 to his first years, he 'found it most difficult to believe with any reality of belief that such a poor and insignificant little worm as I could really belong to, really form a *part* of an assembly which, notwithstanding the prosaic character of its entire visible equipment I felt to be so august.' His maiden speech in 1833 had been on the Slavery Abolition Bill, in defence of the manager of his father's estates in Demerara; later in his own defence he wrote that 'of course allowance is to be made for the enormous and most blessed change of opinion since that day on the subject of negro slavery.'[1] His speech brought him to the notice of important members: George Keppel, Whig MP for East Norfolk was pleasantly impressed by his 'earnest, intelligent countenance, and large, expressive eyes'. Sir Robert Peel congratulated him immediately afterwards in the lobby and even the king, William IV, expressed interest in this charming young man. At this time his father and his brother Thomas were also Members of Parliament but William's parliamentary career would soon outshine theirs and that of his brother John Neilson who had an intermittent and inconspicuous parliamentary career for seventeen years.

He enjoyed working on administrative details and business technicalities and he was forced to realise that he was 'a man in politics', but in 1845 his moral and religious principles were tested to breaking point and he resigned from the government over what was known as the Maynooth Grant. It was a move to endow the Roman Catholic College near Dublin. In principle he rejected it, in practice he supported it, so he resigned from the Cabinet and stayed in the Conservative party. He was seen by many to be perverse and foolish but it did mean that, out of government, he had more time for his family and friends and especially for his children in their formative years.

The Scottish visit was a move to strengthen family ties. Sir John's health was deteriorating after a lifetime of robust vigour. He had given generously over the years to Glynne and Gladstone investments and in return he expected regular attention. This time the stay would be long and arduous. William was expected to shoulder the responsibility of attending to his father's wants, but there were moments of relief when he could romp with his children. He called Mary 'his mountain bird', delighting in her sweet singing. He thought that she was 'the quickest and most forward of all the children'. Stephen persevered at his books while Willy was a quick reader, Agnes was helpful and Jessy was sweet.

Miss Helen Gladstone could only tolerate quiet, well-behaved children. 'It is more than one can humanly expect from human nature to have them always plodding,' Catherine wailed to Mary at Hagley, and went on to describe how her sister-in-law trailed into dinner like a tragedy queen 'with gold crapes hanging by her side'. Helen was thirty-five. She had always been closest to her brother William, but he had gone away to school and left her in the company of her elder sister Anne who developed tuberculosis when Helen was nine. Anne slowly declined over six years, bearing her illness with a patience and stoicism that her family remembered with reverence. Helen, with a passionate intelligence that matched William's, was expected to be companion to her mother who increasingly took to her bed and trailed her daughter along with her from doctor to doctor. Illness, disease and death were inescapable preoccupations for the Victorians. The Gladstone family shared their doctors and cures among each other. When Helen's brother Tom had been suffering from depression and physical debility in his mid-twenties he was put under Dr Jepherson of Leamington Spa. Where the grand tour had failed, Dr Jepherson's rigid routine of cold showers, hot baths, vigorous exercise and strict diet worked wonders. It was now Helen's turn. After Anne's death, she had taken upon herself the guilt of being alive, filled with self-disgust at her own failings. Her education was neglected and what might have been a good brain was left to moulder. When her mother died in 1835

Helen sank into depression and took drugs to obliterate the pain. Doctor Locock, family doctor as well as obstetrician, was one of a string of doctors who tried out imaginative cures for Helen. One of his prescriptions for what was described as her 'tick pain' involved bark and soda to be taken every six hours. On another occasion he advised asses milk three times a day. Laudanum became her means of escape from reality. She could perhaps have found a role as mistress of Fasque, but her father made all the decisions.

A small window of escape had opened briefly for her in the year that she went with William to Ems. She met and fell in love with Count Leon Sollohub who was of Russo-Polish blood and belonged to the Greek Orthodox Church, but his family were against their marriage. She sought solace in the Roman Catholic Church, perhaps as much in rebellion as in truth, and here she found the peace of mind that had been sorely lacking in her life. She was received into the Roman Catholic faith against vehement family opposition. Her father insisted that she came home to Fasque and here she was living most miserably, appreciated and understood by none of her family, least of all by William and Catherine.

William Gladstone's energies found release in the cut and thrust of Parliamentary jousting. In 1847 the Athens home of a Spanish Jew, Don Pacifico, had been seized and ransacked by a mob; he had been born in Gibraltar which entitled him to British nationality. He sought compensation through the courts and the affair dragged on for three years.

In 1850 Foreign Secretary Lord Palmerston despatched a fleet of ships to blockade the Greek coast without consulting with France and Russia, co-guarantors with Britain of Greek independence. The Parliamentary debate that followed was long and lively. Gladstone's masterly speech from the high moral ground attacked Palmerston's actions:

> When we are asking for the maintenance of the rights that belong to our fellow subjects resident in Greece, let us do as we would be done by; let us pay all respect to a feeble state and to the infancy of free institutions, which

we should desire and should exact from others towards their authority and strength.[2]

His rhetoric gathered momentum as he went on to attack Britain's stance as universal moral arbitrator:

What Sir ought a Foreign Secretary to be? Is he to be like some gallant knight at a tournament of old, pricking forth into the lists, armed at all points, confiding in his sinews and his skill, challenging all comers for the sake of honour, and having no other duty than to lay as many as possible of his adversaries sprawling in the dust?[3]

Disraeli joined in the condemnation but the House of Commons voted for Palmerston's action which received a majority of forty-six. The debate heightened not only Gladstone's reputation but also his distrust and dislike of Palmerston. The day after the debate ended he lost his mentor of many years; Peel was thrown from his horse and died three days later after forty-one years in Parliament. He was mourned by the nation as the greatest statesman of his day.

There were some bright moments for the Gladstone family gathering at Fasque – a bonfire party and, later in the month, Mary's second birthday, but winter storms must have made it a bleak inhospitable stay. Snow lay on the ground as preparations went ahead for the family to leave. It was the end of January 1850 and time for Mary's first brother to leave the family nest. Nine-year-old Willy was off to boarding school. Everyone rose before dawn to get ready for the train journey south to Birmingham. Here the family would split. Willy, in peaked cap and short jacket, portmanteau in hand and tears on cheek would travel on with Papa to a private school in Geddington, Northamptonshire. The grounding in classical Latin and Greek was excellent preparation for Eton and Oxford, but the curriculum was limited and Mr Church's temper was short and could be savage. To be shut away from the stimulating worldly contacts that were open to Mary and her sisters in these early years makes one wonder who had the better education.

Catherine moved on to Hagley where there were now seven little ones and another on the way. The Lyttelton children had whooping cough and two-year-old Mary was soon coughing, but what was causing more concern was the inflammation of her eyes. The Hagley doctor diagnosed an ulcer and anxious parents sought further medical advice from a London special-ist. But attention suddenly shifted to Mary's sister Jessy, four years old, who had become listless and lost her appetite. Doctor Locock was called. He prescribed Dover's powders and calomel for what he said was a stomach disorder. Jessy's pain and fever grew worse. Visiting daily, Dr Locock changed his opinion to tubercular inflammation of the membranes of the brain, but still he sought to reassure that the case was 'far from hopeless'. For another week Jessy struggled on the borders of conscious-ness until, on 9 April 1850, her father was able to write in his diary, 'It is all over, and all is well. The blessed child was released at two o'clock in the morning compassionately taken by her Saviour into the folds of his peace. I dwell on it no longer in this place'.

Anguish, rebellion and anger at what had happened were curbed by strong faith, and obedience and acceptance fol-lowed. It had been a hard lesson and now William must guide his children's tears and fears. At morning prayers he tried to explain to the older children but Mary called over and over for her 'Detty' and scolded 'naughty Papa for taking Detty away'.

There was a sad and tearful family parting as Papa and Willy left for Euston station. Willy was returning to boarding school and father was carrying his daughter's remains to Fasque, to the family vault. As he headed north the heart-weary man pulled down his carriage blind 'to have no other company than the thought of her who seems incessantly to beckon me and say "Come Pappy, come".'

CHAPTER FOUR

'Naples Mary' (1850)

$\mathcal{T}$he death of four-year-old Jessy seemed to highlight the vulnerability of those left behind. Mary now became the focus of parental concern. She was prone to coughs and colds and had an eye infection that was not clearing. Her mother gathered her up along with baby Helen (now called Lena to distinguish her from her Scottish aunt) and headed for the sea breezes of Brighton. From here she wrote to her husband that Mr Taylor (probably Charles Taylor, surgeon to the Royal South London Dispensery and expert on infant fevers) said 'it would be foolish to take her from the sea'. He examined the eye which had the film before it and gave his opinion that in time this would go away, but 'strongly urges her not reading and save them in all ways'. She added 'I think I shall be all the better for a bit of sea air'. Mr Gladstone, visiting at weekends, wrote in his diary that he found that 'little Mary now nearly for three months a great invalid had been going back again'. They must be ever more vigilant.

The Victorians had great faith in the health-giving properties of salt air and sea bathing. Brighton and its neighbouring resorts enjoyed a mini-season in February and March, especially favoured by upper-class families who had neither the time nor the money to travel to the Mediterranean coast. In August the Gladstones and Glynnes congregated on the North Wales coast and Penmaenmawr became their summer home. It was only twenty-five miles from Hawarden, and members of the family came and went as their commitments allowed.

Mary's health was much improved yet temperamental; her parents decided that it would be wise to remove her from

England for the coming winter. Of course Catherine talked over her worries with her sister, who advised, 'does it not look as if eyes and croup both come from stomach and it is stomach complaints which Italy seems to be grand for, digestion I mean'.

A bold undertaking was planned. But before it could take shape, tragedy struck again. Catherine had been nursing her sister-in-law Lavinia at Hawarden Rectory following the birth of a fourth daughter. Despite devoted care, Lavinia died within three weeks of the birth, leaving a distraught husband and four motherless girls. She was twenty-nine, and had given birth five times in seven years. William Gladstone wrote piously in his diary, 'Lavinia was a soul singularly pure and sweet, though quite mature; she was infancy and womanhood together. It is well with her; Earth has lost and Paradise gained.'

As soon as the funeral was over, the plan to escape from the cold and damp of winter went ahead without delay. First Mary was taken to Dr Dalrymple, a London eye specialist. Despite her eye problems, she was a lively child, 'captivating in the highest degree' her father thought, and indeed he was anxious that her impetuous ways were disciplined. But as he was accompanying the family group that included his wife, eight-year-old Agnes and two family servants Emily and Edward, he would be able to correct and curb any signs of waywardness. Lady Mary Lyttelton, with seven children of her own, was at Hawarden in charge of six-year-old Stephen and baby Lena.

'Naples Mary'

It was the 18th of October 1850. The search had begun for a cure for Mary's weak eyes. The day that they sailed from London Bridge bound for Boulogne was Agnes' eighth birthday. Perhaps she was the one to tell the captain, who promptly kissed and hugged her. Her father was incensed at his impudence, and he was still simmering with rage when they reached Paris – he wrote to the captain, warning him to mend his ways. A few days were spent in Paris, making the necessary arrangements for the journey south. This allowed time for a little culture for the grown-ups, by way of the Louvre, the Opera and Versailles.

There was a last-minute change of plans because Mary's eyes had already suffered from the cold air. It was decided, despite the expense, to buy a carriage, take it by train as far as possible, and then journey overland into Italy. It was the Victorian custom for gentlefolk to take their own coach on the railway car to avoid having to make the acquaintance of ill-bred folk. The Gladstones did not have such fastidiousness; this was purely a protective measure for Mary's health. From his first rail journey, as a young man of twenty-two, William Gladstone had always found the railway 'a most delightful mode of travelling'. The last day was spent in the study of maps and guidebooks. John Murray's *Handbook for Travellers in France* would be useful for finding inns and becoming acquainted with French customs. The French government's *Livre de Poste* would be indispensable for calculating distances and changes of postillions and horses.

The Orleans train took the family as far as Nevers. Mr Gladstone estimated 190 miles of railway cost '254 francs or £10 3s for the carriage and ourselves in it: or about 13 pence a mile for the vehicle and five third-class places'. He thought this was dearer than in England. 'We did not quite cover 20 miles an hour. We had however a good stoppage at Orleans: and I went off at a venture to see the Cathedral which pleased me a good deal'. He was however far less pleased when they switched to French posting which he condemned as 'sluggish, heavy and extortionate'. He was continually incensed by the charges and the French postillions whom he dismissed as a 'very unsatisfactory and greedy race'. One lad tried to overcharge, costing the children at full adult rate, but the future Chancellor of the Exchequer was more than a match for him. As he wrote in his diary,

He was abetted by the succeeding postillion & kept me half an hour in debate putting again & again the same question & demanding to see the children & judge of their age. At last the post master appeared & put an end to

this impudent proceeding. I promised to complain to the
Director of Posts: & on reaching Roanne about half past
eight I wrote to him accordingly.[1]

He believed that in twenty years' time there would be a railway
either through or over the Alps, and there would be no need for
arguments with postillions and barely comfortable overnight
stops. The inns and modest hotels which they chose were clean
and the food was acceptable, but there was no concession to
luxuries that would have done much to cheer the little band of
increasingly weary travellers. The first fleabite of any measure
was felt at Susa, a little west of Turin, and of this city the
lasting impression was of its vile smells and dank air. How desperately Mary's mother looked forward to the sweet balmy
breezes over the bay of Naples.

Mornings, when they were not on the move, were leisurely.
Eight-year-old Agnes was set to study Italian vocabulary by
her father while he busied himself with accounts and his diary.
Mary was left to play; her sense of fun was irrepressible as she
created jokes for the adults to share. An oddly dressed messenger who brought Mrs Gladstone's velvet dresses she insisted
was Punch, and she must shake his hand, but the purpose of
their journey was never forgotten and Mary's eyes were carefully watched. By the time that they reached Turin she was
able to leave off her bonnet and veil without any recurring
inflammation in her eye. In Genoa they found time to shop for
velvets and books, for a night at the opera and for the obligatory round of visiting churches.

They had been travelling for four weeks. No words could
describe Mrs Gladstone's relief when the last stage of the
journey was reached. Three nights in the carriage, without
taking off her clothes, had left her feeling wretchedly stiff and
at odds with herself. Arrangements were made for the carriage
to be taken by ferry, while they boarded the crowded Marseilles
boat that leapfrogged around the Mediterranean coast on its
journey down to Naples. The weather held fair and, once away
from Civita Vecchia which was the disembarking point for
Rome, there was space to stretch out and move freely.

Naples was reached at last on the morning of 10 November 1850, and they found rooms at the Hotel des Etrangers. They were looking for 'freedom, space and no stairs' and, at last, an apartment, with five bedrooms, three salons and a hall, all on the first floor, was found. William Gladstone was fluent in Italian and the irksome task of bargaining with the Neapolitans for daily supplies of milk and butter fell on him, with an uneasy feeling that he was being outsmarted.

There was snow on the top of Vesuvius. Driving rain sometimes kept them indoors, but the mild sea air seemed to be helping Mary's eyes. December was fine and bright, with a scattering of dramatic thunderstorms. Life settled into a sociable pattern among the wealthy expatriates who were wintering in Naples. Mary's mother gave tea parties, but she was desperately homesick. The highlight of her days was the arrival of the post bringing letters from home. She gave her usual Christmas-tree party on the night of St Stephen's, but it was hard work, with a fraction of the servant help she could have called upon at Hawarden. She must have thought wistfully of the Castle and the Rectory where there were thirteen indoor servants. Here she must manage with Edward and Emily, the two Hawarden servants they had brought with them. There was little space or privacy and, on top of all her burdens, she was pregnant again.

Too much was being asked of Catherine Gladstone. She had buried her little daughter, she had nursed Lavinia Glynne through childbirth and had watched her die. She was separated from her beloved sister and was worried about her brother Henry, who was mourning the loss of his wife while coping with four young children. She herself was pregnant in a foreign land. On 7 January, she began to suffer severe pains. Laudanum with white of egg was rubbed on her back, and seemed to help for a while, but the pain returned. She took twenty drops of laudanum, but there was little relief and two English doctors were called to her bedside. A miscarriage could not be avoided.

Mr Gladstone went about his business. He called on Mr James Lacaita, legal adviser to the British Legation who introduced him to the political scene. He allowed himself to be swept up in a crusade against the Italian government's unjust imprisonment of their political opponents who were kept in the most filthy, crowded and cruel gaols. Naples at this time was part of the Kingdom of the Two Sicilies, ruled by King Ferdinand. Anyone who opposed his rule, which allowed the minimum of civil liberties, was thrown into prison after a mockery of a trial. Lacaita was lucky to be held in prison for only a week. Baron Carlo Poerio, who had been briefly a Minister, was sentenced to twenty-four years' imprisonment and cast into a dungeon where he was manacled to two other political prisoners. Gladstone contrived to visit him in the Bagno di Nisida and learnt of the appalling conditions of thousands of political prisoners, treated like 'common malefactors' in these filthy dungeons. He made it his mission to bring this tyranny to the attention of the British government. Nothing could stand in his way and, as would be the case in future missions, he convinced himself that he must take what he judged to be the only moral path forward.

It so happened that Sir Stephen Glynne arrived in Naples on 7 February. He never left home without a manservant to attend to his daily needs, or a friend to ensure that he reached the right destination; yet Mr Gladstone persuaded himself that Stephen could be left in charge of his family. It was laughable to expect unworldly, unbusinesslike, unpractical Stephen to be responsible for his sister, who was still well below her usual resilience, two small girls and two servants with only a smattering of Italian between them. But just by being family he would be a great help, and it might be the tonic that his sister desperately needed. She was still worried about Mary's weak eye, which seemed to have a film over it, and she feared it might mean a permanent squint.

All haste was made for Mr Gladstone's departure. In eight days he was back in London, where he devoted all his energy towards exposing what he had discovered in Naples, much to the annoyance of the Conservatives, whose side he was supposed to be on. He wrote to Lord Aberdeen who, as ex-Foreign

Secretary, he felt would have the greatest influence in Europe, but events moved so slowly that he lost patience and published his letter as a pamphlet. The first edition sold out so quickly that a second, enlarged edition followed within a fortnight. The two letters were translated into a number of languages and caused a furore in Europe. Gladstone was elevated into a knight crusading against tyranny, a moral force to be reckoned with.

Meanwhile the little family group was journeying homeward where other problems were being addressed. Ten-year-old Willy was suffering with a painful abcess which had to be lanced. For Lent, he had given up butter for breakfast and tea; his headmaster approved of his principles and, not wanting to weaken his resolve, ordered that he should be given porter to keep up his strength. From Hagley, Lady Mary Lyttelton was seeking advice on a governess. Palm Sunday saw the family all together again at last but now the benefits of their wintering abroad seemed less obvious. William thought that his wife looked thin. Mary's eye was showing more marks of weakness. But there was one amusing result of their trip abroad; Mary had a new name. She was being called 'Naples Mary', and it seemed a delightful idea, as she would not now be confused with Aunt Mary or cousins May and Molly, although Papa fondly called her Mazie, and others did too as she grew older. To her mother she remained 'Naples Mary', certainly until well after her sixteenth birthday. It would seem that Catherine Gladstone needed to make this distinction, as if her beloved sister held undisputed first place in her heart. Her letters overflow with love as she opens her heart to her on every conceivable subject, just as if they were together with their arms around each other, as she calls her 'dearie', 'my dearest' 'my sweet' 'my love', and always signs herself 'Yr Pussy'.

So within and without the family it was 'Naples Mary'; even Garibaldi when he came to London, years later, greeted Mary as 'Maria di Napoli'. The winter in Naples had given her a niche in the family that was entirely hers, and its significance would be linked to her father's heroic stand against Italian injustice

which became part of family folklore. Over the years, Mrs Gladstone was often called upon to tell her boys about good Garibaldi and the wicked King of Naples. 'Did you really go down
into the dungeon?' six-year-old Herbert once asked his father,
and the story was told over and over again, to the children's
delight.

CHAPTER FIVE

'Half-witted' and 'wanting' (1851-9)

The 'Year of Revolutions' had been 1848; a popular revolt in France led to the establishment of a republic and sparked national uprisings in Austria, Prussia, Hungary, the German States and the Papal States. France's republic had been short-lived; Louis Napoleon's coup d'état brought in a dictatorship but Foreign Secretary Palmerston's skilful hand on British influence helped to maintain the balance of European power. William Gladstone was still a man-in-waiting; his time in the Colonial office only consuming a portion of his energies, leaving him time for reading, writing, even time for a naively romantic chase across the Continent in 1849 in search of Lady Susan Lincoln who had eloped with Lord Walpole and deserted her husband and five children. With his wife's blessing, his mission was to bring her home, save her reputation and her immortal soul. He chased across France and Italy, scattering calling cards and letters to the pregnant lady, none of which received any acknowledgement, so that he returned home after a month's exciting travel and a good dose of sight-seeing, and gave himself up to his family responsibilities.

1851-9

Mary had grown into a 'manageable' girl, so her father thought. There is a drawing of her aged about four years, a round-faced girl with large dark eyes and rosebud mouth; her thick brown hair falls in unrestrained ringlets on to bare shoulders as her dress slips negligently down her arms. All the girls were drawn at about this age; in her picture sister Helen has neatly curling short hair, dress in place, and a bright inquiring look. Agnes has a sweetly biddable expression on her heart-shaped face. Jessy looks rosy, round-cheeked, the sturdiest of all her sisters, and yet was the one to die in childhood.

The girls were schooled at home by a succession of governesses, who were also responsible for the boys' education before they were old enough to be sent away to school. Mary's achievements in the schoolroom were not considered important. She was not expected to pore over her school books; her weak eyes must be protected at all costs. Her value was weighed in negative terms – not to be a nuisance, not to get in the way, not to make demands, not to take up the adults' time. Stephen, three years her senior, had eye problems too. He was shortsighted and his weak eyes were the cause of much parental concern. There are detailed reports from his schoolmaster at boarding school, assuring that he is quite able to keep up with his class in Latin translation but 'lettering in ordinary maps is quite beyond his strength of sight and it will be quite a puzzle to convey to his mind a clear idea of what it all means'.[1]

Two younger brothers, Harry, born in 1852, and Herbert in 1854, would in turn step out of the nursery to preparatory boarding school and on to Eton, where new experiences and relationships would shape their characters. Mary did not envy them; rather she pitied them. She had heard about their fearfully difficult Latin exercises that had to be mastered before breakfast, whereas her days in the schoolroom at home with her governess were leisurely. No great demands were made on her mind, which was left untrained and undisciplined. Not surprisingly, she believed that Miss Syfret, her governess from the time she was ten until she left the schoolroom at seventeen, thought her 'half-witted'. In all that time Mary could not remember a single word of praise. She believed that she was taught to read by her friend Mary Herbert whom she had watched devouring books with such passionate delight that it dawned upon her that reading was not just a boring lesson, but a delightful means of banishing boredom.

While Miss Syfret read the bowdlerised version of Shakespeare, the girls sewed shifts for the poor and made muffatees (mufflers) for the boys at school. They made trips to the rectory to show Mrs Peake (the housekeeper) their knitting. Along with her sisters, Mary was learning to be dutiful and selfless. Mama thought that visiting the poor and sick was a necessary training for her daughters as well an important part of her own life, believing that 'one ought to be better for all this experience'.

Gladstone became Chancellor of the Exchequer for the first time in 1852; he took over from Disraeli, having destroyed his budget over four nights of turbulent debate. For the next sixteen years the Treasury belonged to these two sparring partners; after this they would alternate the role of Prime Minister. Lessons for the boys were compared to Papa's work which kept him confined to his study or busy for long days in London. Mary wished she could help in his work but knew that she could not, 'except in trying to be a good girl and I know that will please you', she wrote to him. The mere fact that the boys' schooling had to be undertaken away from home separated them profoundly from the girls. It was duty of a different order. Willy wrote in his first week at prep school that, after he had finished his morning lessons, 'I happened to put my elbow on the table and on feeling my head it was quite wet from having tried so hard to master my Latin exercise but I am happy to say that I did conquer it.' He went on to tell his parents that it was thus by perseverance he conquered difficulties and temptations. All the boys were prepared for Eton where not only would Latin and Greek be expected of them but drinking and flogging were common. Their lives led on to Oxford and Cambridge after which doors would open into politics, or the Church, or the diplomatic service, or the army. Their father's appearance at Christmas, on his first appointment as Chancellor, was brief; he arrived home in the early hours of Christmas morning and left for Windsor on 28 December for confirmation of his appointment with the Queen, and then on to Downing Street.

In March 1854, Mary was at Brighton, for the healthy sea breezes, when her mother was called to help nurse dying Lady

Glynne at Hagley. The children were left in the charge of Mrs Talbot, a formidable lady, intelligent, disciplined, forthright, rich and widowed, and a good friend to the Gladstones and the Lytteltons. Whether it was at this time or another is unclear, but she spoke out strongly in Mary's presence about the child's lack of intelligence, calling her 'wanting'. It severely dented Mary's confidence in herself, and she never forgot the remark.

Seaside holidays were shared with cousins, or with family friends, the Talbots, the Herberts or the Leicester-Warrens. Often it would be the North Wales coast, so convenient to Hawarden, but Brighton and Broadstairs were also popular and convenient for London. Lady Glynne died in May, and in August it was time to take the sea air again. This time it was Broadstairs with their good friends the Herberts; cholera was sweeping through the undrained slums of London and the city was no place for children, if you were fortunate enough to have the ways and means to move out.

William Gladstone was unable to get away from Downing Street so his wife wrote to tell him what she had arranged: 'decided upon taking at once one of the houses instead of the two in the best situation, we can just cram in by taking one room for the two undermaids and I am rather proud of this decision. Six pounds a week instead of £10. I write to Mrs Hampton [housekeeper at Hawarden] to send the two under-maids and Thomas.'[2] The children usually shared beds, some-times with each other, sometimes with a nurse.

In the summer of 1854, political minds were focused abroad: it was fear of Russian expansion, especially towards the Medi-terranean, and a desire to uphold the declining Turkish empire as a barrier to this expansion that propelled Britain into the Crimean War. Mary's parents were prepared for war but her father knew, as he explained to his wife, 'I fear it will swallow up everything good and useful' and he warned her that the full horror was as yet unknown. Catherine Gladstone had four cousins in the British army and her two Neville cousins, Grey and Henry, died in the Crimea. She helped as best she could, writing letters, sending parcels, keeping abreast of all news and thoroughly enjoying being at the centre of events.

By January 1855 there were 12 000 men in hospital and only 11 000 in the camp at Scutari and still the shiploads came pouring in. Florence Nightingale wrote that it was 'calamity unparalleled in the history of calamity'. Through the winter months, the fury in England had been growing as the lists of casualties grew and dispatches revealed the depth of misman-agement: 'The men who had stormed the heights at Alma, charged with the Light Brigade at Balaclava, fought the grim battle against overwhelming odds in the fog at Inkermann, had perished of hunger and neglect. Even the horses that had taken part in the Charge of the Light Brigade had starved to death.[3]

The crisis of war destroyed the coalition government; Lord Aberdeen resigned and Lord Palmerston became Prime Min-ister. William Gladstone joined the new government but resigned after only three weeks, wholly supported by his wife who wrote to her sister that 'whatever William decides will be right'. The family sought the fresh mountain air and the sea breezes of Pen-maenmawr on the North Wales coast. Here they heard news of the fall of Sebastol, followed by negotiations for peace, which resulted in the Treaty of Paris in the spring of 1856.

Home life followed its usual peripatetic pattern with trips to Hagley, London, and St Leonard's on the Sussex coast for the winter months, sharing the house that the Lytteltons had taken. They lived in the most cramped conditions with nurse, nanny and maids as well as constant changes in numbers. The girls were taken on trips to London for parties and lessons in music, dancing and Italian. Those left behind were often nurs-ing coughs, colds and sore throats, inevitable when bedrooms and beds were shared. Mary was there in April, when they all went down with scarlet fever. She was confined to the house and thus missed the Queen's Ball that Agnes, Helen, Lucy and Lavinia attended, all dressed in matching 'tartalatane frocks, trimmed with three skirts with wire ruches twined round with some pretty pink trimmings'. White satin shoes and silk stockings completed their attire. Mary may not have minded missing this grand affair as she set little store by pretty clothes and was much happier romping with the boys.

Her mother was not allowed to visit those in quarantine but she used to come each morning and 'regardless of onlookers, dance in front of our windows. I can see her now as we watched, fascinated, every movement full of gaiety and grace'. Catherine Gladstone was quite without inhibitions. Her only rule in life seemed to be that life should not be dull. As soon as she entered a room, people were aware of her presence: 'By the magic touch of her personality she woke them up, made them laugh or sing or dance. She set things going; she made things happen; she got things done.' She had boundless energy, always flying at top speed and leaving a trail of havoc behind her. Many years later, Mary remembered that her mother's daily path to church could always be traced by the letters strewn along the way which she had discarded as she read: 'Explanations, wordiness, "trolls", bored and bothered her.' She left out words or telescoped phrases to such an extent that often only her nearest and dearest could understand her. A private language had evolved in the Glynne family and been brought to a fine art by the two Glynne sisters, who passed it on to the next generation. It gave an exclusivity to their clan; a privacy and a barrier beyond which the outside world could not pass.

Lord George Lyttelton gathered together all their words and expressions and published them privately as the *Glynnese Glossary*, thus providing a dictionary for friends and relatives. He believed that Catherine Gladstone was the chief authority, 'the great Queen of Glynnese', so it is not surprising that Mary's vocabulary came to be sprinkled with Glynnese, not only in conversations but in diaries and letters. Three of her favourite expressions were 'maukin', which covered anyone unknown to her and probably of no importance, 'phantod', pronounced with the 'p' and 'h' given equal weight and meaning stupid or irrational, and 'bathing-feel' which aptly described that palpitating state before any formidable moment, like the fall into the arms of the bathing-woman inside Victorian bathing machines.

Lyttelton babies continued to arrive every year. After 'the tiny eleventh' was born, Dr Locock warned the exhausted mother that another pregnancy would endanger her life; that her heart was weakened from the many confinements. Yet it would seem that Lord Lyttelton was not similarly warned; despite being a man, he was in many ways the weaker partner. The worst news of his wife's declining health was kept from him. Catherine Gladstone was most anxious, and told her sister that her duty to her eleven children should outweigh all other considerations. She herself had stopped procreating three years ago, when she was forty-two, after eight healthy babies and one miscarriage. When she heard of yet another pregnancy, she wrote to her husband, 'Alas, there is a secret at Hagley which has come upon me quite as a blow; what do you think of Number Twelve upon the way?'

Mary was ten when Aunt Mary died, six months after the birth of Alfred. It had seemed that against all odds she would survive but her heart, weakened by years of childbearing, faltered and faded. When the end was near, each child, in its nightgown, was brought to the bedside for a final goodbye. William Gladstone thought she seemed like one 'preparing for an ordinary journey', but forty-three-year-old Mary Lyttelton knew it was not so; she charged him to take great care of his wife 'for it will make a great change to her and after a time she will feel it more.'

Mary was at Hawarden with her sisters when a long letter arrived from their father explaining that Aunt Mary had 'gone to a better and happier place'. He told them that she had said goodbye to each of their cousins in turn and 'you will never see her more in this world'. Both families talked freely about their sadness and loss. Victorian deathbed scenes might seem today to be excessively morbid and sentimental, but religion was as much a part of their everyday life as the reality of death.

Lucy, in her diary, tried to find comfort in the thought that her mother was now 'with Christ which is far better, and all tears wiped away; and the calm of Paradise, and the arms of God'. Lord Lyttelton asked the older children and close relatives to write down their memories of Mary's final days, which became known as *The Hagley Record*. He believed it would help them in their own spiritual preparation for the next world, where they would be held to account for their life's actions.

Years later, Mary described the loss to her mother of her most dearly loved sister as a life-long wound, 'one of those heart-wrenching sorrows from which, in this world, there is no recovery'.

It was by no means Mary's first close experience of death. She was four when she was taken, with Agnes and Stephen, down the cold, damp stone steps into the family vault under the church among the tall fir trees on the Fasque estate. Her grandfather was laid to rest with his wife and daughter and close to Mary's sister Jessy who had died the previous year.

When she was six, her five-year-old cousin Katie Glynne, whose mother had died in childbirth two years earlier, died at the rectory. And in that same year her uncles Grey and Henry Neville, were killed in the Crimean War. Not surprisingly, Mary would wake in the night from nightmares and creep into her mother's bed, seeking her loving presence. It must have seemed to her that adults always wore black with an aura of musty crape. The Victorians had an elaborate dress code of mourning. The social importance of the dead was marked by the length of time of mourning and the clothes and accessories that were worn. Widows wore the deepest mourning and for the longest time, but for parents and children a full year was expected. Twelve months after her sister's death, Mrs Gladstone wrote to Lucy that she might alter her mourning clothes, and that Meriel 'might have the black lace put upon her thick black scarf, her black silk gown should be carefully put by in cases of slight mourning in November.'

A month after the funeral came Lucy's sixteenth birthday; Mary's mother strove to lessen the grief by telling her to think of her mother's face 'as only veiled and from you for a time, think of her as far more beautiful without spot before the throne of God'. She wrote, 'I thought that there was nothing you would love so well upon your birthday as this precious lock with its beautiful tint and curl and so here it is for you to look at whenever you like independent of the little locket which is ordered for your Papa's present to you but it is not quite finished yet.'[4] Fourteen-year-old Charles, the eldest, had been urged to tell Aunt Pussy anything, as he would his own mother. Spencer, closest to Mary in age, seemed to be the most in need of special comfort, perhaps because he felt it most difficult to express that need. After four years, Mrs Gladstone was still concerned that he required 'great care and looking to and more than Eton can give', but she urged Lucy, 'don't fuss your Dad for there is nothing to do'. This might seem strange advice to us today when we are accustomed to counsellors who give help at times of grief and depression. The Victorians were expected to accept their lot and look to the next world for their reward.

Mary was used to the absence of her parents, and now she had even less of their attention. She became the one in the family to keep everyone informed of what everyone else was doing. Letters to 'my own darling Mama' tell of fun and games with her Glynne cousins, 'Nora came today. She will sleep in the Tower room', or of times spent with uncles; 'We made a big fire in the old Castle and roasted crab apples', 'tea at the Rectory, Uncle Henry and Uncle Stephen came to watch charades, we only had time for one and "Pilgrim" was the word'; 'tell Agnes that Stephy took her canary out of its cage, it flew on to Lena's shoulder and then hopped away on to Stephy's hand', 'Stephy and I are digging a hole as deep as Stephy', 'there is a great rat caught in Willy's rat trap. We only played at football today as it was frosty.'

When Hawarden Church was destroyed by fire in October 1857, Mary kept all those who were away from home up to date on the news. The fire was discovered in the night; the governess Miss Syfret woke the girls and led them to the safe flat section of the castle to watch the flames leaping high into the sky. The fire engine raced from Chester. The roof collapsed, and charred remains of beams and smouldering ashes lay around while the air was filled with acrid smoke. The pew seats were carried out. The rector, Uncle Henry, had climbed in through a window and saved the parish registers. The organ was carried out and then it was discovered that the fire had been started deliberately. The poor-box had been broken open and robbed, but the chest that held the church plate was still locked. For months, the night's activities were the sole topic of conversation in the village. Mary watched the rebuilding of the church and kept all members of the family informed.

William Gladstone, a Homeric scholar and lover of Greece, had been appointed Lord High Commissioner Extraordinary to the Ionian Islands, his task being to report upon the future of the islands, whether they should remain British or whether they should unite with the newly independent Greece. He was out of office and although many of his colleagues thought he had made an unwise decision in accepting the position, it had been as much for his wife's sake as for his own. He believed it would provide a welcome diversion after her sister's death and help to restore her health and spirits. In November 1858, Mary's parents and sixteen-year-old Agnes set off via Dresden, Prague and Vienna for Corfu; included in the party were Arthur Gordon, twenty-nine-year-old son of Lord Aberdeen, as aide de camp to Gladstone, and James Lacaita, his friend from their winter in Naples and now a professor at King's College, London. Their arrival aboard HMS *Terrible* at Corfu was greeted by the British officers of the small garrison, the local aristocracy and the Bishop of the Eastern Orthodox Church; here they settled until March of the following year. While they were away from home it was Mary's task to keep up the letter-writing from Hawarden; she wrote to tell them that the restoration of St Deiniol's Church was almost complete and soon there would be a new spire.

In January 1863 Harry and Herbert went off to boarding school. The two had grown quite beyond Miss Syfret's control. Mama had hoped that a tutor could be found so that they could remain at home but Papa was not to be persuaded that they should be treated differently from their brothers. Nothing could have prepared them for the shattering change from indulgence to discipline. Their headmaster assured Mrs Gladstone that they settled down at once, although he pointed out that it was obvious they were not used to helping themselves. How much did she know of the beatings from straps and riding whips? Herbert said that they never complained. The headmaster wrote that at first 'Harry's tears lived very near his eyelids' and it was not long before he was complaining that

Herbert was 'a canny little thing' who told 'direct falsehoods' while Harry 'could talk himself into lies by too much talk and so must be restricted to yes/no answers.'

Mary at home could always be relied on for letters, and the boys confided their miseries to her. Herbert told her that there was no appeal to reason and honour which was how their father dealt with their pranks, and so they found ways to retaliate against their harsh treatment. She was let into the secret of what they did with the earwigs that they collected from old wooden posts. 'With twigs we raked these out into the tin cap-boxes. We emptied the contents in the master's private room. I remember putting a boxful into his sister-in-law's workbox.'[5]

She waited eagerly for the school holidays. Gladstone energies needed outdoor pursuits whatever the weather, and her parents set a good example by their daily early morning walk down the mile-long drive to church before breakfast. The children were free to roam out of doors. Harry, the youngest, described them all as 'wild as hawks'. For their games they 'purloined planks from the timber-yard, straw from the stables, fruit from the kitchen-garden, candle-ends from the pantry, anything we could lay our hands on from the kitchen. After the kitchen garden was locked up it was our happy hunting-ground.'[6] Woodcutting became a family recreation and Mary joined in with her brothers. Her father was handicapped by the loss of a finger on his left hand in a shooting accident before she was born. What he had lost in expertise he made up for in energy, and trees were cut down to ground level wherever possible. He was very annoyed by a *Punch* cartoon that showed him cutting trees a foot or two above the ground, a practice he considered uneconomical and untidy.

Political life was, and is, a chancy business. When Mary was seven, her father lost office and remained out of the government for four years. Then she could be sure to find him in his study, and he would turn from his paper-piled desk to give himself utterly to his children. These times were madly gleeful, when high spirits could burst forth from adult bounds. He would give them rides on his foot, singing loudly, 'Ride a cock-horse to

Banbury Cross'. He would get down on his knees and carry four children at once on his back round the room, while they held on for dear life. He would open one of his desk drawers and show them his neatly coiled bits of string, his stamp edgings, his half sheets of notepaper which he called 'orts', these little economies which became childish treasures. He never talked down to them, or treated them as other than his equals. Mary was never in awe of him: 'Indeed, we treated him with scant respect; argued across him while he was talking; even contradicted him.' Guests at Hawarden were amazed at the freedom from criticism that reigned in the family circle, and shocked when, at family meals, the arguments grew louder and noisier until a child's accusation of 'A lie!' would be flung at their father. The shock of the guests was part of the family fun, and everyone then relaxed and shared the joke. Many years later Herbert wrote that these times that his father spent at Hawarden 'give the truest understanding of him as a man'.

Mrs Gladstone seems to have been especially successful at what was described by mutual friends as 'humanising William Gladstone'. He had learnt to dance to her rhythm, as he did on the morning when she told him the news that the cook from her convalescent home was to be married. Apparently he took no notice, as he reached for a piece of paper and began to write. 'Oh of course you are too full of Homer and your old gods and goddesses to care – stupid of me!' burst out his wife. He went on writing, and then he handed her the piece of poetic nonsense below, saying 'There! That's all I can do, your information was so very scanty.'

The Cook and The Captain
The Cook and the Captain determined one day,
When worthy Miss Simmons was out of the way,
On splicing together a life and a life,
The one as a husband, the other as wife –
Fol de rol, tol de rol, fol de rol la,

The Captain a subaltern officer made,
But the Cook! she was monarch of all she surveyed –

So how could they hit it the marrying day,
If she was to order and he to obey?
Fol de rol, tol de rol, fol de rol la.

Miss Simmons came home and she shouted, oh dear!
What riot is this? What the d——— is here?
If the Cook and the Captain will not be quiescent,
How can I expect it from each convalescent?
Fol de rol, tol de rol, fol de rol la.

And then followed one of their special moments of joy, which the children loved to watch, as they stood on the hearth rug with their arms around each other, swaying as they sang, 'A ragamuffin husband and a rantipoling wife, we'll fiddle it and scrape it through the ups and downs of life ...'.[6]

By 1859 the political pendulum had swung again in Gladstone's favour and he became Chancellor again under Lord Palmerston, a post he held for the next seven years but always, he said, with a letter of resignation in his wallet at every Cabinet meeting. He was in constant battle with the PM over expenditure; as Chancellor he strove for a balance between direct and indirect taxation. He believed that the more people who were made to pay income tax, the greater would be the demand for less expenditure. Indirect taxation fell mainly on the working classes who had no vote, while direct taxes were paid chiefly by the middle and propertied classes who were enfranchised. He saw that franchise should be related to taxation and, as the working man contributed almost half of the national income and, by indirect taxation, about a third of the government's revenue, there was a need to widen the electorate; his budgets were a balancing feat until the second Reform Act of 1867.

CHAPTER SIX

'Rigged, figged and launched into society' (1864–6)

February 1864: time for sixteen-year-old Mary to move out of the classroom and into society. As she journeyed to London at the start of the new parliamentary term, she knew it was going to be different this time. 'Oh! Horrid, horrid London', she sighed. She would far rather be at Hawarden running free in the park or walking down the village street to the church or rectory. In her letters to Lavinia, she often complains to 'dearest Winny' of the dullness of London life as she longs for the weeks to pass until she will be back at Hawarden, 'greater bliss to me than anyone can tell'.

On Easter Sunday she wore her first bonnet, and it helped her thoughts from straying homewards. She had her first watch given to her by her father. As she walked through the city streets, she was obsessed by her new possession. 'Each person that sees me, will say to himself – That girl has got a watch, only think, I thought, each person will think I have only just this moment looked at it.'

There were many 'firsts' this springtime but riding in Rotten Row was not one of them, for the Gladstones had their own stables; riding was considered a healthy and social exercise. The sun was shining as Mary rode on her pony, Fancy. By her side was William, now twenty-five and at a loose end. His Oxford student days had ended with a second-class degree in Greats and a third in Law and History, a disappointment that Papa was struggling to balance with his son's obvious virtues of quiet perseverance and amiability. William had never had his father's energy and ambition, and never would.

Fancy kicked and reared, threw Mary off her guard and tossed her in the mud. She was unharmed and jumped to her feet, caught the pony, and went on with the ride. Many young misses would have been mortified by having their smart clothes muddied and dishevelled, and would have dissolved in tears. Not so Mary, who was not even embarrassed on meeting the Queen in her carriage; she even had enough composure to notice that the Queen looked 'very dear, but rather thinner and paler'. Her Majesty, who was making her first appearance in London since Prince Albert's death, had reluctantly come out of seclusion to attend the christening of the Prince and Princess of Wales' first son.

Mr Gladstone was Chancellor of the Exchequer, but the family were not living in Downing Street. In 1852, when he had reached this high office for the first time, he and Mrs Gladstone had been only too pleased to live 'above the shop'. He had found time to look over the accommodation of No. 12 (later renumbered to 11) Downing Street and reported:

> There is now only one drawing room but a large and *very pretty* room newly done up and looking out over the Park. The dining room rather small but good and comfortable. The living rooms concentrated on the first floor, and all the ground floor appropriated as my office. The bedrooms numerous and airy. The servants' accommodation above stairs good. Below fair: the servants' hall very small. There are official stables – nearer than ours at No. 6, though not very near. The access to the Park is easy and private, through a garden nominally belonging to the First Lord of the Treasury.[1]

Most of the first floor was furnished by the State and, as this was the most expensive part, it was good news. Mrs Gladstone had been well pleased with the arrangements. All that remained to arrange was the housing of his books, the furniture that would be left by Disraeli, and his Chancellor's robes. The last and, you might suppose, smallest item blew up into a famous row and ended with Disraeli keeping his robes and Mr Gladstone having a new set made. He had spent his forty-third birthday working on his first budget, 'the most crowded and hurried birthday that I have ever had' he excitedly wrote to his wife. 'Only think of my sitting at a political dinner *between* Lords Aberdeen and Palmerston and everybody perfectly disembarrassed and at ease.'[2] He had been about to embark on the most satisfying years of his political life, scaling the pinnacles of power as the most dominant Chancellor of the Exchequer of the century and creating, singlehandedly, the Ministry of Finance.

The family had moved into Downing Street but their stay had only lasted for two years. When Mary's father became Chancellor again in 1859, Downing Street was kept for office hours only; the accommodation was not considered suitable with so many young Gladstone and Lyttelton adults, and they now had a spacious and convenient London home at No. 11 Carlton House Terrace.

One of Mary's first ordeals was to be presented to Garibaldi who had arrived in London to a tumultuous welcome from thousands of people and was dining with her parents and guests. He greeted her kindly as 'Maria di Napoli' but she felt uncomfortable in her fine clothes and out of place among 'such swells'. She was happy to get by with the minimum of attention to her appearance. Her clothes have been described as unfashionable and certainly Mrs Gladstone did not encourage her daughters to indulge in extravagant dressing or the latest fashions, which used the most luxurious materials and elaborate decoration. Crinolines were being discarded for skirts with slim, straight, apron-like fronts around which cascaded layers of frills and flounces. Mary's mother engaged a Hawarden dressmaker to make all her dresses and she would ask for a spare bodice to each skirt; it was the kind of economy she delighted in and her daughters followed her example.

But now there was a need for shopping expeditions, in which Mary was included, and eight silk gowns and two muslin shawls were chosen for Lucy's trousseau. Lucy Lyttelton was to marry Lord Frederick Cavendish, younger son of the Duke of Devonshire, and Mary was to be one of the bridesmaids, along with sister Helen and cousins Lavinia and May.

The engagement was very much to the liking of Mrs Gladstone who had faintly hoped that Agnes might catch Lord Frederick's eye, but she soon regarded the match as a personal triumph, and was not Lucy more like herself than any of her daughters? Lucy had captured one of the most eminent bachelors of a leading Whig family with great estates at Chatsworth, Hardwick, Bolton Abbey and Holker. Lord Frederick was not heir to these estates but his elder brother Lord Hartington seemed unlikely to marry. Of course, arranged marriages were no longer acceptable, and the attachment must be romantic but, once romance was in the air, parental approval was essential.

Lord Frederick had been warmly welcomed at Hawarden by Mr and Mrs Gladstone but, it must be said, with less enthusiasm at Hagley. Lord Lyttelton needed to be reassured that Lord Frederick's religious views were not too liberal. Lady Sarah Lyttelton, Lucy's grandmother, expressed her anxiety when she wrote, 'People do slide downhill so awfully when they have begun to doubt or cavil.' Twenty-two-year-old Lucy loved her handsome Freddy, and she was convinced that he measured up to her strong sense of duty and her even stronger religious convictions. Meeting the Cavendish family and household had been a great ordeal for her. 'Be at my ease I cannot,' she had written in her diary after her first visit, and even two years after the wedding, Lavinia observed that Lucy was still 'rather on pins and needles with the Duke' who was a serious, scholarly, silent man. Lucy was full of youthful vitality and tried to bring with her a little of the sunshine from her chattering, boisterous, fun-loving home.

The wedding was a grand affair at Westminster Abbey on 7 June 1864. A few weeks later, most conveniently, Mary was able to wear her bridesmaid's frock again, at the Duke of Sutherland's party at Chiswick House. Alas, it was torn to pieces when she enjoyed a romp with Lord Edward Cavendish, Freddy's younger brother. The Prince and Princess of Wales were among the guests, and in the country dancing, Mary had to take the Prince's hand, a moment of such importance that it had to be recorded in her diary. Gladstones and Lyttel-tons had met and mingled with the royal children throughout their growing years. Mary had taken turns with the others at attending the royal birthday parties and, when she was eleven, her turn had come to go to a fancy-dress party at Buckingham Palace. Dressed as an Albanian peasant, she had led the country dancing with George Herbert; Queen Victoria had seen them getting into a real muddle and had come to their aid, holding their hands and showing them how to pirouette.

Mr and Mrs Gladstone had been frequent guests at Windsor Castle until the sudden death of Prince Albert in December 1861 had plunged the royal atmosphere from gaiety to gloom. Princess Alexandra was glad of Mrs Gladstone's company, enjoying her easy informality and unstuffy way with her children. She found it very refreshing after the Queen's candidly critical interference and her disapproval of her son and his friends, whom she called 'the Marlborough House set'. When the Princess of Wales' second son was born in June 1865, Mary was taken to see the 'little darling princes' and she thought Prince Eddy adorable at eighteen months, as he played with his mother's boots. Her favourite word for the little ones was 'ducks', an affectionate term that pays scant regard to their royal status.

Presentation at court marked a young girl's official entry into society. Mary's turn came in March 1865, only a few weeks after she had said goodbye to her governess Miss Syfret. It seemed a brief and businesslike affair, not as awful as she had expected. She made eight curtsies and the Princess of Wales shook her hand. Now she was, in Lucy's words, 'rigged, figged and launched'. An entry in *The Queen* of March 1870, covering the first court event, pays particular attention to the ladies' attire; Mrs Gladstone wears, 'Train trimmed with lace, white satin petticoat trimmed with flounces of Brussels lace; bodice of blue velvet. Head-dress, diamond tiara and necklace. Miss Mary Gladstone – train of pink silk, trimmed with white tulle, pink bows and silver wheat, white net skirts with bouillonne and flounces, looped up with pink satin bows and silver wheat. Miss Helen Gladstone – the same.'[3] The list of fashionably dressed ladies is long and the Gladstones are placed last, as if of minor importance.

Mary's first ball seems to have been a disappointment. She was not allowed to waltz and she moaned in her diary that there were only five square dances. Now there were strict rules to be observed. A girl must not dance more than three dances with the same partner, or sit out a dance with a young man. Quadrilles and reels could be enjoyed, but the seductive rhythms of the waltz were considered unsuitable for those of impressionable years. There were brief moments of compensation, like the delicious drive home from a ball in an open carriage in the early hours of the morning, but she discovered that dinner parties could be a tedious bore; it all depended on one's partner. 'To dinner hooked to a muscular Christian in the shape of a hunting parson whose conversation is strictly limited to sporting subjects and the aristocracy' was one diary entry and, a little later, at a big, smart and 'hideously dull' dinner she was handed in by a youth 'of whom I found no clue in spite of laborious research'.

'Maukin' became her favourite word to describe a dull, nondescript person, usually male. Oh, for the boisterous, carefree days of Hawarden and Hagley when she was released from what Lucy called 'dressums, ballums, fidgetums and seasonums'. She much preferred the rough and tumble of boys' company, sharing their jokes and escapades. In a typical letter to Harry at Eton she tells him, 'It has been so awfully hot that some of us have been roasted alive and been served up for dinner for those who escaped being boiled. Goodbye. I have emptied my brain of everything there is in it – you see my usual eloquence has been scorched and burnt out by the heat of the sun'.[4]

She was rescued from the tedium of social occasions by attendance at the House of Commons, and London ceased to be dull. The Parliamentary day did not begin until 4.30 p.m. Everyone adjourned for dinner between 7 and 7.30, so that the major debates were played out late at night, and often ended at around 2 a.m. The eighty-six steps to the Ladies Gallery became a familiar climb to her. A small room holding only twenty-four seats had been partitioned off from the Strangers Gallery and was screened from the debating chamber by heavy

brass grilles, designed by Hardman, Birmingham button man-
ufacturer and friend of Pugin, the Victorian architect whose
Gothic churches led to the recovery of all forms of arts and
crafts. This accommodation for the ladies was accepted as
proper although one MP described the new gallery as being
'between a birdcage and a tea caddy' and Lord Brougham
had declared at its opening in 1852 that 'the ladies would be
better employed in almost any other way than in attending
parliamentary debates.'

His views were given scant attention by Mrs Gladstone, who
made the gallery a lively, sociable place. 'I found myself nearly
upon Lady John Russell's lap, with Lady Palmerston and other
wives near. Funny, we began talking, though before unac-
quainted and I told her my husband was to answer hers, which
news she received with the greatest interest.'[5] They tolerated
the abominable grating that distorted the voices so that
rhetorical declamations were lost in ringing echoes. They suffered the unpleasant and unhealthy river smells that wafted
upwards on hot steamy days. What mattered was the performances on the floor of the House; the reputation of their loved
ones. Over the years, Mrs Gladstone polished the dull brass
grille to burnished gold by her gloved hand as she pressed
her face eagerly close. The Ladies Gallery was an exclusive club
that Mary entered naturally, knowing there would always be
family or friends there. It was a club that closed abruptly in
1888 because of 'rowdy behaviour' by the ladies who were
shouting their support for the votes for women campaign,
and it did not reopen until 1909 when ladies had to sign an
undertaking to be of good behaviour; the grilles remained
until 1918.

On 4 July 1864 Mary stayed for five hours in the House, with
sister Agnes by her side, to listen to Disraeli speaking for nearly
three hours, followed by her father whose speech was half as
long. She could hardly wait to tell Lavinia, 'The first was simply
full of stuff and nonsense, ungentlemanlike, and really incon-
sistent. The second was splendid. They say it was his best speech,
and he did look so grand and noble when he got up and spoke,
now with indignation, now with calmest contempt.'[6]

She thought that Dizzy got the thrashing he deserved and she was back again a few days later for six hours but, along with the other visitors, she was turned out for the division, which she thought was the most exciting part. Back home at Carlton House Terrace she asked to be awakened when the result was known and at 3 a.m. she was given the good news that the government had a majority of 18. 'Hurrah, hurrah!' her diary exults, 'And it's mostly owing to Papa's beautiful speech on Monday.' This Schleswig–Holstein debate had not exactly gripped the nation's imagination but it was the drama that appealed to Mary, with her father playing the hero's part.

Mr Gladstone's budgets were set in spring. Political and social encounters intertwined at the political breakfasts that were a feature of life at Carlton House Terrace. Mary attended her first a few days before her first ball. She noted in her diary that these breakfast parties had been started by a Mr Samuel Rogers. He was probably the poet and art connoisseur, a man of independent means and generous reputation in the early 1800s. The Gladstone breakfasts ran from 10 a.m. until midday, or thereabouts, and were more like early luncheon parties with meat dishes and wine being served. Guests sat at two round tables in the drawing room that looked across St James' Park to Horseguards Parade. On the morning of her father's ninth Budget, Mary joined the adult company but the occasion does not appear to have been a great success for her. She was led to observe that 'often the most brilliant components made the dullest breakfasts and vice versa'.

February 1866 heralded in a fresh Parliamentary session; Lord Palmerston had died during the long recess and now Lord John Russell was Prime Minister, with Gladstone as his Chancellor and his Commons spokesman. For Mary, social events were eclipsed by the political. She watched the Queen go by in her carriage for the State Opening and she shared in the people's muted approval, which she called 'a kind of low murmur of emotion' rather than a full-throated cheer. She was in the House to watch the election of the new Speaker; the ceremony of leading him to his chair she declared 'rather absurd'. The first item on the political agenda was the twentieth

Coercion Bill, a sad reflection on the miserable inability of politicians to understand and to govern Ireland, but the main preoccupation of all shades of political opinion was the reform of the voting system. As John Morley wrote in his biography of Gladstone, reform was the fighting question 'and fighting questions absorb a legislature'.

As the spring evenings lengthened, Mary went regularly to the House to watch her father stand up as the champion of the working classes. He had been asked to introduce the Representation of the People Bill which had been drawn up to bring more working men on to the electoral roll. The Tory party and a considerable number of Liberals were utterly opposed to extending the franchise, whereas all the leaders were committed. A Reform Bill was being pushed through an anti-reform parliament. On 27 April Mr Gladstone spoke for two and a half hours and Mary was glued to her seat as she absorbed what she declared was one of his greatest speeches. It was a scene of frantic excitement; her father warned his fellow-politicians:

> You cannot fight against the future. Time is on our side. The great social forces which move onwards in their might and majesty, and which the tumult of our debate does not for a moment impede or disturb – those great social forces are against you; they are marshalled on our side; and the banner which we now carry in this fight, though perhaps at some moment it may droop over our sinking heads, yet it soon will float in the eye of Heaven, and it will be borne by the firm hands of the united people of the three kingdoms, perhaps not to an easy, but to a certain and to a not far distant victory.'[7]

This was the culmination of eight nights of debate; a drama unfolding in gestures and passions as much as in words with Gladstone centre stage, man and cause inseparable. 'Helen and I nearly died of excitement,' Mary wrote in her diary, 'and so absorbed were we in the splendour of the speech that we gave no thought to Division. The Government was saved by five votes. It was four o'clock a.m. when we entered Palace Yard.

A small crowd cheered the Reformers. On the Duke of York's steps we met Papa, Willy, Freddy and Lord Edward [Cavendish], in various conditions of thrilling excitement.'

The narrow victory was short-lived. For two months ideas, opinions and proposals floated in the air until they were defeated in an Opposition motion. There followed a week of agitated excitement as rumour fed on rumour. The Queen was, as usual, at Balmoral, and resignation, dissolution or a vote of no confidence were all options under review for the present Government. Nothing could be decided without the Queen's presence. The Cabinet eventually decided to resign and not to seek a dissolution, which would lead to a general election. Mary was in the House to hear her father's final speech to the House, 'most calm and dignified', in contrast to the cheering, milling crowds outside.

On 28 June there was a huge Reform Meeting in Trafalgar Square, and thousands marched from the meeting to the chant of 'Gladstone and Liberty'. Mary's father, hero of the working classes, was away, but those who were at home went on to the balcony and were received by the cheering crowds that stretched as far as Pall Mall. *The Times*, unhappy with Gladstone's appeal to the masses, reported that 'the ladies of Mr Gladstone's family accepted the honour of an ovation on Wednesday evening from persons of the lowest class.'

On 6 July Gladstone took his seat on the Opposition benches for the first time for fifteen years, but he was not downcast, for he believed that the government's resignation was an important and necessary step: 'In the hour of defeat I have a presentiment of victory.' A summer of unrest followed; the railings at Hyde Park were torn down when the gates were found to be closed against a Reform Rally. This only incited the rough element in the crowds to violence. The Life Guards were called out, which was truly absurd, Lucy thought, 'as they did nothing whatever and the people dispersed in time after some knocks had been exchanged'. Lord Derby and Disraeli took over the reins of government and the Lytteltons and Gladstones moved out of London in search of fresh air and relaxation.

Mary's induction into politics had been highly entertaining and often thrilling. She had seen history in the making; she had watched her father fighting for a just cause with no thought of surrender, and she had shared in his moments of victory and defeat. How could parties and balls compare with these dramas? Nevertheless, she must follow a programme of meeting the right people, with an eye to her future role as somebody's wife. As Queen Victoria advised her eldest daughter, 'Being married gives one one's position, which nothing else can.'

CHAPTER SEVEN

Charities, country houses and Continental polish (1864—8)

*M*rs Gladstone was a working wife in ways that were socially acceptable and praiseworthy by Victorian standards; indeed many times her enthusiasm for her charities was considered too energetic and her priorities a little unbalanced. Mildness and meekness were desirable qualities for Victorian ladies, whereas she valued resourcefulness and independence more highly. Her mother, Lady Glynne had told her when she was nineteen that, 'A little roughing it without a maid makes one both handy and independent' and she probably said the same thing many times to her own daughters but, more importantly, she taught by example.

Mary's father was Chancellor of the Exchequer through the years of the American Civil War. John Morley, in his *Life of Gladstone Volume 2* writes:

> Of this immense conflict Mr Gladstone, like most of the leading statesmen of the time, and like the majority of his countrymen, failed to take the true measure. The error that lay at the root of our English misconception is now clear. We applied ordinary political maxims to what was not merely a political contest, but a social revolution. Without scrutiny of the cardinal realities beneath, we discussed it like some superficial conflict in our old world about boundaries, successions, territorial partitions, dynastic preponderance.

The Lancashire cotton towns suffered great hardships from unemployment as a result of the Northern blockade of the ports of the Southern States from which cotton had been exported to Lancashire looms. Relief committees were set up doling out charity to destitute cotton workers. By the autumn of 1862, when the crisis was at its height, Mrs Gladstone discovered that forty-nine mills had closed and that the number of unemployed exceeded 17 000. She set up soup kitchens in Blackburn, feeding a thousand a day, and, as the Chancellor's wife, she could pull strings very effectively. One small child is said to have taken home the story, 'Mother, who do you think we have had in the school today? The Government's wife.'

She hit upon a plan to bring unemployed factory workers to Hawarden. Six men were put to build roads and footpaths on the estate and ten girls to domestic service; in 1862 the men's wages were twelve shillings a week. The girls were housed in a large refurbished building within the castle grounds and when their domestic training was complete, Mrs Gladstone worked tirelessly to find them positions among her wide circle of friends and acquaintances. The Duke of Argyle wrote to say he would be happy to take a Hawarden-trained girl in one of his houses, 'where she will be in very good and kind care of an excellent housekeeper and a very comfortable rather old housemaid.' She organised a concert at Hawarden and the factory girls in shawls wrung the hearts of the audience and loosened their pursestrings with their singing of 'Hard Times'. She wrote countless letters to newspapers and to anyone she thought might help, and was even bold enough to keep the Queen informed of the condition of the poverty-stricken Lancashire families. Fourteen-year-old Mary helped to sort out the mountains of old clothes collected for the Lancashire people and looked for ways to be useful, but her mother turned first to Lucy whose star shone so brightly that there were times when Mary felt her own worth was almost extinguished.

In the summer of 1862, Mrs Gladstone joined her husband on a tour of Lancashire and the North-East, and both were welcomed by cheering crowds of working people. The Chancellor of the Exchequer was making himself known as a national figure who understood their daily lives. It was in Newcastle that he made his claim that the southern Confederate leaders had made an army, were well on the way to making a navy and 'they have made what is more than either, they have made a nation'. It was not the first and certainly not the last of his ill-judged statements; however, it did him no long-term damage. Meanwhile, Mrs Gladstone continued her tireless efforts in a variety of new charitable enterprises, raising money and forming committees. In 1864 the Newport Market Refuge was founded as a night refuge for the homeless and street beggars; a hundred beds were provided, iron rods holding bedding strips of coconut matting. There were washing facilities, and bread and coffee night and morning. An industrial school was opened and *The Times* carried an article that raised over £3000; the name of Gladstone helping in the purchase of the building's lease for £2000.

Many years later, when Mary wrote a book about her mother's life, she opened with this scene that captures her very essence, 'Who is that lady, and what is she doing?' The lady in question was Mrs Gladstone; she was carrying babies rolled up in blankets from the London Hospital, at the time of the virulent outbreak of cholera in 1866.[1]

Mrs Gladstone opened a home at Clapton for the babies and children orphaned by the epidemic and brought young boys to Broadlane House, Hawarden. The next year she opened a free convalescent home at Snaresbrook in Essex and began an appeal to buy the freehold of Woodford Hall, which was officially opened in November 1869 as Mrs Gladstone's Free Convalescent Home for the Poor. A few years later she opened another home at Hawarden for the elderly and infirm, and whatever they needed she sought to provide, whether it was bread or meat, a piano, or seeds for the garden. Everyone must be asked to help; everywhere must be used for shelter. Mr Gladstone was asked, 'Should you mind three *clean* little children being taken to C.H.T. (Carlton House Terrace)?' and of course he did not. However, when Agnes, inspired by her mother's work, had asked if she might train as a nurse, Mrs Gladstone had become quite agitated; a career or paid work for her daughters was out of the question.

For someone with a reputation for living in perpetual disorder, Mrs Gladstone was singularly organised and efficient

with her time. Her tireless energy drove her in many directions. She never lost an opportunity to help someone, however
out of her way it might take her, and she never hesitated to
inveigle her husband into her endless schemes. A typical letter,
a jumble of requests, reads:

> Could you order some toothbrushes and brushes *cheap* for
> the Orphanage? Have you remembered to peep in on the
> Miss Ds?' [two impoverished Italian ladies that she had
> taken in and found shelter as caretakers in Downing
> Street]. 'Only open the boudoir door and you will find
> them. Did you manage the flowers (or grapes) for Mrs
> Bagshawe? She lives quite near Portland Place. If you
> have time please bring down a present for my three-
> year-old godchild; there are beautiful Bible prints at the
> Sanctuary, Westminster, and also we want a common
> easel from the same place, 5s to 8/6, to hold the big maps
> for the boys.[2]

Mary believed that her mother was only saved from furious
reprimands by her father's sense of humour and his heart of
gold.

All of these charitable exercises taking her mother away
from home meant that Mary was seldom, if ever, at the centre
of her parents' concern. In February 1864 she wrote to 'Dearest
Mama' from the Rectory with news of sick people in the village
and signed herself 'your very loving child Mary Gladstone'. She
often apologised for taking up time with a letter, 'I suppose you
are very busy and will naturally think me a great bore. But I
would not be one if I could possibly help it as I know you are
up to your eyes in work.' And of course she knew that Papa is a
very busy man, attending debates in the House of Commons
and making famous speeches. She wrote to him just before
her seventeenth birthday telling him that she has opened a
letter with no name on the envelope – was it wrong of her?
She is so sorry if it was. She is so anxious to please, and has no
idea of her value as a responsible girl, able to perform village
errands, pass on messages to the servants and keep an eye on
her younger brothers. Her mother was away on this birthday

and asked Lucy not to forget to write to 'Naples Mary', adding 'poor childie, I am almost always away on her b'day and she adores you.' Her mother meant to be kind, but the use of Mary's childhood pet name when she is almost seventeen shows that she still regarded her as a child. Her daughter was growing up and she was not aware of it.

The 27 April 1865 was Gladstone's ninth budget, and his last under Palmerston. There was a July election in which he lost his Oxford seat but was elected for South Lancashire. There was only one Cabinet meeting before the summer recess and the new Parliament would not meet again for seven months. It was time for country holidays where life might be less formal, but the importance of mixing in the right circles remained. Mary accompanied her parents to Drumlanrig Castle, home of the Duke of Buccleuch. Among the guests was the twenty-eight-year-old Duke of Tech who would marry the Queen's cousin the next year.

Mary was now on display as an attractive candidate for marriage, but she was still more child than adult. She thought that Drumlanrig Castle was a glorious place with its splendid terraced gardens but 'where are the park walls?' she asked. Her host's reply was to point to the soaring mountains. She was exhilarated by the fresh air and open spaces, and her high spirits led to a rebuke for throwing leaves and berries out of her bedroom window. The next social call at Inverary Castle, home of the Duke of Argyle, provided her with more scope for her youthful energies, and a handsome son to share them. They walked, fished and rode together, and Lord Lorne escorted her on an exciting otter hunt. He led her horse and was most attentive, so that her young heart was enslaved. It was the kind of holiday that she loved, with challenging walks down steep ravines, across tumbling rivers, jumps and near misses over burns. Nineteen-year-old Lord Lorne would have been less than human if he had not enjoyed the obvious admiration of this sweetly attractive girl.

The Knutsford Ball at Tatton in Cheshire, the home of Lord Egerton, was always a very smart affair. When Mary was invited in December, she took her black silk gown, with a morning and evening bodice, and her one ballgown of white tarlatan. She felt remarkably well-dressed, and this was quite an extensive wardrobe by Gladstone standards.

The next year she was invited to Wilton House, near Salisbury, to spend five weeks of the summer with the Herberts, neighbours from Carlton House Terrace and old family friends. There was 'endless riding, driving and boating and beautiful summer weather, sobered by visits to the sick and poor, and steady reading.' Her brothers and sisters spent that same summer scattered across country houses. Mrs Gladstone was adept at organising them to family and friendly outposts. In such an arrangement the following spring, Mary lists William and Agnes as being at Wicken Place, Lord Penrhyn's hunting place in Northamptonshire, Stephen at Oxford, Helen at Hawarden, Harry and Herbert at Eton while she was writing from Chiswick House, where, with her parents, she was one of the guests of the Duke of Devonshire. Helen wrote to Herbert for his fifteenth birthday and reminded him that she had seen him only once in the past fifteen months and that had been for tea.

By September 1866 it was time for a little continental polish and time, Mary's father judged, to remove himself from politics during the recess.

> In England I should find it most difficult to avoid for five minutes attending some public celebration or other, especially in Lancashire. I think that I have said already in one way or other, all that I can usefully say, perhaps more than all. So far as I am concerned, I now leave the wound of the Liberal party to the healing powers of nature.[3]

It was Mary's first trip abroad since the winter in Naples when she was three; her parents took her and Agnes, one maid and one manservant. It was arranged that William, Stephen and Helen would join them later, and even Uncle Stephen landed on them at Rome. The two youngest, Herbert and Harry were left behind at school. First stop was Paris, in comfortable rooms at the Hotel Vouillimont, in the Rue des Champs Elysees. They dipped into the Parisian shops and churches, the Louvre and the British Embassy, and then headed south over the St Gothard Pass.

It was a perilous carriage journey between the snow-covered, cloud-capped mountains. The road followed the river Ticino, and after two whole days travelling with an overnight stop, they reached Lake Lugano, shining green in brilliant sunshine. Now they could board the train from Como to Milan, where Mary was guided around the architectural wonders and the splendid frescoes. She was overwhelmed by the glories of the cathedral, its vastness and grandeur, the beautiful stained-glass windows colouring the white marble as the sun streamed through. 'My winkie, how lovely it was !' she confided to her diary.

The next train stop was Parma. Here awaited some of the horrors of travel, and they were all cold and tired. 'We got into a very dreary station, the floor all covered with soldiers asleep. Found a single open fly into which we all six bundled, luggage and all. Drove to two inns unsuccessfully, bringing down the poor men in their shirts with a tallow dip, and not half awake! At length found a room at the Poste; very fair, except we were all more or less much troubled with fleas.'[4] This was the year of the Austro-Prussian war, and Europe was politically unstable as Italy staggered towards a unified state. Mary's father, as he assured Lord Acton, did not intend to meddle in politics: 'I consider myself bound to good conduct in a very strict sense of the word.' Next day they moved on to Bologna, and Mary climbed the leaning tower. She declared it was twice as high as the one in Pisa and the ladders were none too sturdy. There was one more long day travelling before Rome was reached by ten in the evening. She was very tired, and thankful that they were spared the searching of luggage and obligatory fumigation. She believed it was due to the Italians' high regard for her father.

For the next two and a half months, they made themselves at home in comfortable rooms in Madame Tellenbach's house, at 51 Piazza di Spagna. Each day began with an Italian lesson, and reading Dante with Papa. Archbishop Manning had written to his Roman friends to ensure that they were shown every kindness, warning that 'Gladstone does not come as an enemy, and may be made friendly, or he might become on his return most dangerous.' Mary's hours were filled with outings and visits, sometimes chaperoned by Stume, her mother's maid. Her first impression of Rome was of filthy streets, a muddy Tiber, and foetid air. But when her father led her, with her eyes tightly shut, under the dome of St Peter's and she opened her eyes to its beauty and grandeur, it was a sight she felt sure she would never forget. They were still within the church when the ringing of a bell told them that the Pope was approaching. They dashed outside and were in time to see him drive up with his outriders and guards. They curtsied low, and were rewarded by a wave.

They were soon invited to a private audience. Five of them drove in a carriage to the Vatican – Mr and Mrs Gladstone, Agnes, Mary and Lady Augusta Stanley, wife of the Dean of Westminster. Mr Gladstone wore formal black attire, the ladies were clothed in black silk with black veils. Each in turn curtsied and kissed the Pope's hand. Everyone sat down, the visitors on stools in a semi-circle, before a kind of dais where Pope Pius IX, robed in the purest white, sat: 'Then he began to talk and trolled on very good-naturedly, laughing a good deal, for about 20 minutes.' It was more of a monologue than a conversation as he moved from one subject to another with scarcely a breath, all conducted in French. His blessing 'Que Dieu vous donne toutes les Graces!' suddenly alerted them that it was time to depart. There were more curtseys and kisses and a personal blessing for each one, and they escaped. Mary thought the whole affair 'excessively ludicrous'.

After a while, one precious marble began to look very like the next, and undiluted culture and learning makes for dreary days. Luckily they had many English friends wintering in Rome; especially welcome were the Duke and Duchess of Argyle with Lady Edith and the dashing Lord Lorne, who had made such an impression in the summer. Prince and Princess Radziwill invited them to tea; Lord and Lady Enfield drove out with them into the countryside; Lord Odo Russell called on them. Mrs Gladstone gave a Christmas party and English traditions were maintained with hymns and carols. On New Year's Day, the great pianist Liszt came and played for them, and Mary found his performance more exciting than anything she had ever heard. But the awful part of it was that she also had to play to him and at first she was quite paralysed by nerves.

She had absorbed all that Rome could offer. She had stood in the Coliseum, and in her imagination travelled back in time to the bloody scenes when thousands of innocent people bravely met their deaths. She had crept down a pitch-dark spiral staircase to a tiny cell, where Beatrice Cenci was held for a year, and into another where Benvenuto Cellini was shut up for two years. She had entered the catacombs and the Jewish Ghetto. She had visited artists' studios and even found time for lectures on archaeology and singing lessons. It was time to begin the journey homewards; they moved on to Florence which was the seat of government of the nearly united Italy: here her father called on King Victor Emmanuel and was invited to dinner by members of the Italian government.

The last stage of their travels, by carriage from Genoa to Nice, shared with the Cardwells and their two servants, was anything but comfortable, but very amusing. Mary enjoyed writing to Harry about how Mr and Mrs Cardwell 'nearly always go to sleep with their mouths *wide open* but first Mrs C's head bobs about all over the carriage and then swings backwards and forwards till at last it finds a resting place – meanwhile we go into fits of laughter and are in a mortal fright in case Mrs C might wake and see us.'[5] Then there was the time when their coachman, driving far too fast, landed them all in the ditch by a sheer rockface. The only consolation was that on the other side was a long drop to the sea.

And so so they headed back to Paris, being dined and fêted along the way, culminating in a glittering evening in Paris as guests of the French Emperor and his Empress. Mrs Gladstone decided that the girls' ballgowns should be simple but very pretty, 'plain white, trimmed with rolls of white satin, no gathers in front, and tremendously long.' The Empress' gown, with only a very little crinoline, was covered with diamonds.

Mary was not impressed by Emperor Napoleon III, 'a short, podgy, little man, very ugly and a very foxy expression, but his little eyes look very sharp and clever.'

Once she was back home at Hawarden she decided that an over-indulgence of riches and high society gave her cultural indigestion. Now she could enjoy cricket and tennis and tree-felling while her mother was dashing round the country from convalescent home to hospital to orphanage, never missing one of her husband's parliamentary debates, fitting in dinners and parties, and mindful of her sons and nephews at Eton. Mary had far more independence than was customary for unmarried young ladies of her time; she never thought to ask her mother's permission before inviting friends to the house, and there was always Uncle Stephen to keep an eye on them.

In 1867 Auguste Schlüter joined the family as maid to Mary and Helen, doubling as chaperone when necessary although she was only seventeen. Schlüter was expected to look after their clothes, pack for journeys away from home, accompany them on visits, dress their hair for special occasions and take care of their everyday personal chores. She quickly became one of the family and 'Miss Mary' was her favourite, her 'darling lady'. 'Schlut' was dependable and utterly trustworthy, with an honoured place in the household hierarchy along with Mrs Jolly the cook, Hyem the butler and Zadok, Mr Gladstone's valet.

Gladstone had been out of the government for two years; the general election of November 1868 swept the Liberal party into power and him to the highest office. He was given detailed advice from the Dean of Windsor on how to deal with the Queen, with great emphasis being placed on a light, gentle touch and when he differed, it would be best to pass the matter lightly over and engage in gentle intercourse. Mrs Gladstone begged him to cultivate 'great dignity, great patience, but not too much humility'. Mary wrote with her own encouragement: 'How wonderfully quick you have been about the formation of the Government.'

Gladstone's new principal parliamentary secretary, Algernon West, has left his first impressions of his new chief in dark frockcoat with flower in buttonhole, neck-cloth slightly disordered round a high collar, amputated finger of left hand covered as always by a black finger-stall. This was the result of an accident in 1842 when he had shot off the forefinger of his left hand while reloading one barrel of a gun with the other fully cocked.

Christmas week found them all at 11 Carlton House Terrace with Papa behind his desk. The family were rallying round Stephen as much as Papa. He had just been ordained curate of St Mary's Church, Lambeth, one of London's poorest churches. He was taking lodgings in a little terraced house with a kindly widow to look after him. Mrs Gladstone invited twenty-one-year-old Margaret Leicester-Warren of Tabley House in Cheshire to join the family. It was a typically kind-hearted gesture and Maggie had often been invited to family parties; the girls were now busy making flannel petticoats in between wrapping toys and presents for her Home of Charity. Maggie was in awe of Mr Gladstone and noted in her diary that she was so glad that he did not care what he ate or drank and never took sauces: 'I was always sure that really great men didn't, and now I have proved it for he is the greatest man I know.'

Brother William had been a Liberal Member of Parliament for Chester in the previous government and Mary had written to Lavinia with all the details of his maiden speech in March 1868.

> You may fancy the sort of state we were in, Mama rushing madly about the box, and now and then hugging her knee. Luckily there was no one else in that box, so that we could freely give vent to our feelings. Meanwhile the congrats have been endless. There is not a single person who does not think it was otherwise than a great success, and they say that it is the best maiden speech that has been heard for a long while. I never saw anything so self-possessed as he was outwardly, though very white, and he never paused or hesitated. They cheered him capitally, at the end of every sentence.[6]

She could not help adding, 'We are going to Dizzy's party next Wednesday, such fun.'

William was re-elected at the November general election; as always, Mary was there to cheer and encourage, her role centred in the family whether she was passing on praise as when she tells Harry, now launched on a business career, that their father had said, 'it would only do to put a fellow with brains into such a responsible position' or giving a mild rebuke, 'considering what Mama is altogether I think it is very disloyal to talk of her so ... as if we were her rightful judges.'

Her twenty-first birthday on 23 November seems to have made little impact on the family; her mother is once again away from home and, in a letter to Lucy, merely mentions the fact. Her father is of course steeped in government business which occupies him over his sixtieth birthday the following month. Mary writes 'one line not to take up your time to wish you many happy returns', adding, 'I wish I had the knack of writing these sort of letters well, but whenever I most wish to express myself well, the words refuse to arrange themselves.' Her letter ends, 'Goodbye dearest old Father. Harry and Herbert send their love.'

Gladstone's diary for 4 December 1868 reads, 'I feel like a man with a burden under which he must fall and be crushed if he looks to the right or left or fails from any cause to concentrate mind and muscle upon his progress.' On his birthday he calls on God to sustain and spare him, 'for some purpose of His own, deeply unworthy as I know myself to be.' Mary and her mother are convinced that he is serving the country by Divine will, and they will do all in their power to smooth his path.

CHAPTER EIGHT

The passionate years
(1868 – 75)

Seeing and hearing Liszt in Rome had awakened a passionate response in Mary. She had been so nervous when the
great man had asked her to play for him that her fingers had
been stiff and awkward. She had her own piano in London
and now she took lessons and practised daily. It was a useful
discipline, helping to concentrate her mind, which might
otherwise have drifted aimlessly. Music touched her deepest
feelings and liberated her thoughts. Her language in her diary
is unfettered and exuberant with phrases like 'saturated in
sublime music', 'all-absorbing as to leave no room for any other
sensation', 'takes entire possession of your whole being',
'dragged all my inside out'. She met the celebrated violinist
Joseph Joachim at one of her London parties. 'Oh, my winkie,
Joachim played. It was marvellous. I was introduced to him
and my feelings were nearly too many for me. An Andante of
Mozart's, but the great thing was a Concerto of Mendelssohn's,
Sullivan accompanying him on the P.F. I am so excited with the
remembrance I can hardly write.'

Joachim was Hungarian by birth, living mainly in Germany
but a frequent visitor to Britain. He became a personal friend
and Mary's diary of 3 March 1873 records that she talked with
him 'about the exhaustiveness of music'; the next week, going
into dinner with him was 'very nearly quite perfect bliss'.

Her musical talent was being applauded by the great musi-
cians of the day. She had at last found people to take her seriously. The world of music gave her freedom and independence
and a growing self-confidence. She went off to concerts in a
group of male friends. What could be more decorous than a

Handel concert in the company of a brother or male cousin? Hubert Parry was an old Eton and Oxford friend and had become one of her musical circle. She learnt a lot about technique from watching him play and declared that anything appealing in her playing, 'anything tender or wistful or passionate', was entirely due to him. She believed 'it was he who first revealed to me how to express in music the emotions of the human heart.' He was her 'Archangel' and his playing carried her 'into Paradise as usual'. He was in love with her great friend, Maud Herbert, but Lady Herbert strenuously opposed his attentions, and even George Herbert sided with his mother. Believing that girls were 'very expensive animals', he thought it quite wrong to marry before he could support a wife.

Mary was the couple's ally and she made sure to invite him to Hawarden when Maud was to be there. When he looked back to his Oxford student days he thought they were the happiest of all, 'the many intertwinings of youthful living souls in music and pure conversation'. Among these young idealists, Mary blossomed. She was having lessons in harmony and her knowledge of musical theory was impressive. In a letter to Herbert she went into details of chords and chants, informing him that the bass, tenor and soprano are in the same key but the alto is in the key of B instead of F. 'Do you know,' she tells him, 'that once the now well-known termination was considered quite outrageous and the first man who dared say he liked it, was received with a howl of indignation and horror?'[1] Then she drew the musical score for him so that there can be no doubt. Her interpretation of Beethoven was very much her own and she would say, with a smile, 'Oh yes, *that's* how Beethoven wrote it, but I like playing it like *this*.'

She turned to books to further her education. In January 1870 she was struggling with Lewes' *Life of Goethe*, hoping 'the substance of the book may stick in my head better than most do'. The next year she studied Morley's *The Rise and Fall of the Dutch Republic*. Her father's library was open to all his children and he taught them to handle books with love and care. Mary knew that it gave him real pain to see a book used carelessly, 'laid open on its face, untidily marked, dog's eared, thumbed'. His books, like friends, must be comfortably housed. She described him as 'a gourmand' in his reading tastes and she too ranged widely over poetry, fiction, history and theology. One week she read Shelley's poetry, another time Mrs Oliphant's *Phoebe Junior*, another time American authors, *The Scarlet Letter* and *The American*, and often she turned to Tennyson's poems. She and her father engaged in after-breakfast literary discussions and evenings were often spent reading aloud. They did not always agree. She thought de Quincey's *Autobiographical Sketches* delightful, whereas he had to confess that de Quincey struck him as 'laboured, long-winded, self-conscious and affected'. Mrs Gaskell and George Eliot were among her favourites. A popular novelist, Julia Kavanagh, was enjoyed but Disraeli's *Lothair* she dismissed as 'snobbish and trashy'. She read Chaucer with sister Helen, and Butler's *Analogy of Religion*.

The first year of Gladstone's first government went smoothly and successfully; he was intent on home affairs and enjoyed being able to alternate London pace with Hawarden peace. At home he could follow his daily morning worship with long, undisturbed time in his study on ministerial correspondence, with a spot of tree-felling in the afternoon and reading in the evening. He explained to Lord Clarendon, 'in point of hours it is much the same here and there though [here] the free hours feel much more free which is the great thing.'[2]

Mary was aware of her father's new status and her best way of helping, she knew, was in keeping family relationships ticking over harmoniously; writing letters to her brothers at school played a big part. To sixteen-year-old Harry at Eton, in February 1869, she writes, 'your Papa is in good spirits though of course overwhelmed with work'. And to Herbert climbing in Scotland the next year she writes, 'We were so very glad to learn that your bones were not bleaching on a mountain top – I was hourly dreading the arrival of your stick dipped in your blood – and being a walking stick it would have walked straight here I imagine.'[3] Her sense of humour is echoed by her father in a letter to his Home Secretary a few months later: 'If you read in the papers some morning that I have been committed to Bedlam, and that a straight waistcoat is considered necessary, please to remember it will be entirely owing to the vacancy in the see of St Asaph.'[4] Bills and Acts were flying around Westminster corridors like confetti; the Disestablishment of the Irish Church, the Irish Land Bill (attempting to settle the thorny problems of Irish rural living), the Education Act bringing elementary schooling to all, competitive examinations for entry to the Civil Service, Trades Union Acts to raise standards and improve conditions for workers, the introduction of the halfpenny postcard, army reforms and Church appointments always preoccupied his thoughts. There was little space left to consider foreign affairs, and the Franco-Prussian war of 1870–1 was left to the European powers to settle diplomatically, which ended in the domination of Europe by Bismarck's Germany.

With older brothers at Oxford and cousins at Cambridge, Mary's circle of menfolk could not fail to be erudite, witty and rich. In Oxford in the summer of 1870, she lunched in Eustace Balfour's rooms, 'so cool and delicious with the best claret cup I ever did taste', then went on to tea at a certain Mr Turner's for music, strawberries and ice, followed by a walk through Magdelen and New Colleges 'which we lionized' (a Glynnese word meaning loved inordinately). The evening held a concert, dinner and a ball where, chaperoned by a Mrs Lightfoot, she was 'surrounded by lions clamouring for dances. It was the best fun in the world and so pretty. I danced three times with King Arthur, also with Mr Turner and Eustace, twice with Harcourt and once with everybody else, a rather nice Mr Littleton among them.'[5]

'King Arthur' was the eldest of the Balfour boys, all of them Eton- and Cambridge-educated. His close friendship with Spencer Lyttelton, sealed by their mutual love of music, brought him into the Gladstone–Lyttelton circle. Arthur Balfour had inherited great wealth and vast Scottish estates. He was uncommonly handsome and could be charming and witty when he so minded, but there was a cold centre deep within him that meant he was often remote, and gave a certain detachment to his behaviour. The word used more often than any other to describe him is 'languid'. As a child, his health had been fragile, and he had spent much of his day resting, a habit which he continued into adulthood. It was as if his high spirits erupted too highly and burnt out too quickly, with no reserves of energy.

On their first meeting, Mary was not impressed. 'Mr B is not altogether a remarkable person to look at, and he talks in a rather too self-confident way,' she wrote in her diary. But her initial criticism dissolved as she delighted in his madcap ways and perceived the sensitive nature beneath. He bought a London home near to them at 4 Carlton Gardens and her father took to him at once. Here was a young man of wit and intelligence who was not overawed in the elder statesman's presence. He was anxious to please, but disliked easy conquests. He had an adoring mother and sisters who fell over themselves to answer his every call. Although he enjoyed the female graces, he had developed from an early age an elusive, vague air to protect his private self.

Mary's newly gained self-confidence wavered. The more she became aware of his wit and beauty, the less she estimated her own. There were three Talbot sisters, Adelaide, Gertrude and Constance, all great beauties and all marrying men in high positions. Feeling quite miserable and inadequate, she spent her twenty-third birthday at Ashridge Park in Hertfordshire, home of Adelaide, Lady Brownlow. Letters from her parents helped to dispel only a little of her misery as her letter to her mother shows. 'Twenty-three seems a lot of years considering how little there is to show for it', she moaned. 'As for minding my manners, I expect the gentlemen here think me a very staid young woman only perhaps rather dull.'[6] And as they were out shooting all day, she probably found them very dull.

She confided to her mother that she had been expecting something that had not materialised, perhaps a hope that Mr Balfour would be present or remember her birthday. Whatever hopes were dashed, her sensible and positive nature reasserted itself. She decided that it was time for her to begin to buy her own clothes and set about persuading her mother, 'I quite agree, you know, about Helen but think it would be far easier for you to give your mind to her if I was off you – at the same time you know I would follow your wishes entirely.' This was a clever line to take and she continued, 'I don't mind how much only I think I ought to know how to manage my money, fancy at 23 not buying your clothes, you see everybody does when they come out – and it would save you a lot of worry as I can't feel any interest in what I wear as long as the money to buy the things isn't my own, and if I took the pains as I should feel it my duty to do, I believe I could dress rather well.'[7] Her mother had promised two years ago and Mary thought it was time to hold her to it.

Two months later, when Mr Balfour came to stay at Hawarden, Mary was equal to the challenge, even feeling a little superior for she noticed that he was rather shy as she was the only person present whom he knew. This was his first meeting with Lavinia and May Lyttelton and their first impressions were no more favourable than Mary's had been. Twenty-two-year-old Lavinia, married last summer to Edward Talbot, academic and clergyman, was already a prim little matron. She noticed with disapproval the efforts being made by Mary and her parents to pin down the erratic Mr Balfour. In her opinion he was basically 'very clever and good and starts in life with an attractive dreamy and sometimes amusing manner' but she thought him 'conscious of his impulsiveness and attraction, as well as of the fact that all the young ladies during his four months' visit have been at his feet.'[8]

May Lyttelton was similarly unimpressed on first meeting Mr Balfour. 'He dangles about and does nothing to an extent which becomes wrong.' May was a highly intelligent girl, not conventionally beautiful but with a warm personality that lit up her boyish charms. Her mother's death had been followed by her father's deep grief, which had overwhelmed him for years until he had at last married Sybella Mildmay, and this had forced upon her an early, reflecting maturity. Since Lavinia's marriage, she was restless and lonely. She turned to Mary for the intimacy that she had once enjoyed with her sister and the two girls shared secrets and gossip on new and old friends – what were called 'trolls' in Glynnese. May knew that her

cousin was falling in love with Mr Balfour and she decided that
the best way she could help was by displaying the rather reckless, exhibitionist side of her nature that would be sure to kill
any romantic ideas he might be nurturing for her.

Through the year of 1871 Mary, her cousins May and
Spencer, and Mr Balfour became a constant foursome. Mary
said that they were all 'perfectly insane on music'. Saturday
concerts at Crystal Palace and the Monday Popular Concerts
almost always found them in the gallery, sometimes joined by
other Balfours or mutual friends. After a St James' Hall concert, Mary wrote in her diary 'The programme was superb, that
mad prelude, fugue of Bach's Mr Leigh plays, delightful Gigue
of Handel's, Sonata of Beethoven's for P.F. & Violin with lovely
Adagio finely played by Halle and Neruda. Aufswung, Warum,
and other little jewels of Schumann's. Chopin's Berceuse
quite perfect, and a drunk Polonaise with marvellous octave
playing.' When they left the hall, even the grimy buildings and
smoky chimneys seemed to be transformed by the glorious
sunset.

Another evening of concert-going began with a visit to
No. 10 Arlington Street, home of Lord Salisbury who was Mr
Balfour's uncle. Then they moved on to Crystal Palace in an
open carriage, Mary seated by May with 'Miss B and a gigantic
amount of music taking up the 4th seat, Mr B and Spencer
behind in a hansom.' The evening ended with tea at Arlington
Street and gossip and giggles. Five days later they were at the
Crystal Palace again, with another absurd meal in the interval
and even the waiters being drawn into their laughter. This time
Mary sat between Mr Austen Leigh and Mr Balfour at the concert and she watched their reactions, 'the former's face wearing
an expression of concentrated attention and unmixed delight,
the latter's appreciation so keen and intense as almost
amounted to pain.'

In July she was invited to Hatfield, as Lord Salisbury's guest
for a weekend house party where it was quite obvious that Mr
Balfour was singling her out for music, croquet and conversation. He was expert on the concertina, known among them
as 'the infernals' and the two played hours of duets. They

sauntered alone through the rose garden and sat undisturbed in long conversations. Mary was one of the last guests to leave on Monday. Trains back to London left without her and the hours drifted by, until a sudden realisation of the lateness sent her escort chasing to and fro like the Mad Hatter.

That summer at the Eton–Harrow cricket match, she declared that there had never been a more glorious luncheon than the one she ate that day. Arthur Balfour had invited everybody 'he knocked up against right and left, till the party swelled to a gigantic size. Spencer and I were jammed up at the end, 10 others inside, 5 on the box, and others about the wheels and steps of the carriage. Our host was in mad spirits, shouting choruses between acts, hatless, with a handkerchief round his head, hair flying all over the place.'[9]

The crowning month was August when Lady Blanche invited her to Whittingehame for a whole week. The Balfour ancestral home of cool, grey stone stood at the foot of Scotland's Lammermuir Hills. Mary was being offered a taste of their most intimate family life that was only given to their closest friends. Surely, after all that they had shared together that summer, it was not foolish of her to hope that Mr Balfour might one day ask her to share his life?

There was a large house party of Balfours and spouses, Mr and Mrs Gladstone, sister Agnes and a couple of lords. There was noisy, boisterous informality of the kind that Mary knew and loved from Hawarden and Hagley. Meals were uproarious. Songs were sung at the tops of their voices and midnight walks in the park were daringly undertaken; in total darkness she 'was pushed uphill and led down dale' by the Balfour brothers. Next day they dashed off to the seashore, seven miles away. They took a picnic, built a fire and sat around singing glees. They built an enormous sandcastle to defend themselves against the sea with such earnest endeavour that they could not bear to leave until it was dark.

And when the weather turned wet and cold, they stayed indoors, composing limericks which were the latest amusement. Mary developed a taste for ghost stories, and of course Mr Balfour told the most thrilling. She was even adopting some of his phrases as her own, 'but that's a detail', 'but no matter' and 'but let pass' entered her vocabulary whether by accident or with sweet purpose.

Sunday was perhaps the most special day of all. The Balfours, like the Gladstones, lived with the habit of daily prayers, the inner discipline of conscience paramount. Mary was a fine judge of church services and she gave the Whittingehame service high marks for prayers and sermon, less for the hymn singing. After dinner she shared more prayers and hymns with Mr Balfour, ending by playing the Messiah right through, 'frantically excited in *Why do the Nations* and, dreadfully exhausted, finished with *I know that my Redeemer liveth*.' She tumbled into bed, once again 'saturated with sublime music'.

Arthur Balfour accompanied the departing Gladstones on the first leg of their journey to Edinburgh. Already he seemed like one of the family. They stayed overnight at a quiet hotel in George Street. It was a low-key evening after their hectic week, 'all lying down, so exhausted, feebly capping verses but ending by composing some first-rate limericks.' In Mary's family these were called 'Penmaenmawrs', echoes of their holiday fun in North Wales. It was obvious to others, and must have been to him, that Mary adored Mr Balfour.

He came to stay at Hawarden and they went together to a concert in Liverpool, both bundled up against the cold. He wore a gigantic fur coat right over his head so that everyone stopped and stared. He was quite aware of the effect that his behaviour had on others; it was always so effortless on his part. He took Mary's affection like a bee takes honey; one sip and on to the next. She was always available, unlike May Lyttelton, who had chosen to distance herself.

May had met and fallen in love with Rutherford Graham, a handsome and rather wild Balliol undergraduate. His father was a self-made Glasgow merchant and patron of the Pre-Raphaelite artist, Burne-Jones. His sisters Amy and Frances were friends of Mary and May. Lord Lyttelton did not approve of his daughter's choice and forbade May from attending balls where she might meet him, but she was a girl of spirit and, although obedient to her father's wishes, she was not prepared to give Rutherford up. She agreed to a year's wait, at the end of which she hoped that her father would have softened his attitude. As the old year ended and 1872 began, May looked ahead with hope and a little trepidation that all would be well, while Mary reflected that it seemed to be man's destiny 'to rejoice little, to suffer much and always to hope'. She did not regret her love for Mr Balfour and her bruised heart was relieved by pouring out her feelings to her mother, 'I do not indeed think I could have helped it for I have tried very hard not to let the feeling grow'. Now it was part of her being, giving 'keener sorrow and keener joy'. She stressed that it must be a secret, but May could be trusted, for she had secrets of her own. She assured her mother that she had plenty of good sense and would be cheerful.

The New Year was spent with Lytteton cousins and after Hagley high spirits, a term of duty was required with her mother, visiting at the London Hospital. Mary found it quite an ordeal to go from bed to bed, chatting with the patients, but seeing the grey reality of lives less fortunate than hers and how cheerfully others coped, she was able to get on with her own days. May had reached a private understanding with Rutherford that they would wait until her father was prepared to give his approval. Family opposition included Lavinia and Lucy but May was not prepared to give any other suitor a chance and when Nora Balfour invited her to Whittingehame in September, she wrote in her diary, 'shan't go of course'.

So Mary and her parents again enjoyed the Balfour hospitality, this time on the Strathconan estate of grouse moors, deer forest and salmon river in Ross-shire. Mary went with no expectations, determined to enjoy the company; indeed, her friendship with Nora was growing while Mr Balfour seemed to be more interested in impressing her famous father. The two men had long philosophical talks and Mary noticed that in her father's company, Mr Balfour's whole being was transformed from his 'usual indolent postures' and her father delighted in their vigorous walks and talks. He delayed his return to a London Cabinet meeting to the last possible moment, which led to a hurried five-mile trek by moor and loch to the nearest railway station. How they were still on the loch when they saw the train pulling into the little station, and how Mr B leapt from the boat and ran through the shallow pools waving frantically to the engine driver has made a delightful and well recorded story. All ended happily, the driver's eye was caught and the train waited for the Prime Minister and his party. Arthur Balfour noticed a pair of wet socks hanging out of the carriage window as the train pulled away. He was not yet a politician but he was soon to be persuaded that this was a life that he could enjoy as well as any other.

Meanwhile, Rutherford Graham was about to travel to America, but, before he could board ship in Liverpool, he caught diphtheria and died within a few days. May was completely heartbroken and crept to Hawarden like a wounded animal, into the comfort of Mrs Gladstone's arms. It was the second time that fate had dealt her this cruel blow. When she was nineteen, her hand had been sought in marriage by Edward Dennison, ten years her senior. He was intelligent, idealistic, well-connected and liked by Lord Lyttelton, but his health was fragile, and he had died in Australia where he had journeyed in search of a cure for his poor health.

May's health had always been finely strung and now she recoiled from others' vitality. Her life ahead looked black and dreary and she dragged herself through the days, often complaining of headaches, cold or sore throats. For many months the only men she could bear to be with were her brothers. She eventually took up concert-going again, but it was never the same.

Gladstone's government was petering out; Mary was in London in January 1874 when the end came and from her diary entry it would seem that neither she nor her father were downhearted: 'Thunderbolt. Dissolution of Parliament. Chuckling breakfast with Papa and copious searching of newspapers. His address (3 columns long) quite excellent. Lucy came and we tore up letters for 2 hours.' Her father was standing for re-election at Greenwich, and the hustings brought plenty of excitement: 'Off in open carriage at 2, arriving on the common at 3. Clambered up into a wagon and there sat in state during Papa's animated and spirited speech, full of good hard hits and very happy turns, received with frantic enthusiasm. Drove off at 4 protected on each side by galloping mounted police, hundreds running along by the side of the carriage, and deafening cheers.' Voting may have been secret for the first time but the rowdy, jostling, jeering and cheering crowds would have intimidated many. Not so Mary, but it was all to no purpose, for the Conservatives gained a majority of about fifty although her father was back in Parliament.

In January 1875 May fell victim to typhoid. She became ill while staying at Hagley Rectory, while the Hall roof was being repaired. For ten weeks her strength fluctuated, and no one dared to think the worst. Eight days before she died, Mary had an impulse to rush down to Hagley. The news had been of some improvement in May and Mary tried to believe that May seemed her old self, but she could not deny that there was a terrible change in her. May was lying with her eyes open, 'quite torpid' and although she gave her a beautiful smile she was quite unlike her old self. When Mary drew close, she said, 'Oh, this is fun. Did you think I wouldn't see you, silly old thing?'. Mary tried to get away but May wouldn't hear of it, and whispered, 'You see, I'm not so very much better.'

Mary returned to London to keep her social engagements, but she could not forget the scene she had just left. She had a wretched time at a dinner in honour of the German ambassador and a party afterwards at Lord Granville's. She stayed on in London, dreading the news that she now knew would come. On Palm Sunday she heard that the end was near, and her only comfort lay in the words, 'All is peaceful'. She believed that her mother's last words to May were, 'God will be with you, darling.'

Once again the family was plunged into the deepest mourning. At the funeral it was said that Mr Balfour was overtaken by uncontrollable weeping. It is a fact that he asked Edward Lyttelton if an emerald ring that had belonged to his mother, who had died three years previously, might be enclosed in May's coffin. He made it plain to the astonished Edward that he had intended asking May to be his wife, but there is no hint of this in May's diary, written up to 12 January after their last meeting and just before she was taken ill. What a contrast to her diary entries of love for Rutherford, secretly written in German and in a tiny script, decipherable only to herself.

After May's death, Arthur Balfour avoided any further emotional commitment. His spirit had been battered by the death of his mother three years earlier and now came this second bruising. In later years he would conduct a loving friendship with Mary Wyndham, who said she would have married him if she had been asked, but he gave no hint to encourage her and she had the good sense not to wait for him. When she was twenty-one, she married the eligible Hugh Charteris, Viscount Elcho, later Earl of Wemyss. Once she was beyond his reach in matrimony, as May Lyttelton was beyond his reach in death, he could persuade himself that he had loved.

For those left behind, the uphill struggle began. Mary's days were grey and endless and she suffered from aches and pains and moods of depression. Three months later she wrote in her diary that for the first time she was thankful for a comfortable mattress so that her weary body felt relaxed and rested. She was glad there was no need to dress up for balls and dances, which were forbidden during their time of mourning. Her wounds seemed sharp-edged whichever way she turned, but others' miseries seemed so much greater than her own. She looked for ways to comfort May's brothers, especially Spencer who had been rudderless since the loss of his mother. None was closer to him than Mary and he now turned to her comfort and love. They were consolation to each other in these darkest days. He had never been able to show his feelings, but he had no need to with Mary who knew exactly how he felt and how to deal with his moods.

Other friendships helped to draw Mary out of her grief. She saw more of her cousin Gertrude Glynne, and Frances Graham took her along to Burne-Jones' studio where they all had tea in his pretty garden. At first Mary was shy in the artist's company but soon they became real friends. New directions and unconsidered occupations lay ahead, that would take her down paths she had not yet imagined.

CHAPTER NINE

Life without May (1875—6)

*A*fter May's death, Mary was swept down a tunnel of grief and despair. She drew closer to Spencer who was inexpressibly miserable, confessing to his diary that he had 'no power whatever of reading or paying continuous attention to anything.' He found bittersweet comfort in reading May's journals, from her first aged fifteen to her last that stopped with her final illness. Memories of his mother's death and funeral when he was just ten years old came flooding back and deepened his depression. He and Mary, more often now 'Mazy', and sometimes forgetfully called 'May', found life again through music.

April brought a week's escape with friends to a music festival in Dusseldorf; Arthur Balfour was one of the party. Over the years Mary had schooled her heart, and love had softened into friendly interest. Her inclusion in the group meant a hurried arrangement for a chaperone. Mrs Gladstone was persuaded that Mary needed a break from her grief but Schlüter could not be spared. Mrs Ponsonby, wife of the Queen's private secretary, was approached and agreed to accompany the party.

They all met up at Victoria station. Mrs Ponsonby noticed that Mary arrived in a flap, and she put it down to worry that everything would not go well. As they settled into their seats, she observed her charges.

Opposite me sat Mr Arthur Balfour, who shut his eyes at once and looked exhausted to begin with − a clever, intelligent face with beautiful eyes and forehead, but lower part not good, a general look of ill-health, gentlemanlike, and the most grand seigneur of the party. Next to him, Mr

Gosselin with a cheery open face and a mass of fair curling hair and much gesticulating of manner from having
lived almost entirely abroad. Next to him, Mr Austen
Leigh, tutory looking, but intelligent and spirituel though
rather an effeminate face. On my side, Spencer Lyttelton,
6 ft 3, curling black hair and beard, good-looking,
abrupt, throwing himself about like his father, and
absent, sometimes scarcely answering when spoken to.[1]

The night train through Belgium brought little sleep except to
Mr Balfour who, Mary declared, was 'the only utterly unconscious one'. Spencer's long legs got in everyone's way and he
had to tie himself into a variety of positions, all with great good
humour. Mary and Spencer bagged the cushions that Mr Gosselin had brought, and she settled against Spencer's comfortably familiar shoulder. The train stopped at Brussels and
everyone gladly took a walk to the Hotel d'Angleterre to wash
and breakfast on omelettes and coffee. They had brought along
a book box and, back on the train, they nodded over their books
until they reached Dusseldorf.

Mrs Ponsonby was not impressed by their accommodation,
a sitting room and three bedrooms in a newly-built wing of a
house where the builders were still at work. It mattered little to
Mary and friends, who at once gathered round a pianoforte
that they had ordered for their rooms, and began to make
music until sheer fatigue drove them to their beds at midnight.

As the days passed, Mrs Ponsonby became better acquainted
with her young people. She thought that Arthur Balfour was
the cleverest, when he could be bothered to rouse himself. As
he never wasted his time on anything he did not consider
worthwhile, she was always afraid of boring him. He seemed
quite unaware of his effect on others, but anyone who could
appear in a long black coat and a large soft felt hat 'like a
disreputable Archdeacon' knew exactly what he was doing.

Mary seemed remote to Mrs Ponsonby, who found her
informality disconcerting. She felt that underneath Mary's
rather vague and dreamy air, which was reminiscent of her
mother, was a latent strength inherited from her father. She

came to the conclusion that Mary was 'definitely not common-place, and a capital musician'. Mary's preoccupation may have been due to her complete absorption in the musical delights on offer. Everyone seriously interested in music was there – Mrs Joachim was singing, Jenny Lind's husband was in the audience, Mr Groves who organised the Crystal Palace concerts was there.

On the first day Mary watched Joachim conducting Mozart's Jupiter Symphony and Beethoven's Mass, and every day there were more delights, culminating in Brahms conducting one of his own symphonies on the last evening. In between they could attend rehearsals and play Bach fugues and Handel overtures and arias in their own room. The queues for rehearsals were tremendous and once Mary and Spencer claimed the last two seats. Mrs Ponsonby thought that, as they were cousins, she need have no qualms about them being alone. Indeed, she was happy for them to go off at any time in each other's company, which meant that she was free to indulge in a little sightseeing and souvenir shopping. Times for meeting up with her young people were sometimes confused but she blamed this on Mary's 'insouciance' and never thought that she was deliberately being given the slip.

Journeying on to Cologne with Spencer and Mrs Ponsonby, Mary turned over in her mind the happiness of shared experiences. Spencer had been 'a peculiarly delightful traveller, his observant eye a clear gain and above all his endless store of epithets always fitting and never stale.'[2] They were on their way to pay respects to Miss Helen Gladstone whom Spencer thought 'decidedly eccentric'. It was a mild enough description for Mary's sixty-one-year-old aunt who had spent the last six years at the Hotel Disch 'and has been going home ever since, but can never quite make up her mind to start. She sits surrounded by books and flowers, and every fortnight her maid packs, and then she changes her mind, She turns night into day, generally getting up at 11 p.m.'[3]

Mrs Ponsonby's unsympathetic opinion was shared by many who failed to appreciate the tragedy of one who had been broken by the iron will of a dominant father and by four strong brothers who wanted her to conform to the conventional mould of dutiful, submissive daughter. She had a good brain but had never been allowed to use it. She was now a physical and mental wreck entirely ruled by opium, completely careless of dress and habits and leaving a trail of unpaid bills wherever she went. The Hotel Disch in Cologne where Mary now paid her call of duty was to be her aunt's last refuge. Even on her deathbed, two of her brothers tried to convince themselves that she had renounced her Roman Catholic faith and returned to the Church of England fold.

Mary's father, aware of his own human frailties, was his sister's sternest judge. He believed that help lay in eternal vigilance, submission through prayer, through daily Bible readings and through regular attendance at Church of England services. His constant exhortation to Mary with every year's birthday wishes was to be on her guard against evil and temptation. He regularly spoke to his children about the need 'to buckle on strong armour' against the snares of easy pleasures.

He had met many young women who had slipped from the straight and narrow path. From the time of his student days at Oxford, he had chosen to work among London's prostitutes, helping to set up 'Homes for Fallen Women', walking the streets to find them and talk with them, even taking them home. He saw it as his Christian duty to help these women in every way that he could; his problem was that he enjoyed talking with them. At times of great personal stress and overwork, he sought out these women ever more zealously and, after long conversations with them, he would find sexual relief in self-scourging. He kept a detailed record of these activities in his diary and they took the form of confessionals, religious searchings of his soul. He held in check his turbulent passions by discipline and constant hard work, and he believed that his sister could do likewise. He failed to appreciate the emptiness of her life and that the channels into which his energies could flow were exclusively male and therefore closed to her. He could pour his passions into political crusades, with the blessing and full support of an affectionate wife and loving home.

There was no bridge of sympathy and understanding between twenty-seven-year-old Mary and her Aunt Helen. She only saw a bitter and selfish woman who riled against her relations and their well-meant advice. After two acrimonious meetings, Mary left for England. Back home, she wrote long letters to her brother Harry who was making his way in business out in India. She wanted to explain why he had not been telegraphed at the time of May's last illness, 'It costs £4, and we thought it scarcely worth'. Indeed they had even been in doubt about sending word to May's brother Neville who was also out in India. To ease Harry's sense of isolation, she shared with him the grief that they have all felt, not forgetting that he has been nursing a bruised heart from a broken romance. She tells him that, when May came to Hawarden for the last time, she 'used to think about you, and be so sorry for you, and wish so intently that life was altogether a more cheerful and bright thing to you.' She set May as an example to follow and yet, she wanted to remember the real May with her failings as well as her goodness. She sent a photograph: 'Do you see the ring on her finger, the one which belonged to Mr Graham? She was so proud of its showing in the photo.' This was not the ring that had been ostentatiously buried with her but the one that was now with Rutherford's sister, Frances Graham.

Mary and Frances went visiting Burne-Jones, whom Frances had known since she was a child, for she had often been taken to his studio by her father, who was his patron. Frances was a lovely girl with wild eyes; Burne-Jones, a romantic dreamer whose dreams spilled into his art, had fallen at once under her spell. He delighted in drawing and painting her and he often used her profile in his paintings. She appears as the young bride in 'The King's Wedding' and as Eurydice in 'Orpheus and Eurydice'. He had sent Frances a Valentine which Mary had thought quite beautiful, 'a big picture of Cupid dragging a maiden through all the meshes and mazes of Love'. Mary was not one of the dreamy young damsels who frequented his studio, her common-sense and straightforward honesty were a refreshing antidote and he would go on painting while talking with her, valuing her opinions, agreeing with her, confiding in her. He let her look through his pictures and his sketches, and the designs that he was working on for his commission to decorate Arthur Balfour's London home. He gave her tea in his big studio and they walked together in his pretty, old-fashioned garden. 'How very nice you always are, aren't you', he wrote after one of her visits.

The Eton–Harrow match that year was endured to breaking point. Everyone was there in support of Alfred, the last Lyttelton in his last Eton term and the best cricketer in the family. Once this loving yet painful family gathering was over, Spencer set sail for New Zealand with Arthur Balfour. The two young men looked forward with relish to uncomfortable physical challenges in wild uncivilised places, a marvellous antidote to their grief. The first stage of their journey took them across the Atlantic Ocean and overland to Vancouver, followed by long sea voyages to New Zealand, Australia and on to India.

Spencer owned an estate on New Zealand's South Island which he had inherited when he was nine from his uncle and godfather, Earl Spencer. His father, Lord George Lyttelton, had been involved in the Canterbury Association in the 1840s, a Church of England settlement whose plan was to buy land from the Maori tribes and to re-sell it to the white settlers at a profit which would be used to build roads, establish schools and university and, of course, a church and cathedral. Thus were founded the cities of Canterbury and Christchurch and the harbour town of Lyttelton. *The Lyttelton Times* never failed to reach Hagley from Canterbury and in 1867 Spencer and his father had made their first journey to New Zealand. Six provinces had been established by this time, each with elected councils; in 1875 the provinces joined together to form a united Dominion, a sign that the British attitude to her Empire was changing with the realisation that colonial self-government need not imply separation but, instead, increasing trade to the benefit of all.

Spencer and Mary kept in touch by long, gossipy letters. In a letter dated 17 October from Lake Rotorua, North Island he sends her details of the weather and the conditions of their travel. On the voyage from Canada to New Zealand, which took twenty-five days, he read voraciously while Arthur Balfour suffered dreadful seasickness. Now in New Zealand, they camped in a deserted Maori hut and rode for seventy-five miles across wild desolate country, leaving him saddle-sore. He gives Mary an idea of the distance between them: 'A telegram from England to New Zealand takes eight days as there is no cable yet between Australia and New Zealand though there will be one in about a year.' He tells her that they plan to spend a short while in Christchurch before setting sail for Singapore and that, when they reach Delhi, he and Balfour will part company, he will be joined by his brother Neville and they hoped to meet up with Harry Gladstone in Burma. A month later he wrote again from Otago, New Zealand and thanked her 'for a really grand letter discursively lengthy, full of gossip and conversational, in fact I should think the opposite of what this will be.'[4]

Spencer was a shy, introverted man, often appearing rude and heartless but he could open his heart to Mary, knowing that she would understand him; feelings were such fearfully complicated things to him that he ran away from any kind of display, yet beneath his bluff guard lay what has been called 'a crystal-clear integrity'. In this letter he tells her, 'No, I cannot talk to B of May, neither of us are persons to whom such a thing would be easy or possible, I don't think it would be of use and I don't seem to feel the want of any such communication. Her memory is green enough indeed for me and supplies a subject of almost unceasing thought.'[5] He has brought with him May's photograph that Mary gave him before he left on his travels.

With Spencer away, Mary returned to the daily round at Hawarden. Brother Stephen had become the rector after Uncle Henry's sudden death, brought about by being deluged and possibly struck by lightening in a violent summer storm in 1872. The two Glynne orphaned cousins had moved into 'The Cottage' in the village and soon Gertrude would be married. The old schoolroom in the rectory had been turned into Stephen's study; it had the advantage of an outside door for visiting parishioners. Albert Lyttelton joined him as curate, taking over what had been the study. Mrs Peake the housekeeper had stayed on to look after the two of them; they were the same age but of vastly different characters; Stephen was capable and organised, Albert absent-minded and eccentric.

Uncle Stephen's death had been abrupt and unexpected two years earlier. He had been looking at churches in Suffolk, their history and architecture, a life-long interest of his, and he was taken ill on his return journey at Shoreditch station. Passersby helped him into a doctor's room in the High Street, where he died. It had been agreed in the family that Mary's eldest brother William would inherit the castle and estate and, by April 1875, all the legalities had been completed. His father had written to give him the news along with much salutary advice,

> You will, I hope, familiarise your mind with this truth, that you can no more become the proprietor of such a large body of property, or of the portion of it now accruing, than your brother Stephen could become rector of the parish, without recognising the serious moral and social responsibilities which belong to it.[6]

He went on to urge him to find a wife and, by end of the summer, William had done just that; he married Lord Blantyre's youngest daughter Gertrude who could count three aunts on her mother's side who were duchesses. Mary was prepared to like her sister-in-law and to make her welcome at Hawarden for she believed she was 'the brightest, pleasantest, nicest and most pliable of the lot' although the family had a reputation for obstinacy, and this would become a problem between the bride and Mrs Gladstone.

As 1875 ended, Mary wrote in her diary, 'the heart-aching parting with this April-like year; each of the three families [Gladstones, Glynnes, Lytteltons] is altered. The blessings will no doubt stand out more vividly as time goes on, but just now, Palm Sunday is more present to me than anything else, and it almost seems today like going through it again. Goodbye poor old year, tearful '75.'

Her life had reached a watershed. She desperately needed a purpose, a daily structure. Alfred Lyttelton knew that Mary would feel acutely the loosening of family bonds, and he had written to her in September: 'I want you, if ever you should feel desolate and in the cold amid the hurly burly of marriages, to try and remember what an immense help you are to all of us. I sometimes think that you fancy yourself "vocationless"; no one can be less so.' He assured her of her value: 'I think, and Edward feels the same, half the fun of visits and such like is the anticipating of recounting the incidents to you.'[7] He shared with her his feelings of how grim and gaunt London could be, and for Mary the city had lost its charms; she did not regret her father's decision to part with 11 Carlton House Terrace.

At this time, Disraeli was Prime Minister and pursuing a vigorous foreign and imperial policy; in 1875 he acquired control of the Suez Canal by purchasing the Egyptian Khedive's shares. Gladstone was out of office, no longer leader of the Liberal party and with a need to economise. The lease of 11 Carlton House terrace was sold for £35 000 to Sir Arthur Guinness with a four-day sale of books, art and china realising over £9000. It was a particular wrench to Mr Gladstone, who described it as 'like a little death'. A more modest house in the Terrace was taken for a season as Mrs Gladstone was quite sure that they could not possibly manage without a London base. These decisions were not important to Mary as long as she could count Hawarden as her home.

Despite a successful second marriage, Lord George Lyttelton was prone to bouts of black depression. The marriages of his daughters Meriel, Lucy and Lavinia had brought crises of melancholia. May's death had deepened the despair that held him captive for days on end. A cloud of sadness and apathy thickened around him and deafness isolated him. In April 1876 the family noticed that he had entered upon 'a different and darker stage, utter lassitude and hopeless distress with occasional paroxysms of misery.' In London on Easter Sunday, at the church service, Lavinia thought him 'fidgety and scared-looking'. The next day Mary was with him at a concert, after which he dined with them all and she felt that he was comparatively quiet. But the next morning, while dressing, he pushed past his manservant and flung himself headlong over the banisters. Within twenty-four hours he was dead. Lucy believed that 'a messenger of release' had seized him. Mary was at hand to comfort her grieving cousins. She broke the news to Arthur and then spent the day with Lavinia, her quiet presence a support. 'Oh God,' wrote Lucy, 'what can we all be without him?'

Through the summer months of 1876, a frantic madness seemed to drive Mary. Life must be enjoyed to the full. She accepted all invitations, went to art exhibitions, the circus, concerts at the Crystal Palace, played tennis and joined in all the latest crazes. She had dabbled in seances with the Balfours, their interest in psychic phenomena going back to their student days at Cambridge. When she had told Herbert about her spiritual adventures, cautioning him not to quote the Balfour name if he should tell anyone, she had marvelled at the unearthly happenings of tables moving, wet flowers being flung in their faces, and words spelled out in raps in the table top, but she had concluded that the medium was 'a silly little woman, who could not for a moment keep up the imposture, from sheer lack of brains'. Now her interest resurfaced, and Harry and Herbert joined in the seances, but she was even more sceptical and more convinced that it was a trick.

A new friend became important. Henry Scott Holland was nicknamed 'Monkey' and Mary added 'the Flying Dutchman' because his brilliance and vitality made her think of wings. He was her own age, educated at Eton and Balliol, and a tutor and priest at Christ Church, Oxford. She delighted in his boyish high spirits and innocent sense of fun. A friendship began that would last for forty-two years until his death, when Mary wrote that, 'Nothing ever happened, no event public or private, no new book I had read, no new friend I had made, was ever complete until it had been shared with him.'[8]

She invited him to Hawarden that mid-summer and he was mesmerised by Mr Gladstone, whose presence he described as 'a gathered store of force. I keep expecting it to go off pop like dynamite in a box.' It must have been a meeting of like spirits, for Mary has written that no one could be in the same room with Scott Holland for five minutes without being conscious of the presence of 'a kindling force'. There were no words too superlative to describe him. He came into Mary's life at just the right moment; his Christian faith dispelled all her doubts. She described him as 'a sea breeze quickening, bracing, sweeping out the dusty corners of the soul, renewing life and love.' He was an original, and being in his company, enjoying his friendship, his sympathy and kindness inspired her to reach out to life and not be afraid. He always made her feel that she was the important one, and he loved to hear what she had been doing, what she thought and what she felt. He was the first man, other than her younger brothers and cousins, who had really had time for her.

After she had been in Oxford in the autumn he wrote that he hoped she would be down again soon, 'and we will have an evening of comic songs, through which we will sadly and soothingly talk.' He had lost a friend from typhoid in 1874, the year that he was ordained, and perhaps Mary entered his life at the right moment for him. There was never any question of romance between them although his mother would have loved Mary as her daughter-in-law. Scott Holland had given his heart to Christ and his life to His service. Mary suggested to him that he should think of her as his dead wife's sister, so that they should not misunderstand each other's motives. It was a shrewd, humorous move and much appreciated by him.

Now that her father was no longer in government and was at home without a secretary, he needed someone to help him with his letters, which were piling up at the rate of fifty a day. Harry was in India, Herbert was at Oxford, Helen was furthering her studies. Mary was the only member of the family drifting aimlessly around, and it seemed an ideal arrangement that she should help with the mountain of correspondence. Apart from being available, she was by temperament the most suitable sibling to become her father's assistant; she knew his loving nature, she could speak openly to him, she understood his ways; as she had told Harry 'Papa idealises his children so much that there is never any fear of his being over-stern with them.' Now she would discover that she had a valuable contribution to make to his political life. She was twenty-nine years old; she wrote on her birthday, 'I can't say there is much satisfactory to look back on.' What lay ahead must be more rewarding.

CHAPTER TEN

The Eastern Question and an Irish visit (1876 – 9)

Trouble in the Balkans had been gathering pace since the spring of 1876. Uprisings in Bosnia and Herzegovinia had sparked a revolt in Bulgaria which became a massacre of thousands of Bulgarian men, women and children by troops loyal to the Sultan of Turkey. The consuls of France and Germany at Salonica were murdered by the Turkish mob. Serbia and Montenegro were up in arms. The only political alliance in Europe at this time was the League of the Three Emperors (Germany, Russia and Austria); their view was that pressure should be put on Turkey to grant better conditions to their Christian subjects. This was known as the Berlin memorandum, and England, France and Italy were invited to sign up to the proposals.

Disraeli dismissed the memorandum and acted independently by sending a fleet to anchor off the Dardanelles, a warning to Russia to keep out of Constantinople where they could pose a threat to the British naval base at Alexandria. As news of the massacre filtered through, public opinion was stirred and Disraeli's cavalier comment in the House on 10 July that he doubted that 'torture has been practised on a great scale among an oriental people who seldom, I believe, resort to torture, but generally terminate their connexion with culprits in a more expeditious manner'[1] sparked moral indignation, but his sights were set on maintaining British power and influence. Within a month he had swept out of the Commons and taken his seat in the Lords as Earl of Beaconsfield; Gladstone's comments reflect his generous respect for his political opponent while condemning his foreign policy: 'Disraeli assumes his earldom amidst loud acclaims. I had better be mute about him and his influence generally, except as to a full acknowledgement of his genius and his good points of character. His government is supposed now to stand mainly upon its recent foreign policy: the most selfish and least worthy I have ever known.'[2]

Parliament ended for the summer recess and did not meet again until February 1877; political debate continued at afternoon teas, dinner parties and country house weekends, even rocking theatre performances. Gladstone was at a performance of *Othello* in Liverpool in late November and his diary records that, when 'the words were reached 'The Turks are drowned', the audience rose in enthusiasm and interrupted the performance for some time with their cheering.'

At Hawarden, Mary took an early breakfast and devoted long hours to her father's correspondence. She made a note of the most interesting letters. There was one from Mr MacColl, later Canon of Ripon, who was writing from the scene of action in Bulgaria. He was horrified by the scenes that he was witnessing and he expressed 'earnest gratitude' to Mr Gladstone for his vigorous involvement, a point of view that Mary shared. Too much tree-felling had brought on her father's lumbago and, while taking a day's rest in bed, he wrote a pamphlet, *Bulgarian Horrors and the Question of the East*. On 3 September he rushed off to London by the overnight train, 'pamphlet in hand, beyond anything agog over the Bulgarian horrors, which pass description,' wrote Mary in her diary. 'The whole country is aflame, meetings all over the place.'

On 9 September there was a huge meeting on Blackheath; Gladstone denounced the Turks as 'the one great anti-human species of humanity' and called upon Europe to bring relief 'to the overcharged emotion of a shuddering world'. Next day he stormed back to Hawarden and awaited reactions, which swiftly followed. Disraeli dismissed all the agitation as 'coffee-house babble'; in Mary's view, he was 'cynical, sneering, vulgar' in his speech at an agricultural dinner. There were letters to the newspapers on the refusal of the government to summon Parliament, and John Bright spoke on the crisis at a public meeting in Manchester. By the end of the month, 200 000 copies of the pamphlet had been snapped up by the public.

Her father was spending more time in London and depending increasingly on her assistance. A London base was needed and a lease was taken on 73 Harley Street. Mary was there in December when a conference on the Eastern Question brought together what she thought was a curious collection of people – 'poet, historian, painter, cleric, dissenter, R.C., unbeliever, and bishop, headed by the Duke of Westminster.' Politicians who called at Harley Street over the winter months discovered that Mr Gladstone's daughter was more than her father's cipher and they welcomed her bright-eyed contributions to their conversations. She was privy to the most recent news and secret information, and quite obviously her father welcomed her good humour and, above all, her discretion.

She took time off to visit Lyttelton cousins Edward and Alfred at Cambridge, staying with the Sidgwicks, Henry and Nora, at their home in Chesterton Road. Nora had been a Balfour before marriage; she and Henry were the driving force behind the lectures and courses for women in Cambridge that had led to the opening of Newnham Hall the previous year. Mary became enthused by the idea that sister Helen should become a student; twenty-seven-year-old Helen was the quiet studious one in the family; she had sorted and catalogued her father's books and was desperately in need of some useful occupation. Mary wrote to tell Lavinia that 'von Moltke' had a surprising plan but not to breathe a word until it had ripened. Her love of organising everyone had led to her family nickname, after Bismarck's young aide de camp. With Nora's encouragement, she returned to London determined to win parents over to her idea. It was no easy task, for neither her father nor her mother were in favour of university education for women, but Mary's arguments won the day; Mrs Gladstone was probably a little relieved that her youngest daughter would be away from home, usefully employed and not constantly drifting irritably around. Helen did not enjoy the domestic life;

as she wrote to Harry in praise of Mary, 'She is almost the only one of us (more shame to me) who really does help Mama – and moreover she does it constantly and lovingly.'[3]

Nora Sidgwick made some revealing comments on university education for women in a lecture at Liverpool University a few years later:

> University education was looked askance at by many, and to break down prejudice it was useful that a daughter of Mr Gladstone's should enter the College. Also in those days there were comparatively few occupations open to women ... except that of teaching; so that there was a certain danger that the College might become merely a place for the education of teachers and so lose the advantage of bringing together women with different backgrounds to their education, different experience of life, and different plans for the future.[4]

When Helen became a student she lived at first with the Sidgwicks and Nora Sidgwick admitted that a Gladstone staying in a Balfour house might be taken as a 'demonstration'. She gave no clues as to what she meant by this; a demonstration of Gladstone's belief in university education for women? The Gladstone name certainly worked both ways for Helen and Mary, both a useful means of networking and a barrier to their own self-esteem.

On 7 May 1877 Mary opened and sorted one hundred and twenty letters before heading for the House of Commons, where her father was to move five resolutions. It was an unprecedented scene. He was no longer leader of the Liberals, yet here he was speaking as though he had never resigned his post, and was threatening to split the Party by his stance. He spoke three times before his big speech, by which time the House was emptying for dinner. He had forgotten his spectacles and had to speak without notes, which only heightened the tension. For two and a half hours his voice rang out, gaining in feeling and conviction, and turning the mood from hostility and impatience to enthralment. The seats quickly filled as word got out of the dramatic turn of events. Mary was elated by his performance which she called 'a triumph of sustained beauty of language and passionate earnestness'.

His words on Bosnia, Herzegovinia and Montenegro were the thrilling climax as he passionately proclaimed,

> Sir, there were other days when England was the hope of freedom. Wherever in the world a high aspiration was entertained, or a noble blow was struck, it was to England that the eyes of the oppressed were always turned – to this favourite, this darling home of so much privilege and so much happiness, where the people that had built up a noble edifice for themselves would, it was well known, be ready to do what in them lay to secure the bene-fit of the same inestimable boon for others. You talk to me of the established tradition and policy in regard to Turkey. I appeal to an established tradition older, wider, nobler far – a tradition not which disregards British interests, but which teaches you to seek the promotion of these inter-ests in obeying the dictates of honour and justice.[5]

Arthur Balfour, a Member of Parliament since 1874, having taken two years to make his maiden speech on an obscure sub-ject at a time when the House could be guaranteed to be ill-attended, now found himself a willing pupil as he listened to a speech that, in his opinion, 'As a mere feat of physical endurance it was almost unsurpassed; as a feat of parliamentary courage, parliamentary skill, parliamentary endurance, and parliament-ary eloquence, I believe it will always be unequalled.'[6]

Gladstone lost the parliamentary debate but, that summer of 1877, the family at Hawarden was besieged by crowds of well-wishers as excursion trains arrived at Queensferry station full of Liberal supporters who then walked the two miles to Hawarden Castle. They were seeking out the man described by one local paper as 'the hermit of Hawarden' and by another as 'a friendly Gulliver at Lilliput'. It was as though Mr Glad-stone, having removed himself from Westminster and the centre of political power, now belonged to the people. Over a thousand people came from Bolton and two weeks later, three thousand arrived from Salford and Darwen. Two days later, two thousand turned up from Bacup, and so it continued. Many did not recognise their hero when they met him in the park, mistaking him for one of the gardeners.

Mary disliked seeing her father so harassed as he dodged enthusiastic well-wishers; she declared that they would have to be kept away while the family was at home. It could be that she disliked the disruption to her own peaceful days; the enchantment of home lay in the green open spaces, the breezes in the branches and the deep quiet that was broken only by the sounds of the countryside. The park had only been open to the public since August; the decision had been made by brother William, head of the family home and estate since the death of Uncle Stephen. Mary thought that a new rule would have to be made to keep out the crowds who even milled round in the church searching for the Gladstone pew. But they were orderly, well-behaved crowds who happily left with chippings of wood from trees felled by the family.

Throughout 1877 the issues of peace and war veered unstably, and who could say what the outcome would be? Mary was often to be found in the House of Commons until midnight, delighting in the noisy debates. She was twenty-eight and, as she told her mother, it was only 'an accident' that she was not married. She discovered a new yardstick by which to judge friend and acquaintance; were they for or against the Turks? There could be no half measures. If you were not with her, you were a traitor to the cause.

Disraeli's realistic policy was carrying the day but Mary stood with her father on the moral high ground. She discovered within herself a strength hitherto untapped. She was not afraid to state her opinion even if it differed from others'; however small the matter might be, she was prepared to stand her ground. One night at a large dinner party, the conversation turned to the subject of what qualities are needed for the ideal dinner guest, and a challenge was thrown down for each to choose the ideal ten for dinner. Everybody else chose the conventional table plan of five men and five women, and were astounded at her choice of nine men and herself, an arrangement that would have caused much gossip in their social circles, and which reveals a modern woman awakening from her Victorian restrictions.

In the autumn of 1877 her father decided, somewhat abruptly, that it was time to visit Ireland; the impression should be put about that the visit was a social occasion. His motives were complex and perhaps obscure even to himself. His passionate public outbursts on the Balkans were making him extremely unpopular in aristocratic circles but the working classes were responding to his rhetoric. Perhaps this trip was part of a plan, not yet fully realised, to find a platform away from London and Westminster on which to launch his comeback. Neither he nor Disraeli had ever set foot in Ireland although he had begun his first premiership in 1868 with the words 'My mission is to pacify Ireland', and he had made a successful start with the Irish Church Disestablishment Bill, followed by the Irish Land Bill. At one time he had thought to solve the Irish problem and the question of employment for the Prince of Wales at a stroke by installing the Prince as Viceroy of Ireland, but he had only succeeded in creating further distance between the Queen and himself.

The problem of Ireland had plagued successive governments since Elizabethan times, and policies had fluctuated between coercion and acquiescence. When Disraeli had observed to the Queen in 1863 that for two centuries the Sovereign had only passed twenty-one days in Ireland, she had replied, 'For health and relaxation no one would go to Ireland and people only go who have their estates to attend to.'[7]

Mary's task was to organise her parents on to the boat at Holyhead. They were taking along two family servants, Hymen to attend to her father's needs and Schlüter as ladies' maid. Mary was not at all sure that she was going to enjoy the trip although she would have the company of Spencer who was home from his world travels. They would act as secretaries, one of their tasks being to keep the reporters at bay; 'the noble army' as Gladstone called them. She thought this would be quite simple, for they were not a particularly fit crew and could easily be given the slip on country walks.

The first stop was in County Wicklow as guests of a distant cousin, the Earl of Meath. They moved on to the Fitzwilliam estate at Coolattin and wound up with a few short stays at other great houses around Dublin. The hospitality was overwhelming and they were showered with invitations, all of which they determined to refuse, although Mary felt sure that her father would have to make a speech when he was honoured with the freedom of the city of Dublin. Steering his way round controversial issues was, he said, like 'treading on eggs'.

The only dark clouds were in the skies on the morning they embarked on the sea voyage back to Holyhead. The wind rose and waves broke over the deck. To add to Mary's misery in the lurching swell, their ship had to change course to answer a distress signal from an American merchant vessel, whose broken masts and sails were flapping helplessly. The crew refused to abandon ship, so they steamed on, only to be forced to seek shelter themselves. All of this added hours to their time at sea. Poor Mary, never a good sailor, spent those wretched hours in analysing her sensations: 'At the moment the ship goes away from underneath you, leaving your inside behind you, there is literally nothing on earth that could compensate, and life is simply not worth living.' And when at last her feet were safely on dry land, there was another ordeal of enthusiastic crowds to struggle through. 'We smiled and bowed as if we weren't dead, and Papa made one of his most spirited speeches.'[8]

It would seem that the trip had recharged her father's energies and fanned the flames of his popularity as people gathered at the stations along the North Wales coast to wave as the train steamed by. For Mary, Hawarden had never seemed more peaceful nor bed more blissful; it would take her more than a night to recover and she woke the next day 'with aching eyeballs'. She wrote to brother Harry about the ordeals of country-house visiting; 'going into dinner each night hooked to a new person' meant that she was 'always to be digging in untried ground'. Spencer's company had been a bonus as they had been working closely together on the day-to-day problems.

He had always been specially dear to her and now he became 'my Spencer'. She wrote in her diary, 'no more rot', with no further explanation. Marriage to her first cousin was out of the question, although her mother became a little worried for a while at their need for each other. Spencer had never seemed interested in women. There was a family joke that when he was asked if he had ever kissed a woman, he had answered, 'Yes. Once, on the forehead.'

The Eastern Question was bubbling over and all else paled in significance. The Russians were camped outside Constantinople. The British Fleet had gone into the Dardanelles. A storm of anti-Russian feeling broke over the Gladstone home in Harley Street while Mary was there with only Schlüter for company. The house was being guarded by the police at the time but a crowd, jeering and hurling abuse, had pushed down New Cavendish Street and broken through the police barrier into Harley Street. About twenty raced down the street, with policemen in hot pursuit. They reached the house and threw stones at the windows, cracking a few panes, before being driven back. Mounted police were called in and Mary and Schlüter watched them parade up and down the street until bedtime when peace and quiet were restored.

Suddenly events moved to a resolution. Her diary reads, '28 March 1878, Everybody's breath knocked out of their bodies by the news of Ld. Derby's real sober resignation on calling out the reserve forces.' She continues, 'The war party are throwing up their hats and the peace ditto letting down their legs.' This was her way of saying that the first were rejoicing and the others were feeling sorry for themselves.

The personal vendetta between Gladstone and Disraeli now reached new depths. They goaded each other nightly in the parliamentary debates. On 21 May Mary heard her father speak for over an hour; Arthur Balfour, who had just been taken on as private parliamentary secretary to his uncle Lord Salisbury, had to reply. Mary felt quite sorry for him as he was obviously out of his depth, being new at the job. She could not help being amused: 'It was funny watching him – much emphatic gesture, too much'. Her father's speech was well received on all sides. Her opinion was that 'people think he has gone so mad on the E.Q. that they are taken by surprise by a speech of that kind, quiet, forcible, strong, careful and telling in its legal points, no bursts of vehemence, but sustained in earnestness and vigour.'[9]

In June, Disraeli and Lord Salisbury attended the Berlin Congress. Arthur Balfour was there as principal private secretary to Lord Salisbury. Mary was staying in Darmstadt at the same time. There had been a sudden family arrangement for her to accompany her Lyttelton uncle who had been appointed to the position of chaplain to Princess Alice of Hesse. Schlüter was included in the party as Mary's personal maid; her diary records their arrival at Darmstadt after a merry train journey. 'We had three nice ladies in our compartment, who joined in Mr Lyttelton's jokes with all their heart. About eight we reached the dearest little house in Darmstadt, four sitting rooms and four bedrooms, a kind maid received us and we all were soon refreshed and enjoyed a good tea.' The days passed pleasantly. 'Mr L bought himself a pepper-and-salt suit and a light umbrella, and it is rare fun to see him come home, from the balcony, for as soon as he sees me he shouts out to me what he has bought, for he always returns with a brown paper parcel under his arm.' Schlüter was given two days' absence to visit her mother in Hanover, her train ticket paid for by Mary and others in the family for which she was truly grateful: 'How good is God to me!' she wrote in her diary.

The stay in Darmstadt lasted almost a month; Eustace Balfour called on them, he was a gifted artist and architect and may have been paying his respects while on a continental tour. They dined several times at the Palace; while Mary was being entertained by Princess Alice of Hesse and Eustace Balfour was playing lawn tennis with the Duke, Bismarck was battling with Disraeli at the Berlin Congress. Lord Salisbury thought little of his Prime Minister's diplomacy. 'What with deafness, ignorance of French, and Bismarck's extraordinary mode of speech, Beaconsfield has only the dimmest idea of what is going on, understands everything crossways, and imagines a perpetual conspiracy.'[10] Yet the wily Lord Beaconsfield secured Cyprus for Britain and returned home in triumph, declaring he brought 'Peace with Honour'. Mary scornfully termed it 'Peace with Diz-honour'.

The Conservatives were riding high, but time was not on their side and as the old year ended, Mary reflected in her diary that 'the country weighed down by hard winter and great distress seems to be losing confidence in their flashy Gov. and who knows what political changes the coming year may bring about.' There would be conflict in South Africa, in Egypt and in Afghanistan before Beaconsfield Toryism had run its ruinous course but, by the end of 1879, Mary would be thirty-two-years-old, the family would be in Downing Street and she would be in the midst of the political hurly-burly, carving out a unique role for herself.

CHAPTER ELEVEN

Mary as confidante and heroine (1879)

Mary had scarcely drawn breath from welcoming her new sister-in-law when it was time to dress cousin Gertrude Glynne for her wedding to Mr Pennant, afterwards Lord Penrhyn. Gertrude had hoped that William Gladstone might have been her sweetheart but he had chosen another Gertrude. Her marriage to a wealthy thirty-seven-year-old widower with seven children would seem a mixed blessing. Mr Pennant was no romantic hero. Mary described him as 'decidedly ugly, short legs and long thick hair, a beard rather like a goat's, good eyes, about five foot eleven inches, good from top to toe I should imagine with a character of simple goodness and straightforwardness and an unquestioning faith.' She tried to make sense of the romance, 'When a man of that sort who is dry and almost disagreeable to the common run of mortals and who you know is sad and lonely and to whom all the world is utterly indifferent, when such a man suddenly wakes up to love you, I believe it does carry you straight off your legs.'[1]

She helped to dress the bride, making her wreath of myrtle from the cuttings grown out of Agnes' wedding wreath made two years earlier. Agnes had been the first to break the family circle and to have a home of her own. She had married the Reverend Edward Wickham in Hawarden Church which was now the setting for Gertrude's wedding; Mary described it as 'a most cheerful wedding', the hymns 'choky', but Uncle Billy Lyttelton tripping over his words in the service and asking the bride, 'Wilt thou have this woman for thy wedded husband?' had caused some smiles. After the wedding service and the happy goodbyes, it seemed to Mary that 'all the brightness from Hawarden' had left with them.

As one after another moved into marriage, Mary grew increasingly aware of her solitary state. She was determined to marry for love, but she knew that others could not always afford this choice. When she heard that her friend Margaret Leicester-Warren of Tabley Hall had agreed to marry Arthur Cowell-Stepney, she told herself it was 'a comfort'. He is 'about 100 years old' she joked with Harry; 'When he dies they will have about £30 000 a year I believe − won't it be fun to have Maggie rolling in gold and giving us silk gowns and opera boxes.' After two brief years of happiness, her husband became quite mad: 'His monomania is hatred of her, he will not stay in the same house with her, he is going off to Japan with a mad doctor.' Maggie was alone in her little house near Ascot 'with nothing to comfort her but her baby and a horrid ugly bulldog called Bill who she worships because he belongs to her husband.' Mary unburdened herself to Harry: 'It does seem so wretched that she who has already led such a clouded life should be called upon to suffer like this.'[2]

There was a new curate, the Reverend Edward Bickersteth Ottley, at the rectory who was proving delightful company. Clergymen made such safe companions, everyone thought. Mary's days at Hawarden were informal, she walked to and from church, sometimes bringing Mr Ottley back for luncheon or dinner, or a game of tennis. She was a good listener and the shy young man felt that he could talk easily to her.

Autumn of 1878 gave way to winter and Mary plotted an exciting house party. She invited Scott Holland, Mr Ruskin and Lord Acton. 'That will make a most brilliant little assembly,' she told her father. Cousin Alfred would be staying, and George Wyndham, a distant relative who lived close by, would come each day. Mrs Gladstone was in London and although her husband wrote urgently that he wished she could be at Hawarden, her sense of duty to her many charities kept her there. She did, however, feel responsible for the sleeping arrangements at Hawarden so, in a typically unconventional way, she sorted out the bedrooms and left Mary in charge as hostess.

Mary had met Ruskin when she had stayed with Frances Graham in the Lake District and had charmed the fifty-nine-year-old with her pianoforte playing. His gentle chivalrous manner delighted her. She wrote in her diary that he spoke just as he wrote, 'the slow and soft stream of beautiful yet unaffected words, the sudden lighting up and splendid laugh. He talked about sins and ugly things in the world all as mistakes or misprints, and utterly condemned the way in which they are dwelt upon.'[3] He had accepted her invitation, more for the delight of listening again to her playing than for her father's erudite conversation.

Scott Holland could hardly believe his good fortune to be invited to Hawarden at the same time. As he watched Gladstone and Ruskin in conversation he was amused at how opposite they were in temperament and opinion, 'the one in despair of all things here on earth, attributing this century chiefly to the devil, the other profoundly convinced that there never was such a good time, never such a hopeful age.' Ruskin accused his host of being a 'leveller', whereas he believed in the aristocracy. Gladstone swiftly responded, 'Oh dear no! I am nothing of the sort, I am a firm believer in the aristocratic principle − the rule of the best. I am an out and out inequalitarian.'[4]

Ruskin had almost turned down Mary's invitation. He was unsure that he could get on with Mr Gladstone, and on the first evening he had once or twice mentioned that he might be called away. Before bedtime he took Mary and Alfred aside, and gave them a long homily on marriage. 'Women are, in general, far nobler, purer, more divinely perfect than men, because they come less in contact with evil,' he told them, a view often held among Victorian gentlefolk. At precisely 10:45 p.m. he announced that he always retired to bed early, and vanished. Mary thought he was 'a dear old blessed man' but there were times when she found the honour of being singled out by him a strain.

The Reverend Ottley was under a similar strain as he preached his Sunday sermon before these illustrious guests. The young curate was in his first post after Keble College, Oxford. He was enjoying the warm friendship offered to him by all the Gladstones, but he was particularly drawn towards Mary. After the service he joined the guests for luncheon, but his meal was spoiled by seeing Mary talking so vivaciously with Mr Holland. He was disconcerted that she did not make more of his company, and he took himself off to 'a sulky coffee at the Rectory'. As for Mr Ruskin, he enjoyed himself so much that on his return home, he wrote to Mary that he had ordered his publisher to cancel the page of his book that contained insults of her Papa, and if she ever saw them she must forgive him. He would come again to stay in the autumn, and even join in the family tree-cutting fun, as long as Mr Gladstone would mark branches, not trees, for him, nothing more than one inch thick. His letters to her become increasingly affectionate, addressing her as 'My dear little madonna' and 'Darling Cecilia'. He signs himself 'St C.', an abbreviation of Saint Chrysostom, fourth-century Bishop of Constantinople; Mary calls him St Crumpet.

Mr Ottley could afford to lie low until the important guests had left; he had Mary's company for another two weeks before she was bound for London. This time she was depressed at leaving Hawarden. London society was self-absorbed and dressing-up was dreary, she told her friendly curate, who was so encouraged by her confidences that he wrote in his diary that he would do anything in the world to make her happier and more blest: 'Oh I can't bear her going away and putting Hawarden's eye out.' He let her read what he had written and she was not angry. She did not love him now but might she later? She was in a quandary and needed time to sort it out, with a little help from long 'trolls' with Maggie and Lavinia.

In London, there was the usual round of art exhibitions, studios, concerts, plays and dinners, and in March there was new excitement in the form of trips to see the latest inventions of telephone and phonograph. In her opinion, the former would be the more useful, but the latter quite took her fancy: 'The phono. keeps your words and voice shut up for any length of time and then repeats them back word for word' she wrote in her diary.

In June she was invited to visit the Tennysons at home on the Isle of Wight. She asked Maggie to accompany her as chaperone, quite a proper arrangement as Maggie was a married lady even if she was separated from her husband. Their first glimpse of Farringford, a comfortably solid, ivy-covered house on the south-western tip of the island, was from an open carriage as they were driven at a fair gallop down lanes of yellow gorse with the blue sea peeping between the branches. They had hoped for a quiet drive but Hallam had been waiting on the jetty at Yarmouth and his immediate presence had done nothing to calm her nerves. It was as though she had some presentiment of what this invitation to visit the family might mean.

It was an enchanting time of year and Mary felt at once that the sun seemed warmer and brighter here than elsewhere. While Maggie rested, she was taken by father and son over the garden. She felt appallingly shy. She liked Hallam who was five years her junior, but this was no handicap; her favourite Lyttelton cousins were up to ten years younger than her, and she was at times remarkably immature for her thirty-one years. But she was not at all sure how to cope with his father who sometimes behaved like a wayward child, and at other times reversed the roles, playing the taunting philandering male and treating her like a powerless maiden. He made remarks that she called 'near the wind' that left her and Maggie flushed with embarrassment. She had never known such difficult moments. She described her first evening as 'like six rolled into one' as the family followed the fashion of constantly being on the move from one room to another for a different activity. They had four moves which to Mary meant three fresh starts to the evening, ending in a room where they played a game of backgammon before bed.

After a poor night's sleep, the day began well with a glorious walk over the Downs, climbing ever upward as the chalk-white cliffs rose steeply from the breeze-ruffled waves. Everywhere was golden gorse; it was, her host said, 'the sun breaking through the earth'. The scented air, the calling gulls, the intense blue-green of the sea were intoxicating to her as they scrambled down to the water's edge. It was all too much, a riot of colour, a superabundance of nature; she described the sea as 'P (assionate)-B (rompton)', a term used critically by some when Pre-Raphaelite art went beyond all bounds of what was expected. She felt a sudden urge to bring some reality to this idyll and despite all protestations, she jumped into the sea 'and felt glowing and delicious'. Whatever became of her dripping self when she emerged was not important enough for her to record, but such impulsive high spirits must have made a strong impression on both Tennysons, father and son.

After luncheon and rest when she read Henry James' *Daisy Miller*, they drove to the nearby shore of Alum Bay, wandered over its strangely coloured sands and watched the sea gleaming silver and grey around the Needles. A ship, bound for distant shores, steamed slowly by. It was such a peaceful afternoon that they found it hard to leave.

Tennyson senior was obsessed with Mary's eyes; he thought they were 'remarkable', 'wonderful'; he had to look closely at them as he could not make out if they were blue or grey. Another time they were driving home in the carriage when his remarks made her blush deeply and there was no escape until Hallam came to her rescue and held up the rug to shield her from his father's gaze. Later that evening it was her nose that came in for scrutiny. The fifty-year-old poet began to stroke it, declaring it was a 'petit nez retrousse' that meant all sorts of naughty things. How fortunate that it was balanced by a strong jaw! She was so unused to being singled out for compliments; she thought that she had quite an ordinary face.

Tennyson told Maggie that his son 'had a great respect for that young woman' and he too was intrigued by Mary's blend of innocence and maturity. She clashed with him on politics that evening and, no doubt, he liked her the more for it. She could charm him with her pianoforte playing and he responded by reading his poetry. *The First Quarrel* and *Bones* she thought were 'splendid and equal to anything he ever wrote' but awfully sad. It was hardly surprising if Hallam was overshadowed by his outrageous father who was intent on pressing his attentions on the two young women. The next day he started straight after breakfast with his teasing compliments: 'Those wonderful eyes of yours. I do believe they are grey.' She scarcely knew where to put herself; she was glad that she had Maggie with her.

'We cling to each other, and the moment one rises the other does ditto,' she confided to her diary. They were measured side by side and Mary was found to be an inch taller, to which everyone expressed great surprise. It was always the foursome of father and son, Mary and Maggie. Mrs Tennyson hardly seems to impinge on Mary's consciousness. Only once does any comment of hers seem important enough for Mary to record, and that is after her husband's 'daunting' remarks to Mary, when she explains that Farringford 'is a Palace of Truth', a thought that could be far more daunting.

Just when Mary seemed to need Maggie the most, off she went to lodgings in the nearby village of Freshwater. This strange arrangement is never explained although Mary was clearly upset by her going. Then to her great surprise (and perhaps this is the explanation), it was arranged that she and Hallam should take a six-mile drive in the dog cart, just the two of them, to the pretty little village of Brook. Together they walked and talked and eventually drove home along the sands and downs. Maggie's departure gave Hallam the opportunity for greater intimacy with Mary. His father could be bold, making a game of his forwardness, but Hallam was quieter and more romantic. Not surprisingly, Mary's emotions were in turmoil, awakened and teased by all this attention, by long poetry readings and by balmy summer days in the lovely countryside. For the last two days of the holiday she had to cope alone and obviously found it a great strain. When she visited the poet's 'sanctum' at the top of the house he had alarmed her by kissing her.

Here on the island, remote from conventional behaviour and propriety, 'ships floating past with white wings shining in the sunny wind', for a time she had enjoyed the escape from life. Now she feared a darker side to this garden of Eden when 'the sun withdrew from the island, leaving us in shadow and chilly winds, and shone in silver far far away over the sea.' With

Plate 1   A family gathering 1875–6.
Back row, standing: Gertrude (daughter-in-law), Willy, Mary in profile, Mr Gladstone. Seated: Herbert, Mrs Gladstone, Stephen. Front row: Henry, Agnes, Edward Wickham (son-in-law), Helen.
Reproduced by permission of Flintshire Record Office.

Plate 2   Possibly taken when Mr and Mrs Gladstone were guests of Mr Stuart Rendel (later Lord) at his Cannes villa in the winter of 1888. Included in the party are Harry Drew in clerical dress and Mary seated with hand to her head; all are dressed in their smartest clothes.
Reproduced by permission of Flintshire Record Office.

Plate 3 Mr Gladstone in his Temple of Peace at Hawarden Castle in the 1880s.
Reproduced by permission of Flintshire Record Office.

Plate 4 Mr Gladstone in spectacles, relaxing with a book.
Reproduced by permission of Flintshire Record Office.

Plate 5   Mrs Gladstone with grand-daughter Dossie Drew. Reproduced by permission of Flintshire Record Office.

Plate 6   The Reverend Harry Drew.
Reproduced by permission of Flintshire Record Office.

Plate 7 Mr Gladstone's funeral procession winds through the crowded London streets, 25th May 1898. Reproduced by permission of Flintshire Record Office.

Plate 8   Jessy Gladstone (portrait by G. Hayter).
Reproduced by kind permission of Sir William Gladstone.
Photograph by Barry Hamilton.

Plate 9   Mary Gladstone (drawing by K. Hartmann).
Reproduced by kind permission of Sir William Gladstone.
Photograph by Barry Hamilton.

Plate 10   Helen Gladstone (drawing by K. Hartmann).
Reproduced by kind permission of Sir William Gladstone.
Photograph by Barry Hamilton.

Plate 11　Agnes Gladstone (drawing by G. Richmond).
Reproduced by kind permission of Sir William Gladstone.
Photograph by Barry Hamilton.

heavy heart she thought it was typical that the sunshine should be beyond her reach. She and Hallam had walked along the sands at Yarmouth; this may have been the moment that Hallam had proposed and she had not accepted him. She keeps her most private thoughts from her diary, but it is obvious that her last evening without Maggie was an ordeal. She was the only one who was making any effort to bridge the silences and, at last, while father and son were playing backgammon, she 'vanished drearily to bed'.

The night was 'unspeakably wretched' for both her and Hallam. She eventually fell asleep at 4.30 a.m. but Hallam tossed and dreamed. He wrote down his dream and at breakfast he gave her a letter and a copy of his dream, and the brilliance of the day outside only served to highlight the dark moods indoors. His dream is unsigned but the date at the end of it is 10 June 1879. It begins, 'I saw one dear to me, weary and worn on the outskirt of a forest – pointing toward a fierce torrent. She cried aloud that she yearned to cross it to some garden of peace on the counter-shore. In vast love and pity I raised a bridge for her above the cataract-flood and she past over it.' He continues with his dream; he followed her but the bridge broke and as he fell an angel caught him up and 'held to my lips a draught of the waters of Home – love and straightaway pulses of a divine strength throbbed thro' my lung – while a heavenly happiness possessed my soul.' He urges her not to worry but to 'rest, rest, rest and may God bless and guide you.'

With the dream was his letter, again unsigned and addressed to no one by name, explaining that he had to tell her openly and honestly about his feelings even if he ran the risk of killing whatever lay between them.

> I beseech you not to throw yourself down the precipice; when you do, there will be a double funeral. There is no high love in it, for there is no true self-sacrifice on either side. It is unconsciously, my brave Mary, as it appears to me, a sacrilege, which may God forgive! The passionate of a strong nature may beget love, but that of a weak nature begets a lifeless abortion. As for me, I find *now* that

the dream, which I wrote, is wholly false and will never be realised. God guide you and bless you and give you comfort. This cannot be answered so please do *not* write.[5]

She sat in the garden for the last time with father and son. Hallam read Plato and broke into tears at the death of Socrates: 'I called me "a hard little thing" for not crying too.' Hallam's tears were for himself as well as for Socrates; it was the death of his dream of love with Mary. As a farewell gift, Tennyson gave her *The Lover's Tale*. She crossed the sea with Maggie and they picnicked in the New Forest before heading back to London. Once again she was forcibly struck by the discordance between the outer world of springtime, glowing with colour and vigour, and her inner world that was 'so like a funeral and worse'. Her last words on the week at Farringford are 'Such is life, oh dear!'

She explained to Lavinia that it was really her week's holiday with the Tennyson family that at last opened her eyes. 'Farringford did me one good turn, it was a test and it showed me more clearly the real nature of what I felt for Mr Ottley.' She realised that her friendly advances had been misunderstood and, as she told Lavinia, all that she had wanted was 'to comfort him in the right way'. Now she wrote to him, dashing any nurturing hopes that she could learn to love him.

Home again at Hawarden, despite a houseful of guests, she found time to reflect over these past months when she had been 'confidante' and 'heroine' and even both together. She had learnt from her talks with Hallam at Farringford that she could only marry with love on both sides. She saw that her 'stupid feelings' for Mr Balfour over too many years had killed any chance of any other friendship deepening into love. While everyone enjoyed a reading of Jane Austen's *Emma*, Burne-Jones drew her portrait; studying her face in repose, he may have caught fleeting expressions that others failed to notice. There is an undated letter from him in which he asks, 'What jarred or hurt you that happened? Anything I did? I always want friends to tell me for it does hurt to find out afterwards ... So if it was I that vexed you, you ought to tell me and either I could explain it or be very sorry for it.'[6]

It could be that Mary had decided to settle for friendships and life would go on much the same; there were always her Lyttelton cousins and Scott Holland and Maggie could be relied upon for walks and gossip. Once again she was needed within the family. Her father had accepted an invitation from Lord Acton to stay at his family home in Germany. Mrs Gladstone, Herbert who was now a don at Keble College, and Mary were included in the invitation.

Mary had already discovered how much she enjoyed Lord Acton's company. He had a flatteringly attentive way of listening to her every word. Generally he was a man who liked to dominate but, having been brought up in a household of women, he understood female ways and quickly summed up Mary as one who needed a little encouragement. He was sixteen years older than her, stocky in build with a receding hairline and a dark bushy beard. He was Lord Granville's stepson and had led a privileged life, his only handicap in England being that he was Roman Catholic and so barred from Oxford and Cambridge. Following his mother's dearest wish, he had married his second cousin, Countess Maria Anna Ludmilla Euphrosyne Arco-Valley whose sister Baroness Arco owned the beautiful Villa Arco at Tegernsee near Munich where they would be staying. As ever, Mary was the family organiser for the journey, shepherding parents and luggage from Harley Street to Victoria station, on to Flushing and hence to Cologne. The start was not auspicious; 'Papa looked rigid and Mama hot and excited' although 'Herbert's coming improved matters a bit'. The first stop in Cologne was a call on Aunt Helen at the Hotel Disch and their reception was acrimonious. The evening seemed endless to Mary and she noted that Aunt Helen 'was beyond words contrary at first'.

She put the episode behind her as the train carried them eastwards to Munich and to the Hotel Belle Vue where she had to suffer through the night one of the familiar trials of travel as a persistent flea bit into her every time she extinguished the light. Lord Acton, accompanied by his brother-in-law Count Arco, travelled from Tegernsee to welcome them and took them sightseeing round the King of Bavaria's palace, rich in jewels and ivories and some lovely Cellini paintings. Then they all piled into carriages, Lord Acton choosing to sit beside Mary, for the ten-mile drive to the Villa Arco, a picturesque chalet nestling under tree-covered hills that rolled downwards to a small blue lake. She felt the tensions and aches of travel dissolving; her room was snug, her bed comfortable, and her bath a joy. The house rules were informal and she felt free and happy. After meals it was the custom to linger over coffee and conversation in the garden.

There was quite a large house party. Lord Rosebery was there, and Dr Dollinger, Lord Acton's old tutor and mentor whom Mary described as 'aged eighty, black hair, lively expression, upright figure, powerful face'. She forgot to add that he took a daily swim before breakfast and was an old and intimate friend of her father's. Mr Gladstone had met this Roman Catholic theologian back in 1845 when he had been so impressed by his liberal views and theological argument that he had delayed his return home for a week.

While Mr Gladstone sought Dr Dollinger's company for the pleasure of his conversation, Lord Acton sought out Mary. 'I always sit next to him at meals,' she wrote in her diary for 19 September, 'and from eleven to half past twelve, when all had gone to bed talked to Lord Acton, at least he talked to me, with occasional questions or comments. It went like half an hour.' She could not help but be absorbed by everything he said, for he had met all the great politicians, philosophers, teachers and rulers of his day. Next to her father, he was the most well-read man she knew. She even went so far as to say that 'in fundamentals they were identical'. He made a point of telling Mary of his very high opinion of her father. Every day and every evening they talked together, often joined by Herbert. They sailed on the lake or sat in the garden or drove together while the older ladies kept to their own company. Mary was glad to be included with the gentlemen but one little wistful wish escaped into her diary: 'How nice a honeymoon would be here.'

The last morning was spent in taking photographs; one shows Lord Acton leaning on an iron garden seat, his round black hat on his crossed knees, his left foot resting on a little woven mat that has been placed on the raked gravel. In the background sits Dr Dollinger. An air of ease pervades the scene.

It was time to move on to Venice. They travelled by carriage first to Innsbruck, down what Mary called 'a steependous hill', and after an overnight stop, on through the mountains over the Brenner Pass. This was no way for the faint-hearted to travel. Mary and Herbert wanted to walk the final fifteen miles to save the horses who were fatigued. They started off on foot, but, as Mary put it, 'the older birds insisted on our getting on'. It was a mistake. After about half a mile the carriage suddenly swerved, the axle broke, they tumbled out and Mrs Gladstone landed on her nose; luckily the path was free of stones and there was no serious damage. Mary thought it was all a huge joke, the worst of it being the long weary wait for a replacement carriage.

They were four days on the road before they reached Venice. Burne-Jones had given Mary detailed advice about this part of the holiday. They entered the city by moonlight in a gondola as he had suggested. 'It all felt like magic,' she wrote in her diary, 'and surpassed all my highest and wildest expectations.' They stayed at the Grand Hotel where conditions were just about on par with the Belle Vue in Munich. Her mattress was 'like a tough roly poly with a bullet for a bolster, and there was a beetle and fleas, and mosquitoes buzzed and stinks.' But all was forgotten as she soaked up the wonders of Venice. Burne-Jones had advised her to 'get men to row you in and out of all the byways and watch every corner you turn; windows and arches and gateways of the utmost beauty are ready to greet you at every turn.'

She and Herbert went to St Mark's to meet 'the little Rookes perched up among the shady corners of the temple', not birds at all but Burne-Jones' assistant and his wife, 'entirely unobtrusive and simple and good natured and impossible to offend.'[7] They guided them around the old mosaic floors, the golden domes, the saints and statues, then on to the Academia where she was quite overcome by Titian's *Assumption*, 'the lovely G. Bellini with the 3 musical Angels, the Titian *Presentation of the Virgin* with its unique glow of colour and the Carpaccio *St Ursulas*, made so famous and precious by Ruskin' until she was quite exhausted. Burne-Jones had told her that she must row out to Torcello and see as many islands as she could 'and lunch on figs'.

After a few days, Lord Acton arrived with his wife and family and at once Mary moved within his orbit as though no time had separated them. In fact, only two days after her departure from the Villa Arco, he had felt compelled to be in touch by a letter which ends ambiguously 'and believe that I can promise all things good and true except the wished for signal of distress. I remain dear Miss Gladstone, very faithfully yours, Acton.'

As well as his wife and children, he brought a couple of Italian politicians and Mary joined the men for political gossip as well as socialising with English friends who happened to be in Venice. She ate ices with Robert Browning, was invited to meet the Crown Princess of Germany, lunched with Countess Marcello who took them to see the lace-making at Burano, and dined with Lady Marian Alford. After dinner she promenaded, in the way of continentals, and was overjoyed that Lord Acton should single her out to spend the whole evening talking to her. 'He thinks me a mystery,' she wrote in her diary, and the next day, 'What an extraordinary man. He told me I had a mask of a face without ever showing any emotion upon it. Alas, alas, our last night. Venice grows in beauty and charm and mystery.'

There were goodbyes to be made to all her new friends and as she glided down the Grand Canal for the last time, heading with her family for the station, she felt 'in desperate dumps'. There was a final talk with her 'faithful friend' at the station; Lord Acton had chased after them in a gondola. It would seem that he too was desperate for one more conversation, one more confidence. These few last moments she described as 'the very greatest break in the world.'

It was not surprising that Mary now found the next night wretched, Verona dull, Munich wearisome, Paris very cold and travellers 'a bother and a nuisance'. Her spirits rose at the sight of a letter from Lord Acton, who wrote that he was finding Venice a duller place without her. He ends with the lines, 'I don't know why you disbelieve in my letter writing, but you must not be contradicted. Letters are, no doubt, a snare for evil speaking, and what is worth saying is worthy to remain unwritten.'[8] Perhaps what said more to her than the letter was his gift of a volume of Dante replacing one that she had lost on the journey to Venice.

Back home in England there was no time to pine. She was soon off to spend a whole fortnight with Maggie at Ascot for long heart-to-heart talks, and on to Oxford to hear Scott Holland preach at St Mary's Church. Herbert and Edward Lyttelton were there, as were many old friends. Once again she was the only woman in the group, and she had a marvellous time. By the time she reached Hawarden, Spencer was there, so there was more gossip until eventually she was alone, and reaction set in. But the Midlothian campaign was about to take off; it would provide all the excitement she could possibly need and would help to chase away futile dreams.

CHAPTER TWELVE

Campaigning brings victory (1879 – 80)

The Midlothian campaign began the day after Mary's thirty-second birthday which, not surprisingly, passed almost unnoticed. There were two full weeks of political meetings in the most frenzied carnival spirit that lifted her father's reputation sky-high. They came home to Hawarden on 8 December, to a welcome from friends and family, singing 'Home sweet home'. Mrs Gladstone was exhausted and took to her bed, whereas Lucy thought that her uncle was 'as fresh as paint; his huge personal success had recharged his batteries'.

Christmas at Hawarden was always enjoyed but everything now seems to be in a minor key; the pace of family life slowed and Mary indulged in gossipy correspondence with her cousin Spencer who is once again on his travels, again in New Zealand. Both are concerned about Uncle Billy Lyttelton who is considering a second marriage at the age of sixty. Spencer writes that he is 'all for Uncle B's affairs, the money is the drawback, but she will probably save him a lot and she has been accustomed to poverty.' Mary's reply gives lots of news: Charles and Mary Lyttelton's baby is expected in August, Arthur Lyttelton's marriage is fixed for September and the newly-weds are to live in Oxford lodgings for a year, Edward is settled at Wellington College and Uncle Billy's wedding is next month and, by the way, his bride has a fringe.

In January 1880 her father was called to the deathbed of Aunt Helen in Cologne. He went with his brother Thomas and Tom's wife Louisa and they brought the body back to Fasque for burial; this would entail a service under Episcopalian rites and William Gladstone spent many hours poring over the religious

pamphlets and books that he found among his sister's possessions in a life which she had shared with her devoted maid for
over thirty years. His last thoughts on his deeply troubled and
tragic sister, recorded in his diaries, were that in the end 'in a
wonderful manner youth and beauty came back upon her
worn face for the moment and she looked half her age. With
death returned the looks of Death. God accept her. Christ
receive her.' While this painful family duty was underway,
Mary stayed at Hawarden; she mentions in her diary playing
lawn tennis on 12 January, her partner was Scott Holland
against cousin Edward and brother Herbert, adding 'wonderful fun considering circs' (by which, presumably, she is
refering to awaiting news of Aunt Helen's death).

A by-election win by the Conservatives led Disraeli to judge
that the time was right for a general election and, on 8 March it
was announced that Parliament would be dissolved. When
Mary reached Harley Street, after a very brief train trip to
Oxford to show Lavinia and Herbert her Burne-Jones drawing,
she found 'a state of indescribable beastliness, even worse than
my darkest expectations', her mother looking 'excited, worried,
depressed' all at the same time. Next morning she was
awakened by Schlüter telling her that she must attend a Palace
Drawing Room Function. 'I get up in a rage and find Mama
meek and almost in tears but inexorable. I fly to shops for
ready-made gown at Jay's and train at Heilbronner's (black
stamped velvet).' By the evening both Mary and her mother
had splitting headaches and the maids were rushing around
muttering oaths under their breath. At the large dinner party,
she drowned all her cares in champagne and didn't think about
the next day.

Everyone expected her to go on the second Midlothian campaign. Her father wanted her to stand in for her mother. Mrs
Gladstone was determined not to be supplanted. 'Papa imagined himself en garcon in lodgings' and Mary backed her
mother, for she was equally determined that she would not give
up her Easter week celebrations 'all for the sake of fidgeting at
Dalmeny between Hannah (Lady Rosebery) and Mama for four
days.'

It proved to be more difficult for her to stand firm against the united persuasion of Lord Rosebery and his wife. Mary wrote to Lavinia, complaining about her 'Mad World'. 'It makes me so cross, it's so silly the exaggeration of it, they talk as if the whole election depended on my coming or not. They have got a ridiculous notion that I am the wire-puller about everything in my family, such nonsense.'[1] Nonsense it was not. She had become a formidable person, with more authority than her mother, who was inclined to fuss and overplay the situation. Mary was more inclined to soothe and diffuse the tensions and sort out the right people to the right task. At length a compromise was reached. She could still enjoy her glorious Bach concert, the Passion Music at St Paul's and the Brahms Requiem at St James' Hall.

Her parents departed for Dalmeny, and Mary was glad that she had stayed behind in London for the next day Herbert was adopted as candidate for Middlesex in the forthcoming election. She was, she declared 'in a boiling state of excitement' while Herbert 'all day stared with big eyes into vacancy'. She was just the person to steer him through the political discussions and interviews with the private secretaries, Messrs West and Godley. She felt that his first speech at the City Liberal Club went well and that he made a good impression. For the next few days her feet barely touched the ground. There was so much to do – her father's correspondence to deal with, notes to answer, flowers to arrange, Herbert to organise and, in the midst of it all, who should turn up unannounced but Mr Ottley. 'I thought I should have died,' she wrote to Lavinia, 'I had to have F(rederick Cavendish) and A(lfred Lyttelton) go to him and pack him off at once, so wretched wasn't it.'[2] On top of all this, Hallam Tennyson turned up one evening, uninvited, to press his attentions and Mary had to speak plainly to him. He wrote an apologetic note, 'Do not fear. I shall *not* vex you again. Your course seems to be quite clear, and so I can only pray you may be happy. There is little real friendship in the world.' He would be content and 'let us be friends'.[3]

Friends they did indeed remain, but there were no more confidences between them. It was to Lavinia that she told her dream, how Lord Acton had confessed that he had fallen in love with her and was tired of his wife. *His* dream, that he had shared with her at Tegernsee last year, was that he would write a great *History of Freedom*. At the time, she had thought it extraordinary that he could sit 'patient and quiet over wife and children and wait and wait another year before he writes. What an odd man.' His constant tardiness became a joke between them and the book of his imagination was given the name of *The Madonna of the Future*, after a Henry James short story where the artist's model ages and dies before the artist has put brush to paper. Perhaps Lord Acton doubted his own considerable abilities to achieve his dream. Like Dorothea's husband in George Eliot's *Middlemarch*, he went through the motions of scholarship, collecting knowledge for its own sake, accumulating a library of erudite books and filling numerous boxes with copious notes.

It was a pleasant diversion for them both to share thoughts and opinions. He was writing her long intimate letters; she was flattered by his obvious interest. One of his letters covers six pages, closely written on both sides, on politics, history, literature, and slipped in between lofty thoughts were hints of his feelings, 'When all the world has its rendezvous in Harley Street admit me perdu in the crowd.' He knew how to charm a lady: 'If we are beaten I shall be ashamed to let you see my grief.' He wrote, 'I believe you know how to be generous' and he begged her, 'Be generous before you are just. Do not temper mercy with justice.' He ended his letter, 'Believe me always very truly yours'.[4] Mary was important to him, she valued his opinions, she filled the place that his wife, preoccupied with children and family and her own interests, might have held. And Mary was uniquely placed to filter his ideas and opinions to her father.

Palm Sunday was the fifth anniversary of May Lyttelton's death. Mary felt at odds with the world and could find no inner peace. So much had happened since that awful day. 'What would May think of it all?' she wrote in her diary.

It was a relief to turn to politics and leave aside her emotional quandaries. She was swept up into Herbert's campaigning. In a brougham they flew 'through quiet country lanes and budding hedges to Harlesden'. She was quite astonished by her brother's fluent speeches and his charming manner. She believed that he must 'win all hearts' and make a great name for himself in the House of Commons. Meanwhile her brother William was campaigning for the Liberal seat in East Worcestershire with Lyttelton cousins to help him. He wrote to Herbert, 'How plucky of you to go in for that fearful piece of work in Middlesex.' He wished, 'God speed you. I am sick of this already, though it has only just begun, but I think our chance is good.'

Elections were rowdy affairs despite the private ballot that was now the practice, and fights often broke out. Mary enjoyed the dramas. At Enfield, pepper and snuff were tossed around that had everyone coughing and sneezing and Hallam, who was giving his support, lost his watch or had it stolen. At Southgate the speeches in a tent were almost drowned by tremendous hail-stones and buffeting wind beating on the canvas. 'Very amusing as our opponents made such fools of themselves,' she remarked in her diary. On to Mill Hill in a carriage and four, then to Hendon and from there to Hampstead where a 'tremendous rabble outside and disturbances inside were expected, but it turned out best of all next to Hounslow, and the groans for Ld. [Lord] Beaconsfield were the finest things I ever heard.' Campaigning at Dalmeny was going wonderfully well and family spirits were high.

Mary then took a day off duty. She lunched with Frances Graham before visiting Burne-Jones, now affectionately called 'Ned', at least in her diary where she describes the scene.

> Found Ruskin and Mr Hamilton, they were quite mad, and BJ flitting like a ghost in and out, and Mrs Birks in her scarlet shawl, and gold lockets, and May Morris with her beautiful straight features and parted unfuzzed hair, and little Margaret with her blue frock and blue eyes, and Lady Ashburton panting enthusiastically, and H Tennyson never uttering. All very amusing. Mr Ruskin's chaffing of 'Ned' very gracefully funny.[5]

She dined with Maggie and went on to the Tennysons for a party where she was called upon to play the pianoforte.

She was sure of Herbert's success, for had she not heard his rousing speeches and the way that the people warmed to him? She was not the only one to feel so confident, and Mr Ottley, who breakfasted with her along with Mr MacColl on the day of the results, was even preparing telegrams and paragraphs for the papers. But bad news came at midday. Mary went with Herbert to Red Lion Square for the result of the poll. 'I couldn't say what a sickening moment it was when H came in with a grave, white face. "I'm nowhere. Two or 3000 behind." I slunk home feeling inclined to bite off everybody's nose, and everybody was on my nerves.' And then came a telegram from Midlothian with good news. Mr Gladstone was in, and more and more Liberals were gaining seats. William had gained his seat at Droitwich. Lucy announced that she had eight relations in, and within a few weeks she could add another for Herbert was taken up by Leeds, and returned unopposed, and stayed MP for Leeds for the next thirty years. The Conservatives had been routed; they had lost over a hundred seats. Gladstone's ringing call to the working people to use their electoral power to rid the nation of a discredited government had proved irresistible; England 'has found its interests mismanaged, its honour tarnished, and its strength burdened and weakened by needless, mischievous, unauthorised, and unfortifiable engagements and it has resolved that this state of things shall cease and that right and justice shall be done.'[6]

Disraeli, now Earl of Beaconsfield, would have to lead the Opposition from the House of Lords. In a letter to the Duke of Argyll Gladstone declared, 'The downfall of Beaconfieldism is like the vanishing of some vast magnificent castle in an Italian romance.' Mary's congratulatory letter was brief: 'Dearest Father, One line of joy on your splendid victory. England does not yet quite know what she owes to you, but she will.'[7]

She went off to Cambridge for a few days with her sister Helen; it was delightful to forget for a little while the state of the nation, and to have great arguments on the most ridiculous subjects with the Balfour brothers. There was, however, a great debate going on about conferring degrees on women; a few

Girton students had dared to ask for what had always been upheld as a distinctly male preserve. But this was a storm in a teacup compared with the hullabaloo she found on her return to Harley Street, where bargains were being struck and deals done for high political office. The Queen had threatened to abdicate rather than send for Mr Gladstone, 'that half-mad firebrand who would soon ruin everything, and be a dictator.' Through her private secretary Her Majesty warned Lords Hartington and Granville that Gladstone would not be acceptable to her. She sent for Lord Hartington and asked him to form a government. He replied that no government could be formed without Gladstone and he would not serve in a subordinate role.

Mary decided that a little pressure applied to Lucy might bring about the desired result. She wrote:

What I really want to write about is the great question as to who heads the next government. Every person I meet, every letter I open, says the same thing, 'He must be Prime Minister'. But no one seems to see it is no good saying it to *him*; they must say it to the Queen, Lord Granville, and Lord Hartington. There is one small thing I am certain of and that is that Papa will never take the smallest step *towards it*. The steps must be taken *towards him*. I have never doubted that in the event of a huge crisis of this sort he would never let personal longing for rest and retirement affect his coming forward again if he saw that the general feeling was in favour of it. You will think it so silly, my writing to you and saying all the things everybody knows by heart, but I have always rather understood Lord Granville was the difficulty, that he longed to be Prime Minister. And now I hear he would dread it excessively. And so I don't see what the obstacle is. Lord Hartington would no doubt be considered very much aggrieved by a certain party, but he's too big a man to suffer by that in any way. I mean, he is the man after Lord Granville and Papa have gone, and he would never lose by behaving with splendid humbleness, so as to speak. I think it would be glorious, Papa forced by England to become Prime Minister, and bringing the ship once more into smooth waters and then retiring in prosperity and leaving it to Lord Hartington.[8]

She has clearly made her point and adds that this is 'a private ebullition', knowing that her mother is writing in similar vein and that Lucy will make the contents known to her husband who will discreetly pass them on to his brother Lord Hartington.

William Gladstone was now seventy. For the past three or four years he had been telling his family and his closest friends that he longed to retire from politics, to devote his remaining years of health and strength to religious scholarship and to his Hawarden estate. Yet when he considered his remarkable health and strength, he could only believe that he was being sustained for God's purpose, which had now been revealed. He believed that he alone could speak 'for millions who themselves cannot speak' and that he had been 'morally forced into this work as a great and high election of God'.

Mary told Lavinia that she felt 'that Heaven has called him back to this post'. She had mixed feelings about her future role; she enjoyed the confidences and the intrigues but she shrank from the boring and stuffy social functions that she knew lay ahead. 'Isn't it dreadful to think of beginning all over again, cards and parties and things, it makes me sick to think of, but I suppose one ought not to let those sort of things weigh at all.' In true Mary fashion, she would look on the bright side. 'The garden at Downing St will be a great break, and the coolness and the room.' She knew that working for her father would be exhilarating and that managing her mother would be a great test of her tact and character. She had thought of herself as 'vocationless' despite reassurances from her cousins Spencer and Alfred of how much they all valued her. Now she would have a special role in the political business of Downing Street. She would provide a good informal conduit through which opinions would reach the prime minister. She would need friends whom she could trust and Scott Holland's help would be invaluable to her. She wrote to Lord Acton, asking for his true support and friendship. He replied that she should trust nobody, for all will flatter; such a warning could hardly be a comfort, but at least she would begin work with her eyes wide open.

CHAPTER THIRTEEN

A room of her own (1880—1)

*T*uesday, 27 April 1880 was house-moving day. For the first
time, the family was going to live above the office. Mary
went all over the new home and reported to her diary, 'saw
Dizzy's bed and imagined him lying therein, and his portmanteau all be-coroneted was just going out. Such is life. They have
spoilt the garden and half spoilt the house.' There was no time
for more musings; all the rooms had to be arranged and decisions made on furniture. Schlüter bustled about following
Mary's directions and decided that No. 10 Downing Street was
'a jolly old place'. Her room looked out on to the Parade, a far
better spot than Mary's work space, which had no window
and was really a housemaid's cupboard intended for brooms
and mops. Mary turned it into a cosy, private hideaway with
just enough room for a table and a couple of chairs.

Mrs Gladstone was not at all happy at this recognition of
Mary's definite role on the political scene, and insisted that
her daughter should be close to the family and domestic life.
Lucy was horrified at what she considered her cousin's lack of
propriety, but Mary was adamant that she needed a space to
call her own if she were to be taken seriously, so this inadequate compromise had been reached. The family lived and
slept on the first floor, while the ground floor was given over
entirely to government work. Mary compared it to a rabbit
warren, as people popped in and out of rooms and scuttled down
corridors. With so many people in the house in such limited
space, the air in summer-time was anything but fresh. George
Leveson-Gower thought the smells on the staircase could be
traced to faulty drains, but as the government had come in on

a programme of economy and retrenchment, his view was that he and his colleagues could well be marked down as 'unnecessary expenses'.

Mary's opinion of her father's new Liberal Cabinet was that it was 'highly respectable, rather aristocratic, with a democratic dash in the shape of Mr Chamberlain'. On the whole she thought it 'a good working Company'. There had been such comings and goings until all the posts were filled, the bell and door-knocker sounding all day long. Joseph Chamberlain and John Bright were the only two Radicals included in an otherwise Whig cabinet.

Gladstone was going to be Chancellor of the Exchequer as well as Prime Minister. He was seventy and his energies, however formidable, must have been on the wane. His thoughts on his seventieth birthday suggest that he felt that there was no one up to the task of stepping into his shoes, while within himself there was 'still something that consents not to be old'. He has been criticised for not keeping himself free to take an overall view of the government and international issues. When the Dean of Windsor asked him why he had given himself the Treasury, he replied that he did not trust the financial judgement of his colleagues. But he did encourage young members of his own family; Freddy Cavendish was given the post of Financial Secretary and Herbert's political ambitions were encouraged with the job of Secretary to the Treasury. The family recognised that William's political ambition had run its course and, as eldest son, he should be allowed to give more of his time to the Hawarden estate. Mary knew that cousin Spencer was tired of his aimless wanderings round the world and was looking for a proper job; her taunt that he was a half-hearted worker had hit home. Eventually it was decided that he should be under-secretary to Lord Granville at the Foreign Office, and his younger brother Neville would be with Mr Childers, Secretary for War. Lord Hartington's ambitions were moderately soothed by the office of Secretary for India.

Mary had been on tenterhooks to learn who would be her father's secretaries as she would be working closely with them. Her diary notes, 'Went through horrors as to Sp(encer) and secretaryship and had a Nail driven into my Coffin.' Whether she was terrified of seeing too much or too little of her cousin she does not disclose. She was relieved to learn that Arthur Godley who had been private secretary since 1872 was to be her father's senior secretary, with Eddy Hamilton, son of the Bishop of Salisbury, to take over from him later. Horace Seymour, brother of Lady Spencer, known as 'the cob' because of his cheerful, hardworking disposition and strong, compact figure, Henry Primrose, sporting a fine moustache, and nicknamed 'the Colonel' and George Leveson-Gower, Lord Granville's nephew and just down from Oxford, were assistant secretaries. Mary was the only woman in a team of five. Her inclusion shows her father's high regard for her abilities and his complete confidence in her.

On top of political business there was daily entertaining; the social wheels must be well oiled to keep all transactions turning smoothly. Mrs Gladstone liked to invite friends and interesting people, not those who should be invited for political gain. She never played the conventional role expected of a Prime Minister's wife. Her unpunctuality was notorious in the family, because her days were always stretched beyond the limits as she tried to help too many sad cases or to rally support for too many lost causes. Her complete lack of formality was part of her feminine charm, and Mary had inherited it, but she was a much more organised being than her mother.

Lord Acton was in town and deluging her with attention; in a letter from Downing Street she tells Lavinia, 'He frightens me rather, he talks as if there were such a lot I could do here, but he is a good friend and gave me many kind hints and is going to write most freely. We talked politics the whole time.' Soon he would return to Tegernsee and he warns her to trust nobody; in his first letter he tells her to beware of her 'nicest cousin' and of 'lending herself to horrible intrigue' (he is referring to Lucy and her loyalties to her brother-in-law Lord Hartington). All would flatter and see her as a way of gaining her father's ear and, naturally, he insists that his friendship is not of that kind, but he is critical of Lord Rosebery. Perhaps he senses a rival. Mary responds by asking him to be nicer to Lord Rosebery, to

encourage rather than criticise, for his was a particularly sensitive nature. She even points to failings of his, as seen by others,
'There is in some quarters a general idea that you do nothing
but criticise with folded hands – that you are always negative
– that nobody knows anything at all about your real opinions
– that you continually pull down and tear to pieces, without
raising up or edifying (in the true meaning of the word). I
cannot say that you have ever been so with us.'[1]

Mary speaks plainly; her straightforward honesty was
a quality valued by both friends and colleagues. Was Lord
Acton using her friendship as a means to her father? A letter
in the autumn reveals her unease: 'Somehow I feel as if I had
no right to it, and had got it from you on false pretences –
that you really wrote it for my father, and I think I ought to
confess to you that I am not at all a good pipe or sieve or whatever it should be called, not nearly as good as any one of the
secretaries because neither his eyes or ears are open to me as
they are to him.'[2] In a letter in October he urges, 'Don't show
my letters to others – I need to write freely.' There is a sense
of underlying strain that must have affected their relationship; Mary will come to realise her value as a specially privileged gatekeeper into her father's presence and enjoy the
role.

There was plenty of work for everyone. All letters were
handwritten and copies were made of all correspondence and
business transactions, then stored in cupboards and on shelves
as these were the days before filing cabinets. Sir Henry
Ponsonby, the Queen's private secretary, estimated that while
in office, Gladstone and his private secretaries wrote about
25 000 letters per year, and there were no typewriters. Tables
held paper, blotters, ink pots, quill pens, pencils, envelopes and
telegram forms, notebooks and tapes for binding up bundles
of papers. The only desk that could be guaranteed always to
be tidy was the Prime Minister's, where every drawer was
immaculate, every page was neatly arranged. His daily life
must run as smoothly and as regular as clockwork while his
minions scurried and scuttled to ensure this was so. He was
blissfully oblivious of their efforts on his behalf.

Mary quickly discovered that her father had complete confidence in her; she told Lavinia he had left 'the Airlies, Lowes and Trevelyans specially in my hands to soothe.' She found it:

> ... rather appalling finding myself this time so much in the position of 'a political intriguer'. I mean people like Mr MacColl, Ld. Rosebery, Ld. Reay & Lord Acton write me heaps of letters, suggestions, questions, things to mention if possible to 'the Dictator' as Ld. R calls him, papers, general opinions, etc., etc. Just now I was saying to Papa I wd. retire to another table at the breakfast and he answered I was not to as Ld. Rosebery wd. be disappointed. Mama said, Oh no, he only uses her as a 'pis-aller' when he can't get our ear.[3]

Mrs Gladstone's comment may have amused her husband but it does reveal her irritation at no longer being the queen bee in the hive. The young ambitious men who once had flattered and confided in her, as a way to the Prime Minister's ear, now turned towards Mary. It was a two-way process, for she was also a useful conduit for her father to filter his approval or his caution to the young and ambitious. She could suggest a slightly different line of action, or make friendly but forthright comments which, if issuing from the P.M., would have carried far too much weight.

Lord Acton may have sought her company to gain easy access to her father, but he stayed for the delight of her youthful gaiety and refreshing non-conformity. Lord Rosebery was discovering that she was a comfortable and comforting friend as well as a useful contact. He was Mary's age and a rising political figure, immensely rich, immensely talented and with great personal charm. She knew that he was ambitious and liked him for it. She knew too that her father regarded him as too young for a Cabinet post. Some thought he was inclined to laziness, preferring horse-racing to politics, and it was true that horses were his passion. He had a lovely home, the Durdans, near Epsom where he kept his string of Derby winners. He owned another home in Buckinghamshire that had been part of his wife Hannah Rothschild's dowry, a huge, turreted mansion full of glorious works of art and priceless pieces of furniture.

Mary was invited to Mentmore for a weekend of pleasure and of course, political talk. She met other members of the Rothschild family and was invited to Leopold Rothschild's for strawberries and cream. She described his home, built on land that had once been part of the vast Rothschild estate and a pleasant walk from Mentmore, as 'a palace-like cottage'. She drove back to London alone with Lord Rosebery in his phaeton, and they dawdled in the garden for confidential talk on his political future. He assured her that he would never have undertaken the task of presenting her father and his policies to the people of Midlothian if he had not been absolutely sure in his own mind that he would not take office in the government. She was quite devastated by his next confidence, that he had been ordered abroad by his doctor for three months. The one person that she felt she could trust was to be out of the country just when she needed him. She felt more at ease with him than with Lord Acton, perhaps because they were the same age. She could encourage him when his spirits flagged, tease him and openly invite him for her own sake just as she did her Lyttelton cousins. Now he was off to the Continent, and she thought it 'horrible'. Their last meeting for a while was at the Ascot races where he had seven horses running; Mary wore his colours to bring him luck.

Even from the Continent Lord Rosebery continued to offer advice which he was confident she would pass on to the right quarters. In a letter from Homburg dated 30 June, he warned, 'If you treat Scotland as the last government did and take no Scots bill until after midnight there will be great dissatisfaction in Scotland. Do treat Scots bills as if you considered Scotland a part of the United Kingdom.' More advice followed. 'Would it not be a good plan for the dictator to call a meeting of Liberal members of the House of Commons and address them on his Home and Irish bills? Call it in Grosvenor House or the Reform Club.'[4] He warned her that he could see no loyalty and no enthusiasm in the party and it needed to be welded together; Mary wrote to Arthur Godley about Lord Rosebery's concerns, explaining that she would have told her father the substance but she was staying with her sister at Wellington College for a few days.

Her two favourite married men were out of the country, but Scott Holland would always be single and was safely anchored at Oxford. She could gossip and scheme with him. He could always be relied upon for the right advice which was always so clearly and lightly given. 'Why can't the others help more?' he wrote when Mary had poured out her woes on how she was expected to run in all directions at once. 'Why does Lord Hartington never talk? Could he not take something off Mr Gladstone? or Mr Childers?' She invited him to Hawarden as often as he could spare the time. He impishly replied,

> I shall creep along under Cheshire hills and Flintshire chimneys ... somewhere about the 25th or the 26th of September by the help of a Fenian pass. If you meet anyone in close disguise about then, creeping along the Hawarden roads, it will probably be me ... If this is too venturesome, you will frankly tell me, because I am thickly pressed by relations, and have alternatives at hand. Only if the vigilance of the police did insist on penetrating my disguise and cutting off my escape, how delightful it would be![5]

In August came the long break. Her father was desperately in need of a rest, having narrowly escaped typhoid fever. Mary had been busier than ever as an avalanche of cards, letters and telegrams poured in from well-wishers. Thousands of people turned up at Downing Street to offer gifts of fruit, home-made remedies and prayers for his speedy recovery. She had been touched by a new tender regard and reverence shown by his colleagues as they gathered round his armchair on their first evening together, after he had missed four Cabinet meetings. Sir Donald Currie offered his luxury yacht for a recuperative cruise and Mary went down to Gravesend to wave her parents off. 'The brown- and red-sailed fishing boats, excursion steamers, flags, cheers, flowers and sunshine' almost made her feel like going aboard, but she decided that this trip round the British and Scottish coasts would be 'a seasick trip'. Sir James Lacaita, old friend and one of the guests, was no sailor either, 'he is sick always in a gondola in Venice' she told Lord Rosebery.

She went home to Hawarden and 'was assailed by a whole army of Blue Devils the first evening. It was endless and forlorn.' She reflected upon how much more exciting and absorbing her time in Downing Street had been than she had ever expected. She had met so many interesting and influential people who welcomed her as their equal, and when her father was ill, she had dined alone with the Cabinet. Her sudden removal from the centre of events left a vacuum that could not be easily filled with more gentle country values.

Sometimes it was difficult to balance the extremes of her private and public lives. In which of these worlds did she truly belong? Or was she destined to move from place to place, answering whatever demands were put upon her by her family with no real life of her own? It was pointless to dwell on might-have-beens, and this was not her style. 'How often it has happened to me lately to find reality so far outdo expectations in enjoyment of life,' she told herself as she struggled free from her depression. It was only a fortnight before the 'Great People' would be home again and she knew that then the pace of her life would quicken.

She worked in her father's study, known to them all as the 'Temple of Peace'. There were three writing tables, one for politics placed between two long windows overlooking the park, one for literary work and one for correspondence. At this last table she kept abreast of foreign affairs. She described the situation in Eastern Europe as 'very ticklish'. She thought the Turks were worse than ever 'promising and evading and postponing'. Cipher telegrams flew hither and thither keeping her busy.

Her father did not stay home for long. He had to return to Downing Street, to seek a resolution of the dispute over the frontier of Montenegro. He ordered a naval demonstration against the Sultan off the coast of Albania and luckily for him the Sultan took fright, for France, Germany and Austria refused to cooperate with Britain. His jubilation at the Turkish yielding was, to a large extent, relief that he had not been left stranded by his own action. The brinkmanship was played out over a number of days and Mary, at Hawarden, waited tensely for news. As always, her father trusted in divine providence and was not disappointed. On 11 October his letter from London sang out, 'Praise to the Holiest in the Heights', followed by Arthur Godley's more moderate telegram which read 'All satisfactory'. The news lifted her spirits, making her feel like a new person.

The new Parliamentary Session of 1881 got under way and she had to agree with Scott Holland that it was indeed 'a dark and wild opening of the year'. She was in the House of Commons to hear Parnell make an 'astute' speech, she thought, while Lord Randolph Churchill spoke 'in flippant and unreasoned terms'. These two new personalities in the House were sending ripples in all directions, and Mary thought they were making her father's life very uncomfortable. She never liked Lord Randolph, and her criticisms of him grew harsher. After witnessing one of his attacks in the House she wearily wondered, 'what is the use of crushing a reptile who thrives on crushing?' Her respect for Parnell, however, grew with the passing years as she felt the magnetic attraction of his personality, 'the refined, delicate face, illuminating smile, fire-darting eyes, slight tall figure.'

Soon all other events paled in significance as Irish affairs grew menacing. Mary was educating herself on the Irish problem by reading WEH Lecky's *Ireland in the Eighteenth Century,* and she discovered 'the most terrible story surely of injustice and misgovernment that ever happened in a civilised corner of the world'. Growing agricultural depression had caused over 10 000 Irish tenants to be evicted from their farms for non-payment of rent. In 1879 the Land League had been formed to secure tenants' rights and to work towards Home Rule. Parnell was now President of this League. Gladstone knew that people were close to starvation in Ireland, and that it was useless to try to enforce the normal laws of property. He had tried to rush through a Bill to give compensation to evicted tenants, but it was thrown out by the Lords, and violence had erupted across Ireland. Captain Boycott tried to take over a farm from which a tenant had been evicted and was overnight treated as a leper – no one would work for him or speak to him; his crops lay in the fields, unharvested. The idea spread, and a new word came into use as the way to treat anyone who tried to take over a holding from an evicted tenant: to 'boycott'.

Meanwhile the Secretary of State for Ireland, WE Forster, was behaving, according to one of the secretaries, 'more like an inebriated or demented man than one who had merely lost his nerve'. In February 1881, the Coercion Act was passed after forty-one hours of debate. It virtually gave to the Viceroy the power to lock up anyone he wished. This gave Gladstone time to introduce his new Land Bill in which every clause was fiercely fought over the next few months. John Morley said of the Bill that few British MPs understood it and none mastered it. 'The Whigs were disaffected about it, the radicals doubted it, the Tories thought that property as a principle was ruined by it, the Irishmen, when the humour seized them, bade him send the bill to line trunks.'[6]

Mary described the Irish issues as 'the 3 Fs – fair rents, fixity of tenure and free sale'. Visits to both Houses became family outings and anyone who happened to be in London sat in on the noisy debates. She crammed in two or three visits a day between concerts, before and after dinner.

The third of March 1881 was a typical day. Mary was in the House of Commons, then the House of Lords, then she scuttled back to the Commons 'just in time to see Healy suspended for violent language'. In the evening, she dined with Sir Knollys in the company of the Princess of Wales, the Duke of Cambridge and her mother, who was the innocent cause of much merriment. When Sir Knollys said good night to Mrs Gladstone she offered to go with him, thinking he was returning to the political debate when, in fact, he was off to bed. It was Mary who slid back to the House in time to hear Lords Derby, Salisbury and Northbrook, and her comments in her diary on all three are harsh: 'The former is singularly ineffective. He read his speech, but the matter was of highest excellence. Ld. S(Salisbury) was violent and not happy in any way. Ld. Northbrook too much excited for weight.'

The next day she was in the House of Lords with a concert at St Anne's Church with Spencer singing the bass solo sandwiched in between. This was the pattern of her life for the next few years; exciting dramas in the Houses of Parliament interspersed with marvellous musical treats and enormous parties with all the great and the good. 'A portentous party of Cabinet Ministers, Ambassadors etc.' on 23 March is followed the next day by a family visit to the House of Commons to support Herbert in his maiden speech and three days later, a trip to the art studios where she saw a new portrait of Lord Beaconsfield and thought it was hideous; 'I only mean it was so dreadfully like him'. Her last sight of him had been in the House of Lords when he had spoken in the debate on Afghanistan. On the last day of March she noted in her diary, 'Poor Ld. Beaconsfield is very ill'. His death three weeks later did not make her less antagonistic towards him, 'all the consequent rush of highest flown praise. First-rate nonsense rampaged for a week' she wrote in her diary. Over the years she had absorbed her father's criticisms and now she wondered why he should propose a national memorial for his arch enemy. Her father explained to her that Disraeli had held high office by the willing support of Parliament and the nation and 'history must eventually judge as to the result'.

Almost as an antidote, there had to be moments of sheer madcap fun, like her 'harum-scarum drive' to Salisbury with a group of male friends. They stood on the top of the hill where the old Moot Parliament used to sit and looked down the grassy banks to the still pool. 'Everybody was quite mad, we stole lilies, and coming home over the downs, galloping recklessly where no road existed, was the most wild and perilous business, Mr O driving quite madly. Mr Holland was mad too. They just got me back to Salisbury in time for my train, all seeing me off.'[7] A mature and confident woman, thirty-three years of age, she was travelling by cab and by train entirely alone and unchaperoned.

Back in the House of Commons, the Irish Land Bill was given a bumpy ride. She was there to follow the arguments through every clause and amendment. On 16 August she went to the House of Lords, 'knowing that they had finally resolved to swallow the Bill, Ld. Arlington in a fine rage with Ld. Salisbury, came and swore at him in my hearing and even worse. The Ld. Chancellor was sick on the Wool Sack.' There were times when the family needed police protection during these hot steamy days of debate, and constables were sleeping in the garden of No. 10 Downing Street.

At last the parliamentary term ended. Mary accompanied her parents to Walmer Castle, weekend guests of Lord Granville. How different it was for her now that she was accepted as a person of some consequence. There was an assortment of guests and, at dinner, she was placed next to a rising young politician by the name of Anderson. 'He knows about everything and is well up in magic. We got on merrily though his manners and looks were much against him.' She could not help but recall her visit eleven years ago when she had been shy and gauche. Now she could write with some satisfaction in her diary, 'Altogether it was a very different thing to the snubbed MG of 1870.'

The last of the long summer days at Hawarden were for lawn tennis, tree-cutting and walking in the woods, but politics were never far away and there was plenty of secretarial work for her. She had 'a good deal of copying and deciphering these days, such anxious Transvaal news, the Volksraad fighting over the Convention, wretched Irish things going on, besides many Continental clouds.' The Irish issue was a long way from being resolved. The nationalists were trying to wreck the new Land Bill by making the rent tribunals unworkable and so extracting further concessions from the government. Parnell was making inflammatory speeches in Ireland and, under the terms of the Coercion Bill, he was arrested. Others soon joined him in Kilmainham Jail. Mary and her family were again given police protection at Hawarden as well as in London. Herbert, who arrived in Dublin on the day of Parnell's arrest, immediately bought a gun and learnt how to use it. He described the city as being like one in revolutionary Russia, with soldiers patrolling the streets everywhere, two field guns positioned just inside the castle gates and 25 000 available troops in barracks.

Mary spent long hours with her father, talking over what she described as 'the great vexed question' of his retirement and who might succeed him. She listened to his thoughts and passed on to him others' opinions. She told him that Lord Acton believed that retirement while in health and strength might ruin the Liberal Party. Her father reminded her that he had only returned to high office conditionally and temporarily, and that once the Irish issue was settled, he could safely go. He spoke warmly of Lord Hartington, 'a man of unusual strength and ability', but said that he needed more training before he could take over as Prime Minister. Mary objected that he might at any moment go to the House of Lords and who would then lead the House of Commons? The plain fact was that there was no one who could unite the party as her father could. He confided that Sir Charles Dilke was probably the best man to take his place, but that he would need 'Cabinet training' first. He told her that there was little opposition from the Conservative Party, who were 'demoralised and degraded'. They had 'inherited all the vices of Ld. Beaconsfield without his tact and judgement' and jingoism would be their ruin. Mary again quoted Lord Acton that he could resign place but could not resign power.

She stayed on at Hawarden for her thirty-fourth birthday. It was 'snug', with a tiny house party. Lord Rosebery arrived for the weekend with a lovely book for her, but she was more enthusiastic about another present. It was Charles Darwin's newly published *Formation of Vegetable Mould through the Action of Worms*, a strange present but just what she wanted, describing it as 'such a break', Glynnese language for something of great pleasure. Cousin Spencer arrived in time for her father's seventy-second birthday, and the house was flooded with congratulatory letters, telegrams and flowers. A telephone link to the Rectory had been installed a year ago so that they could talk 'as if in one house', which she thought 'great fun'. Lord Acton arrived on the last day of the year and cousins Edward and Alfred came in time for dinner, and to see in the New Year with her. Mary was content. It was a blessed and peaceful ending to 'a great year in the annals of history, but of no special importance to us privately,' she wrote in her diary.

CHAPTER FOURTEEN

Irish matters dominate, with tragic consequences (1882–3)

When the new Parliamentary session opened in January 1882, Mary made a move from her housemaid's cupboard into more businesslike quarters, no less than Herbert's old room. She felt that she would like it very much 'because of the definiteness supplying some little backbone to one's life'. She had her special role as her father's honorary secretary, but now had added responsibility for ecclesiastical patronage. On the cover of one of her diaries for these years in Downing Street, she has written, 'Thou hast a friend, thy friend has a friend, thy friend's friend has a friend. Be discreet.'

Her friendship with Scott Holland is particularly important at this time, and it works to both their advantage. Between them they were contriving to get JR Illingworth, tutor of Keble College and fellow of Jesus College, Oxford, elected to the chaplaincy of Lincoln's Inn. Scott Holland thought that Edward Talbot, Lavinia's husband and Warden of Keble College should write a testimonial, 'and would you restrain his strict and accurate regard for the truth as much as possible. Mr I will be steady in London, I think, and it will be good for him; the lawyers will be the last people to suffer from a little paradox.' The chaplain would be expected to say Grace at dinner in Hall, 'but it is really the *only* duty required of him, so that I think he might pull himself together and nerve his courage for the effort.' Their little plan came to naught and Illingworth continued in his academic career with a little help from Mary in the publication of his *Sermons in a College Chapel*.

Another time, Scott Holland recommends Mr Dunkerley of Hoar Cross to a vicarage in Liverpool, 'he is an excellent worker-up of a new district, a thorough *Missionary*,' but he warns, 'Of course he had better not go into a nest of "gentlefolk" because he was apt to talk too much on religious matters. But I was assured that he would work up shopkeepers quite well, as well – of course, as the poor.' And if ever Mr Gladstone should be looking for 'a good, simple, broadish creature, who would read theology if he had a quietish country place, very thoughtful and interesting,' he knows just the man. In a letter dated March 1882, Scott Holland assures Mary that he is not using friendship 'in any way as a useful back door, sparing me the natural squeeze on the big staircase up which the world is pressing and pushing'.[1]

As well as the clerical correspondence, Mary took over other duties that once belonged to Herbert – 'the daily orders for the H. of Commons – the petitions to H. of C. – all paper relating to Queen Anne's Bounty, Charter House, Trinity House nominations.' Other secretarial duties included keeping the engagement books, filing an alphabetical record of all calling cards, and answering invitations. Another good friend was James Stuart, Cambridge Professor of Applied Mechanics, who was an MP for a while before marriage took him into the Colman family's mustard business. Their friendship flourished during Mary's time in Downing Street; he flattered her that she had 'a happy ability of introducing good people to one' and he thanked her particularly for inviting him to Hawarden and into her father's company.

Her own room in Downing Street made her position more official but she had to assert herself to both her mother and Lucy who were once again strongly voicing their objections against her receiving visitors far away from what they called the 'feminine' part of the house. Her mother was having to give ground to the next generation; she was losing centre stage to her sociable and able daughter. Mary confided to Harry that Mama was 'curiously dependent on excitement, it acts just like a tonic on her – when she is without it, she rather slips down the hill.' It seems hardly credible, but Mary counted twelve writing tables, where her mother spent 'endless time and strength in walking from one to the other, and hunting for papers or cheques which she has put down on one of them', and 'she scarcely ever answers any business letters herself and never reads anything but the newspapers'.[2] How circumstances had changed since her letter ten years ago in which she had taken Harry to task for criticising Mama, lecturing him that the family should try to cover her faults rather than expose them.

Of course, her mother gossiped with Lucy about Mary's new life among the menfolk and Lucy, equally critical, gossiped with Lavinia.

> It's impossible to ignore that she has out-of-the-common intimacies with various men that really *do* make it necessary & right for her to be circumspect; and I can't wonder that the Gd. D. [Grande Dame, i.e. Mrs Gladstone] has the cares of the thought of all these comers & goers turning up *entirely* out of her ken.

Lucy continues at great length:

> It's no use to tell me that I am bristling with Mrs Grundy fads: the intimacies *are* unusual & shd. not be carried on without any check or red tape. Did not Burne-Jones himself tell me 'I love her' & does not Mazy herself describe Ld. Rosebery's endless tête-à-têtes at Mentmore & Ld. Acton's confidential letters & interviews! I *do* wonder off & on how the wives all like it!

Mary's reputation continued to preoccupy Lucy and the next month she wrote to Lavinia that the friendship with Lord Acton may not be a scandal but it would go down in history: 'All I want is for her to realise that all such friendships require circumspection – the more when the friends' wives are little meek things in corners like Mrs BJ or failures sitting abroad making children and poor relatives like Ly. Acton.'[3] She really did not have to worry. Mary was finding too much excitement in the daily political hurly-burly for her to be dependent on any one friendship. Her experiences with Mr Ottley and Hallam Tennyson had led her to think that it was safer to make friends with married men, but there was nothing like the secure affection of her unmarried Lyttelton cousins Alfred, Edward and Spencer.

Irish matters were bubbling. The English authorities had absolute power to imprison on suspicion alone, and this was being enforced in Ireland by soldiers and armed police. The Prime Minister decided that the time had come to make use of Parnell, languishing in prison. Joe Chamberlain would act as negotiator. Captain O'Shea was used as intermediary. It was agreed that Parnell and two other Irish MPs should be released on condition that Parnell would support the Land Act and on the understanding that Gladstone would introduce an Arrears Bill to cancel debts for certain poor tenants. When these secret schemings came to light, the Chief Secretary for Ireland resigned. It was Herbert's opinion that Forster's resignation was not confined to the secrecy issue but was related to the policy of concession and conciliation that was now to replace his coercion policy.

'What an agitated day,' Mary wrote in her diary on Tuesday 2 May. She flew to the House of Lords to hear Lord Granville's speech and then to the House of Commons to hear her father. Who should walk into the Ladies' Gallery where she was sitting with her mother, but Mr Forster! 'Oh what burning cheeks' she had when he sat next to her, 'and growled out now and then to know more exactly what was being said.' Of course, it was always difficult to follow the speeches, which were muffled by the grille, but she was used to this. She felt sure that the Tories would make 'a hero and martyr of him'. Two days later she was back to hear his farewell speech from the floor of the House: 'It was not a happy one.' As he spoke, the released prisoners came in one by one, 'Dillon looking earthly, O'Kelly fat and jolly, Parnell different. It all looked very nasty. The Tories had all their stings out.'

Gladstone was not the man to be deterred by mere unpleasantness. His secretary Eddy Hamilton said that he had 'implicit confidence in himself', with 'a strength of conviction amounting almost to a sense of infallibility.'[4] He now made the decision that Lucy's husband should replace Forster and would brook no argument. Freddy Cavendish, feeling far from qualified for the job, went to the Foreign Office to talk it over with Lord Granville and returned home to report, 'Well, I am in for it.' His father, the Duke of Devonshire, hated the appointment so much that Freddy believed that he would not have accepted if he had known how upset he would be. The Cavendishes were Whigs, owning land in Ireland and against the land reforms. This appointment could only be seen as one of Gladstone's desperate measures to harness together his party of Whigs and Radicals. Many years later Herbert looked back and thought that, if Chamberlain had been given the job, the Irish story would have turned out very differently.

The sixth of May 1882 began in a normal enough way. For Mary, the day began and ended with Lyttelton cousins. Lucy Cavendish was the first to call, a little lonesome after waving her husband off on the Holyhead train bound for Ireland. It would be only a brief visit; he only planned to stay one night. She dropped in to gossip with Mary about his appointment. In the early evening, Spencer came to dine and Alfred arrived to chat as they ate, before they dashed off to Her Majesty's Theatre for Wagner's *Die Walkure*. Afterwards the two of them walked slowly back to Downing Street. It was half past midnight when Spencer said goodnight at the garden gate.

'There were unwonted lights in the windows, and seeing a number of people up and Smith stammering "bad news" at 1st I thought it was Papa. Then they said Ireland and Ld. Frederick [Cavendish], and I rushed to Eddy and learnt the too-terrible truth. He was stabbed and killed about half past seven in Phoenix Park close to the Viceregal Lodge.'[5] Mr Burke, the Irish Permanent Under-Secretary, with whom he was walking, was also killed. Mary went straight over to Lucy's home in Carlton House Terrace and found her parents there with Lord Granville, Lord Cavendish and Lady Louisa Egerton. Meriel was comforting Lucy. There was a profound sense of shock and disbelief. Lucy turned to her uncle and begged him never to blame himself for sending Freddy. 'Oh no,' came the reply, 'There can be no question of that.' Such powers of self-absorption were enviable, and his conviction that his chosen path was the only one, and that everyone on that path could be used to the attainment of its end. Some have called such conviction 'the egoism of genius'.

In the small hours, Mary returned with her parents to Downing Street for what remained of that nightmarish night. Next day was a Sunday. She was awakened by her mother bringing in 'a glorious letter' that her father had written to Lucy, and straight after breakfast she went over to Carlton House Terrace. When she saw Lucy, she knew that 'her splendid goodness and faith had indeed triumphed in this bitter hour'. Lucy clung to the belief that Freddy's sacrifice might prove the saving of Ireland. Brothers and sisters rallied round, giving their overwhelming support. As always, Mary and Spencer clung to each other in their need. Together they went to St Paul's, carrying Lucy's prayers for salvation through sacrifice.

There were many trials to be endured through the coming days. Gladstone had to announce Lord Frederick's death to the House of Commons. Mary was there to hear his brief statement: 'He could scarcely get through, and never mentioned his name.' The funeral took place at Chatsworth in Derbyshire. The Cavendish estate looked heart-breakingly beautiful in its glorious early Summer blossom. As Mary sat in Lucy's room, intent on making a great cross, 'seven feet long, deep red roses in the middle, the only colour', she comforted herself with the thought that 'the peacefulness and tranquillity took away all horror'. A special train brought two hundred mourning MPs. Many quietly approached Mr Gladstone to offer sympathy to their seventy-three-year-old colleague who, overnight, looked his age.

Back in London, the daily round must be endured. Mary was glad to be available as Spencer, Neville and Alfred sought her company for music and conversation. How often they had turned to her in terrible dark hours, each new death reinforcing their deep sense of loss and their need of each other. She stayed with Lucy on her first night back in London, sleeping in Freddy's dressing room. She helped with all the ghastly practicalities, clearing drawers and removing all coloured clothes from her cousin's wardrobe.

Lucy must wear only black clothes weighed down by black crepe for a year and a day, and for another year only the crepe would be removed. She was expected to remove herself from society for a minimum of three months, and she chose to seek refuge in a retreat at St Mary's at Stone, comfortingly close to her old home of Hagley Hall. Here she gathered strength to face again the world. She and Freddy had been married for eighteen years and, although she had desperately desired children, there had been none. She remained alone in her life, steadfast in her belief that Freddy's death had been a price worth paying for the ultimate prize of Irish peace. She would always be in the Ladies' Gallery whenever any Irish question was being discussed, following fervently all endeavours towards Home Rule.

Mary took a break at the Durdans, one of the Rosebery family homes. Watching the Rosebery children play among the flowers 'looking like mushrooms in their white linen bonnets' soothed her tired spirits. But most of all that summer it was music and cricket and tennis and the Lyttelton boys. The Australian cricket team was over and she was at the Oval every day. Alfred Lyttelton had been selected to play for England and she clapped and gasped through every over. 'It was never hopeless till the very end, as at any point they were capable of making a stand,' but when England's final wicket fell they were still eighteen runs short. Alfred's contribution was 'a slow and patient 12'. After it was all over, she and Alfred dined together at Downing Street. Neville had gone off to Egypt on Lord Wolseley's staff. Spencer was back as one of her father's secretaries, a paid job this time, just what he needed.

A witty unsigned scribble in the margin of her diary at this time reads,

'Proud Masie, bright as a fairy,
Will she give lunch to the Sub-Secretary?'

It could be Spencer's doing, but another possible candidate is Lord Rosebery who was Under-Secretary of State for the Home Department. When he was overlooked for a government post at the start of the new Parliament, a coldness had grown between the two families that Mary had resolved to melt. She had written to 'My dear friend,' and asked him, 'do come and break the profound silence wh. has reigned for so long between yr.

family and ours', adding 'You cannot imagine how much you are wanted or how disappointed my father will be if you refuse'.[6] A month later she tells him again that he is dreadfully missed; this was her constant theme through this year and the next. There is an undated letter from her to her father, marked 'Very Private' in which she is liaising between Lord Rosebery and the P.M. She tells her father that Lord Rosebery would accept the Under-Secretaryship for Home Affairs, and she thinks that it would quieten Scottish agitation for their own Secretary. The letter, intended only for her father's eyes, was not sent via the secretaries. Lord Rosebery became Under-Secretary for Home Affairs in 1881.

The rift between the two families was healed and when an invitation came for Easter 1882 Mary playfully penned this rhyme,

Imagine me, O friend,
And a kind ear pray lend
To my sad and sorrowful rhyme,
My parents are bent
On keeping home Lent
And spending a dutiful time.

I am sorry to say
A visit they pay
To the Rector of Hawarden their son
To pass Easter Day
In a holier way
Than at Epsom they could have done.[7]

It was a continual struggle to keep her prickly friend within the party fold. When he threatened to resign from his post, she tried to explain her father's seemingly cavalier behaviour. 'To him in a way political life is very simple; follow the man you trust and wait till that man sees the perfect moment to re-arrange.' Another time she urges, 'I am sure the more openly you speak to him the better, as he is not exactly quick at understanding people's insides.' This is the nearest Mary ever comes to a flicker of criticism against her father.

The problem was that Lord Rosebery felt that he had been overlooked, even slighted, and Mary's sweet urging, 'And yet even if it is you who has most to forgive, most to give in, then to you falls the higher part in forgiving', could only delay, not prevent, his eventual resignation. Her father tried to hold on to his young colleague; 'if you thus go wandering through fields of earth air and sea what is to become of Scotch affairs?' he argued, but he had no definite offer of promotion for him. Rosebery decided to go, and Mary had to accept his decision. She wrote to him that 'each must be responsible to himself and to Heaven to his actions and his friends should trust him. The blow we have all dreaded has fallen much more gently than I ever hoped – And I want to say to you I do trust you all the time – I think Roseberys and Gladstones ought to do something public together at once – don't you? Fisheries Exhibition?'[8]

Good old Mary, forever practical and positive; she wrote in her diary that they had had the 'inferior' subject out and he had given her a beautiful crucifix as a farewell offering. She does not elaborate and a few years ago, she might have been referring to herself but now it is more likely that Lord Rosebery is the one who is suffering from a feeling of inferiority, unable to secure a position in the Cabinet.

Mr Gladstone was beginning to feel the strain of office. Mrs Gladstone noticed the signs, and resolved to ask nothing of him, but only to soothe and placate. Outwardly he seemed his usual self as he faced his demanding routine. His doctor, Sir Andrew Clark, believed that with his careful habits, he had the best chance of living to a hundred.

At moments of great personal stress and emotional intensity, Gladstone always increased his night walks and his practice of searching out prostitutes and engaging them in conversation in the hope that he might rescue them from their ways. Mary's mother knew and shared his concerns. They were both members of the Church Penitentiary Association for the Reclamation of Fallen Women. Over twenty-five years ago they had founded the Clewer House of Mercy near Oxford; seven years later they founded the Newport House of Refuge in Soho

Square and two years later the St Mary Magdalen House of Refuge in Paddington.

How much Mary knew of her father's activities is not clear. Her opinion, like her mother's, would without question be one of absolute faith in his integrity. There is an undated letter to her father, probably from 1880 as it mentions Herbert's feelings about the Leeds constituency, in which she mentions a long letter of congratulation from Mrs Thistlethwayte, and an invitation to dine with her; she adds, 'I thought not worth forwarding'. Mrs Laura Thistlethwayte had been a London courtesan until her marriage in 1852 to a wealthy gentleman with a house in Grosvenor Square. Gladstone made her acquaintance in 1863 and they became close friends with many letters passing between them (now published in *The Gladstone Diaries*, volumes I – XIV). She cannot be bracketed with the prostitutes whom he sought to save. She was beautiful and religious, a fascinating combination to enthral Mary's father who believed in her purity of heart. Whether Mary had been instructed, or knew instinctively how to deal with such invitations, is open to speculation. There were times when gossip was rife in the London clubs, and the more sensational newspapers delighted in smearing scandal across their pages. She must have come across anonymous letters calling for his resignation, as well as mudslinging in his correspondence.

Mrs Gladstone was well aware of the physical risks for her husband as he walked the streets alone, and he assuaged her worries by carrying a stout stick. He often walked home from the Commons, and on the night of Lord Frederick's murder, he had chosen to walk home from the Austrian Embassy where he had dined with Mrs Gladstone, leaving her to go on alone to another social function at the Admiralty. Here she was met by her host who warned her of bad news and arranged her immediate return to Downing Street. Eddy Hamilton broke the news to her, and only then did Gladstone turn up on the doorstep, having been seen talking to a prostitute on the Duke of York's Steps, a favourite stop for their trade.

After the Phoenix Park murders, the Prime Minister was given a plainclothes policeman as bodyguard, but he would

often give him the slip. His colleagues worried that an unscrupulous member of the force might be tempted to sell his story to
the press. Stories were circulating again and Lord Rosebery lost
the toss with Lord Granville to undertake, on behalf of the
Cabinet, the delicate task of impressing upon him the unwise
risks he was taking to his person and to his reputation. It would
appear that he could not be persuaded to give up his habit.
Eddy Hamilton tried a few times over the years and he did
eventually extract a promise that he would stop. From Gladstone's diaries, where his private soul-searching is painfully
honest, it is clear that he was aware that he was sinning
morally in his rescue work; his sin was that he allowed himself
to be tempted by the pleasures of the flesh, even if at the last
moment he would not give way to the temptation.

Mary never mentions her father's night walks, either in letters or in her diary. Lucy refers obliquely to the Tory disbelief in
Gladstone's public and private morality. Mrs Gladstone scorned
all worldly advice; her only thought was for his safety. Lord
Rosebery remarked to his colleagues that it was not as if he
were achieving much, after all, he had only 'saved' ten women
in all his years.

Henry Mayhew, in his book *London Labour and the London
Poor*, estimated that in the 1850s there were about 80 000
prostitutes out of a population of about a million. Most of the
women that Gladstone tried to help were common prostitutes
and, for such women, their rehabilitation into society was
often harsher than the workhouse. The most famous one was
Mrs Thistlethwayte, whose profession was on a different level;
another was Mrs Dale whose portrait he commissioned from
William Dyce who painted her as 'Lady with the Coronet of Jas-
mine'. It cannot be possible that this was undertaken in secret,
unknown to others in the family. His friendship with the
actress Lily Langtry was another sensitive issue that had to be
discussed. Henry Labouchere, MP and editor of the magazine
Truth, stated publicly, 'Gladstone manages to combine his missionary meddling with a keen appreciation of a pretty face.'
What Mary's mother really thought of her husband's work
with prostitutes is unknown; if her sister Mary had still been

alive, there would have been letters between them, sharing any worries that she might have had.

August brought the end of the Parliamentary term. Everyone was exhausted and desperate to get out of London but respite was short and, at Hawarden, there were weighty ecclesiastical decisions to be made, following the deaths of the Archbishop of Canterbury and the Dean of Windsor. Both Mary and her father took soundings on a successor for Canterbury and Mrs Gladstone again showed her irritation at Mary's involvement being greater than her own. 'I think it is wisest not to puzzle Papa with every passing wind and pigman,' she wrote, as though Mary were a trying ten-year-old. Mary hoped that her father, who was sleeping so badly that he sought a bed and a good night's rest at the Rectory, would soon regain his health and spirits. She wrote to Lavinia that her father's loss of sleep had affected his nerves, 'I mean he got quite afraid of the nights.' A planned Midlothian campaign was cancelled. After a series of sleepless nights, Gladstone was on the brink of resignation and Dr Clark again ordered him abroad. He did not return until the first week of March 1883 and for a while, the country was governed by an absentee Prime Minister.

On her return to the dust and heat of London, Mary showed signs of weariness, a cynical questioning of what before had been utterly absorbing and exhilarating. It was not just over politics but covers all her London activities. She grumbled that the sermon at St Margaret's on liberty was 'a flood of rhetorical nothings and truisms', that Gounod's 'Redemption' to a crowded Albert Hall was 'the poorest thinnest music' and she was 'really frightfully bored'. A large party at No. 10 for the victorious general Sir Garnet Wolseley she regarded as 'disgusting' and she tried to wriggle out of it. Attendance at the House of Commons was losing its magic; the long dull speeches far outweighed the flashes of wit. Her visit to the new Law Courts with Spencer was marred by the sight of the slums and the impoverished crowds along the way. The Lord Mayor's annual procession was merely an 'absurd relic of former ages'.

There is a great sense of her aloneness, and a gulf between herself and all the beautiful people madly pursuing dreams, ambitions and delights. Even Cambridge has lost its charms, and one diary entry reads, 'By the end of the evening was rather depressed, with a tired feeling of having wasted good brains and earnest minds and frittered the time away in ceaseless chaff and chatter.' It is eight years since May Lyttelton's death and Mary calls all those left behind the 'Maryladen', with their sad sense of loss. The terrible murders in Dublin had drained all energy. Matters in Egypt were deepening into a chaotic muddle while the Cabinet was crumbling; Mary knew that her father was exhausted and longing for peace.

CHAPTER FIFTEEN

Cruises and country holidays (1882 – 3)

At the end of the Parliamentary term of 1881 a ten-day, round-Britain cruise in Sir Donald Currie's ship had restored energies. The next year, a short trip in Lord Wolverton's yacht along the south coast gave a brief injection of fresh air to jaded minds and bodies. Mary's father joined the family at Cowes after delivering his end-of-term report to the Queen at Osborne House. Much to Mary's horror, her father elected to sail on to Portland in what was termed 'a fresh breeze' and she knew that she was in for hours of misery. Schlüter was with them and wrote in her diary, 'Portland. Here we are in a yacht, Mr and Mrs Gladstone, Miss Mary and Mr Herbert and my humble self. We anchored here last night, after six hours journey from Cowes, and what a journey! How the boat rolled and pitched and made me feel so bad I had to go to bed.' Mary was never more thankful to reach 'firm Mother Earth', still feeling giddy and lightheaded.

They spent Sunday visiting the prison and sharing the church service with about 1400 convicts; one had recently killed his jailer and was under guard and another, the organist, was a convicted murderer. Mary found it a harrowing experience, especially the dining routines. She had thought that mealtimes were enjoyable, sociable occasions, but not so in prison. She gives details in her diary:

> A loaf and cheese stood on the floor in front of 250 cells. At the word of command the doors opened as if by magic and 250 convicts stood on the thresholds. 'Pick up yr. dinners.' They all stooped. 'Back to yr. cells. Shut yr. doors',

and with a crash of thunder they all vanished, and every door was double-locked. They may never speak to each other. They lose all identity and are only known by their numbers written on their backs.

Of course, holidays were not always tied to her parents, and in September she was invited by Frances Graham, her last unmarried friend, to join a house party on Skye, along with Herbert and Spencer. They were to be guests at the Grahams' Scottish home. The journey from Hawarden was by train to Glasgow and then on to Greenock. There they boarded ship in filthy weather, and travelled through the Crinan Canal's numerous locks to Oban where they stayed overnight at the Great Western Hotel. When the manager knew that they were Gladstones he would charge them nothing 'out of love for the P.M.' Mr Graham, wealthy Glasgow merchant and Liberal MP, met them to escort them on their final leg of the journey and, as the boat got close to Armadale, a little sailboat, dancing in the sunshine, with Frances and Amy Graham and some of their house guests on board, came out to meet them.

They had a marvellously mad time at Armadale Castle, in 'oldest clothes, shortest petticoats, thickest boots', recapturing the innocence of childhood for a few precious days. Katherine Wortley (who was to marry Neville Lyttelton), Ken Muir-Mackenzie and Charlie Wortley were in their party. They went crabbing and climbing, sailing and exploring, working up ravenous appetites, their adventures savouring more sweetly because childhood was in reality well past. Frances was Mary's last close friend to become engaged, and her future bridegroom was a forty-year-old barrister, Sir John Fortescue Horner. Mary, at thirty-five, would be the only one of her crowd left unmarried. She was still determined to marry for love, feeling sure that nothing else mattered when love and trust were present. Frances was marrying for love and Mary believed that she had a great prospect of happiness.

After two relaxing weeks, they left Armadale in late afternoon and watched the sun setting over Rhum and Eigg as they sailed away to Tobermory where they took on extra passengers; four hundred sheep bound for Oban. There was one last weekend and this time they were guests of the Tennant family at their Scottish home 'Glen', thirty miles from Edinburgh. Mary was fascinated but not exactly approving of the four Tennant sisters. She was rather afraid that Herbert might fall in love with Laura, 'as everybody else does who goes there, those sort of girls get proposals every day and they get so used to refusing it costs them nothing'.[1] He certainly was much attracted for quite some time. Laura was just twenty-one-years-old and was, as Mary had to admit, 'the sharpest little creature, like a needle, delicate and yet able to do everything beautifully, like riding, lawn tennis, playing etc., full of life and fun and up to anything in the world, and yet some 'Weltschmerzen' in her eyes and full of aspiration in her graver moments.'[2]

Although the two young women were very different, they grew to appreciate each other's qualities. Laura described Mary as 'a far more collected spirit and a better balanced mind. I wish I had half her qualities, which are rare ones, I think, bless her.' Mary blamed the Tennant parents for not bringing up their daughters in a more responsible way. As children they had been left to run wild, quite beyond the control of a succession of governesses. When they came out into society, they were left free to run around London 'never dreaming any kind of protection or guard was necessary'. Laura's three sisters married young but she had held out until the right man came along, although this did not stop her flirting outrageously and leaving a trail of broken hearts before she decided upon Mary's youngest and most perfect Lyttelton cousin Alfred.

January 1883, instead of the proposed Midlothian tour, Mary found herself in Cannes. Her father had been sleeping badly, even going to the Rectory in search of a night's sound sleep. Her mother too was suffering from sleepless nights. It could well have been that the tragic death of Lord Frederick Cavendish earlier in the year was undermining their normal resilience. Foreign affairs during the year had been particularly nightmarish and not just in Ireland; British involvement in Egyptian affairs in the Sudan, Boer expansion in the Transvaal and British handling of territorial borders between India and Afghanistan were a ragbag of success and failure. Queen Victoria was proving very trying, sending constant letters of advice and complaint to her Prime Minister as though he were an inexperienced junior.

When Dr Clark arrived at Hawarden, having been summoned from London, he found Mr Gladstone was talking wildly of retirement; he ordered a complete change of scene and rest from political problems. The Cannes trip was arranged. Mary was staying with the Actons while her parents were guests at Lord Wolverton's chateau. Royalty, the rich and the famous were all escaping London's chills and fogs, exchanging one set of dining-rooms for another. The Prince of Wales was here, the Duke of Argyll, Sir Charles Dilke; Mary ran into Mr Cross, George Eliot's widower, finding him 'a pleasant chatty individual, not at all the kind one would have imagined'. It seemed to be just what her father needed, and the weeks drifted aimiably by.

Mary described her day in a letter home to Lavinia: 'I have a little breakfast in bed about 8, and do not leave my room sometimes till 11, so can do what I like. Then luncheon comes about 12.45. My room is delicious, catching every ray of sun from its rise to its setting, looking 2 ways, one way to the olive-clothed hills, the other to the Mediterranean.'

Lady Queensberry's young daughter wondered how the Prime Minister could govern England while drinking tea at Cannes. Mary thought it a pertinent question, and perhaps it was an indication of how little the ageing Gladstone was really in control. Back in London, Lord Granville was holding the reins and Herbert was working hard on Irish affairs.

They enjoyed six weeks of delicious leisure at Cannes and unlimited time with Lord Acton, but somehow it was not quite what it had been. Mary was conscious that her relationship with Lord Acton was changing; perhaps she no longer needed his affectionate interest in her or to be needed as his confidante. She tried to explain to Lavinia:

Isn't it like life, that now I have unlimited opportunity of talking to Lord A I do not *quite* appreciate it enough. I think I want a third person to prevent my feeling responsibility. The ladies dribble out to bed, one by one all evening, and by 9 o'clock I generally find myself and Lord A sole occupants of the drawing room. Last night we had a real good go and did not go to bed till 10.30. Isn't it funny that that should be late? But with an evening starting at 6.30, by the time you reach 8.30 it feels like Dead of Night. Well yesterday we talked about sceptism and its future, and how to prepare children for it. He has thought so deeply about it all, especially on account of his 12-year-old son, who will go bang out of the bosom of the family into the Oxford Vortex. I talk as much as ever I can to all the dim females and jabber a mixture of French and English with the utmost freedom.'[3]

The strain of spending so much time with him was diluting the fascination that she had first felt in his company. Now it was not enough for her to be the demure acolyte, grateful for each drop of wisdom that Lord Acton let fall. After one evening she felt 'quite odd, gaunt and flat'. Brother Stephen joined them for some of the time and Spencer was there, making himself useful as the P.M.'s secretary.

They all went on a wonderful outing to Grasse and on to Gourdon, a picturesque 'tumbledown-looking' little town perched some four thousand feet high on a rock. This was certainly a great day but it was the evenings that could seem so interminably long. Her mother and Spencer admitted that they were bored to death; only Mr Gladstone seemed 'content to sit still in this spot as long as they can get on without him'. It was the end of February before he was ready to go home. They were given a flower-strewn farewell at the station and away they went; as the train sped through the night, she shared one side of a wagon-lit with Spencer, sleep giving way to endless talk.

The change of scene and the slower pace restored their energies briefly. Gladstone rejoined his colleagues, and discussions continued on the reform of local government, not an issue to set his missionary zeal ablaze; he left the details to his Home

Secretary. The government was three years old and in the doldrums. The Irish problem was unresolved. Egyptian affairs seemed to have quietened. Mary plunged into her days again, ready to meet friends, fit in lunch and shopping and errands, a Wagner concert at the Crystal Palace, the Rossetti exhibition at Burlington House, rehearsals at Arthur Balfour's for the Handel Society, Berlioz at the Albert Hall; so many glittering occasions that sent her exhausted to bed. It was as if there must be no time of tranquility, no space for quiet reflection or her thoughts would dwell on loved ones no longer with her, and let in the gremlins of despair.

Summer holidays came round again and Mary was delegated to organise another sea cruise, guests once again of Sir Donald Currie on a cruise around the Scottish coast in the *S.S. Pembroke Castle*, his newest and biggest steam ship, which had been designed to carry passengers on the South African route. She was given just a week to arrange the guest list. She aimed to provide a good mix of young and old, bearing in mind that her chief concern was her father's rest and relaxation. She knew that he would be miserable without stimulating conversation. Within the family, Herbert was free but William and Helen had already arranged a mountaineering holiday in Switzerland and cousins Arthur Lyttelton and Constance Gladstone were asked to fill the gap.

Mr Algernon West would represent the Cabinet. Lord Dalhousie and Sir Arthur Gordon were stimulating company, the latter had cruised with the family before and long ago had fallen in love with Agnes when she was only sixteen. He was now fifty-four and unmarried, having spent his life in colonial appointments. He had just completed a three-year stint as governor of New Zealand and would be moving on to Ceylon, from where he would keep up a regular correspondence with Mary, using her to gain the Prime Minister's ear. In one of his letters he asked for her support in his schemes for reducing the military presence in the colony, 'which we have to pay for, which we cannot afford and which we do not want'.

Dr Clark was invited, to keep an eye on Mr Gladstone's health, while his wife could chat with Mrs Gladstone. Sir William

Harcourt with Lewis, his eldest son, known to all as Loulou, could only be prevailed upon to join the ship briefly from Oban to Mull. Mary decided to invite the Tennysons, father and son, who were pleased to accept. After a nudge from Herbert she happily invited Laura Tennant, 'a madcap, a dare-devil, she was literally brimming with joie-de-vivre; nothing was safe in heaven or earth or under the earth from the sallies of her wit.' Yet she could turn in an instant from being the life and soul of the party to a frail wistful child, longing to please.

Mary would have liked Scott Holland to be on board, but he had to be at Truro where he was to be installed as Canon. He had to admit that he was not sorry to be otherwise engaged, for he was a terrible sailor. 'How could I hang on the lips of the P.M. while my whole physical self was itself hung in dreadful suspense, on the edge of each hanging wave?' he wrote; he was 'entirely green' at sea. It would have been immense fun if only it were on dry land. 'Why do these ships go to sea? They are such fascinating things in themselves – so bright & clean & gay. They spoil it all by going on water.'[4] Mary half-agreed with him and she could only pray for calm weather on seas that were notoriously stormy.

The family set off from Hawarden on 8 September, meeting up with the Tennysons at Chester station in their specially reserved saloon carriage that would carry them to Barrow-in-Furness, where the ship was anchored. There was a gale blowing as the little tug carried them on board and the outlook was ominous for the squeamish. Schlüter and Zadok the butler had been chosen from the Hawarden servants to go with the family but, until she got her sea legs, Schlüter was treated like an honoured guest, with chicken and champagne served in her cabin. Once the gales had spent themselves, she eagerly joined in the fun with those on board.

The plan was to circle Scotland and sail back down the east coast as far as London. Laura Tennant came on board at Barrow and logged her first impressions of her fellow guests. 'My 1st introduction to Tennyson was this: standing looking at Scawfell, I said to Herbert, "Isn't it lovely?". Tennyson walked up. "Yes, and cold too, like some women I know." And then silently walked on in a hat!! and a cloak!!! I note the ideal Poet's garments.' That evening she sat next to Hallam at dinner and was not attracted by his looks, but liked him all the same. She weighed up Arthur Lyttelton from across the table: 'A fine head and so unselfconscious.' Mrs Gladstone was at once 'a darling' and she was soon calling her 'Auntie Pussy', but Mr Gladstone was 'the Holiest of Holies'; Laura could never get beyond his sacred aura although she could call him 'Gladdy' in the privacy of her diary.

Other characters would reveal themselves as the days passed, but Laura knew at once that she was having a wonderful time. On second day's acquaintance Tennyson asked her to kiss him, 'Which I promptly did and would any day! I love him. We talked of Swinburne & Rossetti – of fame – and cabbages and kings.' He was enchanted by her, calling her 'the little Witch'. They flirted together endlessly, each enjoying the game and daring each other to greater pranks. 'You will not kiss Mary's hair next time we pass her,' Laura tested him one day as they promenaded on deck. 'Shouldn't I? You will see', he teasingly growled. He passed close behind but made no move towards Mary. 'I could not, it was sacred for the sun was kissing it,' he mischievously parried. The scenery as they sailed past the Hebridean islands was spectacular. It was 'the bluest, sweetest day,' Laura thought, 'with an opal sea and baby islands, and ruby heather, and golden ferns, and seals and porpoises and sails of Indian red, and the sun kissing the world.'[5]

Tennyson needed little persuasion to read his poems and his sonorous voice rang out across the waves. Mary organised a concert for everyone and, with a piano on board, there were always requests for her to play. The cruise was proving a huge success, so much so that Sir Donald proposed that they extend their route to Norway and Denmark. They sailed by way of the Orkneys where the islanders cheered the arrival of the Prime Minister and the Poet Laureate, giving them the freedom of the city of Kirkwall. They drifted leisurely on to Christiana and here they dropped anchor for a day and a night. They took an excursion out into the Norwegian countryside and then next day sailed on to Copenhagen.

It was as if they were on an enchanted journey that knew no end. They entered the crowded harbour to the astonished gaze of nearly all the European heads of state. It was an extraordinary assembly that included the Kings and Queens of Denmark and Greece and the Czar and Czarina of Russia. There were princes and princesses, counts and countesses, dukes and duchesses. Even the Princess of Wales was there with three of her daughters. What had been a private holiday now took on international implications, and yet strangely remained so delightfully informal.

The Danish King and Queen invited them to dine at their country palace at Fredensborg, and a small select party gathered on deck at 3 p.m. – Mr and Mrs Gladstone, Sir Arthur Gordon, Sir Donald Currie, Tennyson and Mary. Sir Arthur Gordon had insisted that, as government representative, he should be included to keep an eye on the P.M., and Mary was absolutely essential as the one most able to shepherd them all safely ashore and back again. She wrote that, 'The whole thing was rather amusing and interesting, loads of crowned heads, an immense country house, great simplicity of life, 80 at dinner.' She wore her black velvet and Laura sweetly lent her jewels and a fan.

There was little pomp and ceremony in the Danish court, and all nineteen royal children danced into the room ahead of the adults and rounded off the evening with a display of gymnastics. Of course the invitation had to be returned, and on the very next day, Mary found herself seated between the King of Greece and Prince Eddy while Laura sat by the Danish king's brother and 'one door off', as she put it, from the Queen of Denmark. After the meal Tennyson read to them, or as many of them as could cram into the tiny smoking-room. He sat between the Czarina and the Princess of Wales 'and patted them just as he does us,' wrote Laura, 'I wonder he did not embrace them.'

Little did the holiday party realise what ripples were reaching out to the far-away British shore. Mary's father was no ordinary man accountable only to himself. He had not thought to ask permission before he left his own territorial waters. However much Herbert might protest that their detour to Copenhagen was 'pure accident', 'a private affair, a biographical incident', it was reported by all the European newspapers as a foolish escapade, a political blunder, a reckless scandal.

Queen Victoria was not amused. She wrote to Lord Granville, 'The Prime Minister – and especially one *not* gifted with prudence in speech – is not a person who can go about *where* he likes with impunity.' Herbert knew that his father was as likely to discuss politics with the royal heads as 'a schoolboy on holiday when meeting one of his schoolmates would be to discuss the text of Aesychylus.'[6] It was a minor storm in a teacup to Mary and her fellow travellers, who reached Gravesend with many happy memories of memorable times. Laura gave everyone a small white copy of *Hamlet*, inscribed 'in memory of Elsinore'. Tennyson was asked to give a verse that could be engraved on a presentation plate for their host and for the ship's officers. He duly obliged:

> 'Grateful guests to gracious host,
> To and from the Danish coast.'

Not exactly great poetry, but it conveyed everyone's sentiments. Mary and Laura remembered another engraving that they had seen on a castle window near Fredensborg, 'O, keep me innocent, make others great.'

Mary was reluctant to leave the ship and break the spell that had encircled them, but daily routines must be resumed. Each said goodbye and returned to their familiar path. Hallam followed the advice that Mary had given him while they were together on board, that he should find himself a girl rich in love if not in material gifts. 'She is a noble-hearted girl who has devoted herself to her sick Father for the last sixteen years,' he was soon writing, 'It all came to pass over *In Memoriam* and I want you for my sake as well as hers *always* to help her and be loving to her.' He went on to tell Mary that his bride-to-be had 'endless brothers but they will none of them know anything about it till Xmas.' He confided that they would be as poor as church mice and if Mary with her connections should hear of some lowly post, 'a political crossing-sweeper's place' would suffice, then they could live in the country and he would go up to London each day. He ended his letter, 'God bless you Mary. Ever your affect. brother, Hallam Tennyson'.[7]

Another of Mary's friends settled in matrimony and, in the same month, Neville Lyttelton at last married his love. Mary had given her opinion to Alfred that £1200 would be ample for any couple 'who didn't mind living rather humbly – going 2nd class and in a bus and inhabiting an unfashionable part of London and not going in for smart cooking.' She had watched her friends as they approached matrimony and she believed that there were two options. If they went into marriage with their eyes open there was no excuse for ignoring such obstacles as poverty and ill-health that can strain the bonds of love to breaking point. It was entirely another matter if love came as a blinding flash and the couple rushed headlong to the altar. 'Heaven sometimes takes much of the responsibility by allowing the two to fall so gloriously in love with each other that it will float them over the roughest sea,' she told Alfred. She had decided that she would not walk into marriage with only friendship on offer; it must be headlong passion for her, or she would remain everyone's favourite maiden aunt.

When twenty-seven-year-old Harry Drew, Stephen Gladstone's new assistant at the Rectory, came to dine at the Castle Mary merely noted that he was 'very quiet and shy and thoughtful' and that she liked him. Harry was the second son of John Drew, land agent to Lord Devon of Powderham, near Exeter. He had left Keble College Oxford in 1878 with a second-class degree in history, having paid more attention to sport than to his studies. He had rowed for his college, shot and fished and been popular with everyone. A fellow student described him as 'the ideal of manliness, modesty, beauty and fun. Strikingly handsome, erect, lissom, with strong square shoulders,' his eyes were 'so blue, so luminous, with their dark lashes'. Yet it was his niceness that first attracted Mary, who was usually appreciative of the physical charms of others.

His arrival was a small event in Mary's life. He was just a comfortable figure who fitted snugly into the dear old

Hawarden scene. She looked elsewhere for excitement, and liked a dash of fire and exuberance in her men. Another Harry – Harry Cust, Lord Brownlow's charming heir and six years younger than her – was one of her glittering, fun-loving London crowd. She described him as 'a nice boy in the cynical stage'. She enjoyed flirting with him, indulging in lively talks on matters of the moment, their ideas sparking off each other. In complete contrast, Harry Drew blended perfectly into the Hawarden landscape, blissful for refreshment but far too bland for a constant diet. She was not yet ready to turn her back on political intrigue and high-society partying, and how would her father manage without her?

CHAPTER SIXTEEN

The swings and roundabouts of politics (1884—5)

*A*fter the summer break that stretched through autumn into winter, Mary went eagerly back to London for the new term loaded with greenery to fill the Downing Street rooms. She found her clerical papers piling ever higher, and decisions were awaited on new bishops for Southwell and Chester. She knew that her father had given Scott Holland a canonry of St Paul's Cathedral, but it was not discussed between the two of them until the official offer was made. Then he joyfully wrote to tell her how wonderful it was to be no longer 'a casual performer hired by the night' but a member of the family under the beautiful Dome.

Living at No. 1 Amen Corner did not strip away his puckish humour. He called the splendidly dressed Cathedral clergy 'glorified armadilloes'. He and Mary still gossiped over the best man to fill a clerical vacancy. In one of his letters he asks her, 'Do you not sometimes want a really good man?', and goes on to recommend a young rector who is 'too good a man to be left in the country. He could undertake an important town cure with great success.' Now that he was a canon of St Paul's he could invite promising young clergy to preach, always assuring them that his congregation were 'not purse-proud gents who sit on rich farms dealing largely with horse-flesh: they are all humble folk who could take the message from you.'[1] His own sermons were passionate outpourings, a whirling of ideas that burned into her soul and recharged her energies.

Her life was 'bewilderingly stuffed with deep and dazzling delights', she told Lavinia. She was always on the move, London or Oxford or Cambridge, and her diary is littered with the names of the keenest minds, the most radical thinkers. On one crowded day she made the acquaintance at a luncheon party of Octavia Hill, active campaigner for housing and social reforms, and William Stead, journalist of the *Pall Mall Gazette*. She recorded her impressions of the two in her diary: 'She talked a good deal of her experiences and was perfectly simple and unaffected, her head well screwed on her shoulders ... Talked a bit to Stead after and liked him tho' his head is certainly not well screwed on.'

Dinner later in the day brought her into the company of other glittering names and she was placed next to Henry James, the American novelist who had been living in London for the past eight years. At supper, she sat next to 'Tenniel, the Punch cartoon man, dear old thing with hair brushed straight from the back of his head towards his cheeks, don't you know.'

In Cambridge, she was her cousin Arthur's guest at the new Selwyn College where he was Head, and she saw a lot of her sister Helen at Newnham. Three years ago, after much family discussion, Helen had taken the position of secretary and assistant to the Vice-Principal, Nora Sidgwick. (Nora Balfour had married Henry Sidgwick, Professor of Moral Philosophy, in 1876.) It was a salaried post, and Helen had needed Mary's support to persuade their mother that it was suitable. Mrs Gladstone had felt slighted that Helen had not come home to explain it to her personally, which would have given her a chance to make her case more forcibly. Mr Gladstone wrote to give his thirty-one-year-old daughter his blessing. He had no objection as long as she gave consideration to two points – that she would be in a subordinate position to Mrs Sidgwick, and that she would keep her independence on religious questions.

Helen had been transformed by Cambridge; Mary had seen how she had blossomed thanks to her first real friendships and the intellectual stimulus that surrounded her. In a letter to Harry, she told him that Helen's life was so much fuller and richer, 'so useful, so much influence. You see the change in her at once and I really think it has stimulated her interest in everything.' She was now Vice-Principal with responsibility for ninety students in residence at Newnham.

Mary dined at Trinity College and met Mrs Josephine Butler, 'that much heard of, much enduring, struggling and noble-spirited woman'. Her husband was headmaster of Liverpool College and Mrs Butler, nearly twenty years older than Mary, had spent her life fighting to improve the status of women in Victorian society, especially the lot of prostitutes. She had fought against the laws that allowed women to be arrested and forcibly examined for VD; all were presumed guilty until they could prove their innocence. These women were seen as temptresses, as harbourers of sin and disease, whereas men were merely responding to their baser natures. Even those women brave enough to talk openly on the subject were considered contemptible. George Butler openly supported his wife and many thought that he had sacrificed his career for her work. When Scott Holland met Josephine Butler he saw 'the look of the world's grim tragedies in her eyes'.

Mary adored the fast and furious debates taking place in Cambridge on such matters as female suffrage, land nationalisation, 'vivisection and vaccination nuts'. The man of the moment was Mr Henry George, with his new book *Progress and Poverty*, and she was deeply impressed by his earnestness and convictions. 'I don't think we made the slightest impression on him and he was very quick and clear in argument,' she wrote in her diary, 'I was almost converted to his views, but not quite.' She felt bold enough to speak out and give her side of the argument, growing as red as her gown. 'I was frightened at my own remarks,' she told Lavinia, 'and nobody backed me up till he was gone. So of course I always felt I must have said the wrong thing', but at least she had the courage to speak out when others had stayed silent. The talk was all about how to improve the lot of the poor, how to bridge the gap between the few who lived in luxury and the majority of the population, who lived in misery and squalor. She went to listen to Mr George's lecture to an undergraduate audience at the town hall. He fared better than she expected and she marvelled at his impassioned performance as he answered hostile questions with 'great spirit and manliness'.

She carried his arguments back to London, and tackled her father and his colleagues on their views; they might sympathise in private but were too astute to support the cause publicly. When Stead's articles on child prostitution in the *Pall Mall Gazette* burst upon the horrified public, she tried to stir the consciences of those with power and influence, urging Lavinia to speak to her husband who, as Warden of Keble College, could influence others. She was ashamed that she belonged with the silent majority who were afraid to fight against this evil 'and we leave almost the whole battle to one or two nervie individuals'. The picture of Mary that emerges from these years is hardly one of a timid, silent soul; she is stirring the waters in her own pool and hoping that the ripples that she creates will spread out and carry to others beyond her reach.

Josephine Butler wrote a pamphlet, *Rebecca Jarrett*, which gave details of how Stead had procured a child prostitute and exposed the ease with which she could be smuggled to Europe, where the age of consent was much higher than in England. Mary supported the cause and bought fifteen copies of the pamphlet to distribute to friends and family. She intended to get her parents and brother Stephen to read it, and she asked Lavinia to try to make Lady Salisbury read it too. There was such an outcry following the publicity that a court case followed, Stead served a prison sentence of three months for his involvement, and Rebecca Jarrett was sentenced to six months; the only good that came out of the case was that the legal age for prostitutes was raised from thirteen to sixteen.

Feminist issues were becoming the main topic of discussion at society dinner tables. Lucy and Alfred agreed that the differences between the sexes were great and each had their different sphere, disagreeing with Mary who held out for equality in law and equal opportunity between the sexes. The discussion led on to whether women should have the same educational opportunities as the men. She was all in favour, for had she not been the one to encourage Helen to go to Cambridge seven years ago? Her father declared that he was all in favour when Oxford, three years after Cambridge, voted by a majority of 140 out of 700 to admit women to their examinations. Nora Sidgwick had realised the usefulness of appointing a Gladstone at Newnham College as she sought to raise the college's status; Mary, in her present position in Downing Street, with access to many sources of power and influence, could be even more useful than Helen in her academic world.

She kept up discussions on moral issues. Her Cambridge friend, Professor James Stuart, wrote to her, 'To make women more independent of men is, I am convinced, one of the great fundamental means of bringing about justice, morality and happiness both for the married and unmarried men and women.' In another letter he declared that it was 'a time-honoured lie that men have irresistible passions, and that women must be sacrificed to them'.[2] Alfred Lyttelton did not approve of these airings of what he regarded as private wrestlings. He wrote that he could not see the purpose of speaking of them 'in ordinary life as ordinary phenomena'.

In Parliament, Gladstone was pushing ahead with his Reform Bill which proposed extending the principle of household suffrage to country-dwellers, eventually giving every able male citizen the vote; but still not women. He argued that he did not want to give the Opposition any opportunity to split his reforms by numerous amendments. The Commons were in favour but the Lords were anxious to protect the interests of the Conservative Party and wanted a deal over redrawing the electoral map. Joseph Chamberlain was incensed by what he saw as Tory delaying tactics; he threatened to lead a march on London of 100 000 Midland men, and an eight-mile procession in support of reform wound through the London streets. The Queen believed that Mr Gladstone was inflaming the situation and called upon him to restrain his 'wild colleagues and followers'. Charles Dilke, MP for Chelsea, was given the task of hammering out a compromise with Lord Salisbury, and the agreement eventually reached was that the Liberals would gain on the franchise and the Tories on the redistribution of seats.

While the Prime Minister was trying to manipulate the extremes of his party, Mary was occupied with her own manipulations over the appointment of Lady Principal for Girton. Her idea was that this was a worthwhile job for Lucy that would help her in her sad and lonely widowhood. It was not one of her better ideas; Lucy was in no way qualified for the post and was not the slightest bit interested. Lavinia told Mary that she would as soon think of proposing her nine-year-old daughter. Undeterred, Mary moved on to her next scheme: Eton was looking for a new headmaster and Mr Welldon seemed a likely candidate. He sought out her opinion on whether he should stand and she had what she described as a nice talk with him one Sunday luncheon. He did not get Eton but he did get the headship of Harrow.

Through this year and the next, political events moved swiftly. Mary was assiduous in her attendance at the House of Commons debates, where Irish matters had been pushed from centre stage by the Egyptian disasters. Her father had concentrated so completely on resolving the Irish problem over the years that he had neglected foreign affairs, which were never his strongest interest. Mary's diary for February 12, 1884 reads:

Today and yesterday have been tremendous in Egyptian anxieties, fall of Sinhat this morning inflaming passion already exaggerated, fears for Gordon, telegrams arrived, Ministers rushing to and fro, the P.M. alone calm and resolute and keen as to his speech. Sir Stafford's was milky mild, the greatest contrast to its object, a Vote of Censure being the strongest move an Op[position] can make. His accusation of indecision and dawdling was made mince-meat of by the P.M. in a magnificent speech of nearly 2 hours. I never before saw the House absolutely crammed between 8 and 9; there was a wonderful play and variety of emotion, indignation, scorn, earnestness and a certain amount of banter even, but for force and feeling I never heard it surpassed; he held the House in his hands and did with them what he would.

The Liberals had inherited their foreign policy in Egypt from the Conservatives with Disraeli's purchase of Suez Canal shares in 1876. Since coming to power in 1880, there had been growing unrest leading to mutiny and massacre. In 1882 there had been an Anglo-French naval demonstration at Alexandria as a means of protecting and evacuating Europeans, but France did not want to become enmeshed in Egypt. Gladstone took action, sending British troops under the command of Sir Garnet Wolseley, his mission to restore order. When they disembarked at Port Said in August 1882 the ever-loyal John Bright handed in his resignation from the Cabinet, describing the intervention as 'a manifest violation of international and moral law'. As always, Gladstone surveyed the Egyptian scene from a high moral ground, always holding on to the rightness of his decision to invade, and at first victory was with the British.

December 1882: Mary was thirty-five and had lived all her life in the shade of her father's rise up the political ladder; he was now celebrating fifty years of public life. John Morley in his biography wrote that he believed 'he had wrought his early habits of severe toil, method, exactness, concentration, into cast iron. Whether they had sharpened what is called knowledge of the world, or taught him insight into men and skill in discrimination among men, it is hard to say. He always talked as if he found the world pretty much what he had expected. Man, he used often to say, is the least comprehensible of creatures, and of man the most incomprehensible are the politicians.'

Throughout 1883 the Egyptians were struggling unsuccessfully to gain control in the Sudan. The British government sought to withdraw their troops and General Gordon was chosen to carry out their policy. He was a disastrous choice, and yet was favoured by Conservatives and Liberals and by the people. He has been described as:

> ... a soldier of infinite personal courage and daring; of striking military energy, initiative and resource; a high, pure, and single character, dwelling much in the region of the unseen. But as all who knew him admit, and as

his own records testify, notwithstanding an under-
current of shrewd common-sense, he was the creature,
almost the sport of impulse; his impressions and pur-
poses changed with the speed of lightning; anger often
mastered him; he went very often by intuitions and
inspirations rather than by cool inference from carefully
surveyed fact: with many variations of mood he mixed
faith in his own rapid prepossessions while they lasted.[3]

He was sent out to report on the situation on the understanding that his task was to evacuate; within days he had
appointed himself Governor-General. By April he was surrounded by the enemy but the British Cabinet believed that he
could save himself if he wished; no reinforcements would be
sent to aid him. They saw it as his duty to withdraw, which
was the last thing in Gordon's mind. Gladstone persuaded himself ('and above all he can persuade himself of almost anything', declared Forster) that Gordon's life was not in danger.
It was only under threat of Lord Hartington's resignation
from the War Office that at last, on 5 August 1884, a grant of
£300 000 was requested in the House of Commons to equip a
rescue expedition.

During November 1884, there were constant comings and
goings in Downing Street where Mary was an all-seeing, all-
hearing shadow. She peeped in at doors, listened to raised
voices, provided luncheons and caught up with the latest deals
over tea with her father. The twenty-third of November was her
thirty-seventh birthday, but far more exciting for her was the
state of play between the parties; political minds were focused
on domestic matters – franchise and redistribution of seats.
Gladstone was aiming for a third Reform Bill before his government ran out of steam and he could retire to his books and the
peace of Hawarden. Mary explained to Mr George Russell who
came to tea, that if the present delicate balance could be held,
'We get our F[ranchise] and R[eform] Bill plus booking the Op.
leaders not to oppose it, plus its being a more Radical bill than
we could have brought in alone, plus its being eventually
impossible to dissolve before Jan. '86.'[4]

Time was badly needed, and it was time that now ran out. When relief finally reached Khartoum on 28 January 1885 the city had fallen and General Gordon was dead. Mary was at Hawarden and did not hear the news until Sunday 6 February. She was on her way to church and felt 'wretched and quite sick'. Even then, she did not know the whole story, only that Khartoum had fallen; there was no news on Gordon's whereabouts. 'All feels most dark,' she wrote in her diary. Her parents were staying at Holker Hall as guests of the Duke of Devonshire. Two telegrams reached them, one in cypher from Eddy Hamilton giving the terrible news, the second a public and humiliating rebuke from Queen Victoria. Her father hurriedly returned to Downing Street with the nation's howls and boos raining down on him.

Friends rallied round. As ever, Scott Holland was quick to give his support, writing to Mary, 'You will be feeling the strain in its bitterest force. Men's hearts are tingling and their minds are rocking, there is a great swaying to and fro. One hardly knows to what it will come.' He was candid in his criticism of her father and the government, believing that they should not have sent Gordon in the first place but, having done so, they should not have failed in their mission. He told Mary that he must write truly so that his sympathy might be sincere and worthwhile. He knew that the fury in the land, just and unjust, would rage until it had spent itself.

She went to London prepared to give all her support to her parents. She had to drive through the jeering crowds who gathered every day in Downing Street. On 19 February she saw her parents off to the House of Commons 'amid a storm of hisses and groans drowned in cheers'; she soon followed, only to be made completely miserable by her father's speech which 'utterly failed to cheer and strengthen or comfort any human being'.

It was the first time that she had not seen him rise to the occasion and crush his foes. It was the first time he had failed her. On 27 February she did not go to the House; 'It did not seem worthwhile,' she wrote in her diary. She thought that they were about to be kicked out, so much so that she had calmly discussed the subject at breakfast that day. It was only the

Opposition's ineffectiveness that prevented a vote of censure against the government, but their majority was slim.

All the next day her mood swung from acceptance to despair. Were they going or staying? Her spirit seemed to have gone out of politics. Not so her father, who was fighting for his political life against the general opinion in the country that he had 'trampled upon the flag and tarnished his country's honour'. From mid-April he received nine resignations in one form or another; in Cabinet he rallied his troops, and carried them with him in his determination not to be ousted.

The end came on 9 June over a paltry Budget issue. Mary declared that it was absurd that they should be defeated in this way; they had 'so persistently watched the wrong rock'. It may have been a minor amendment that caught them unawares but the real stumbling block was the enormous one of how to proceed through the quagmire of governing Ireland. The Cabinet had been torn apart on the issue of local self-government; the radicals were in favour and the diehards against. The new plan had been outvoted and Chamberlain and Dilke impulsively resigned. The Irish were no longer willing to accept the situation and were working behind the scenes on many fronts. Chamberlain was talking to Willie O'Shea, who was talking to Parnell, who was talking to Lord Randolph, while Mr Gladstone was talking to Mrs O'Shea, who was talking to Parnell, who was playing both sides to his own advantage.

Parnell decided that for the moment there was more to gain by siding with the Conservatives and that the Budget amendment would catch the government unawares. He took thirty-nine of his supporters into the Conservative lobby. Seventy-six Liberals abstained; Mary blamed the weakness of the Whip. She could hardly believe that this could be the end of her father's political life. 'And the worst of it is,' she wrote to Lavinia in the middle of that fateful night, 'I don't wish it not to be, and yet I know I shall mind horribly if it is', adding, 'Well, it is all very odd.' Her father being ousted from Downing Street might resolve a quandary before it had to be faced. He was nearing his seventy-sixth birthday and could not continue indefinitely; others were flexing their muscles and manoeuvering for the top position.

When the end came on a hot June night, Mary could not help but see the humour of the government being caught napping. She wrote to Lavinia, 'Well, it is so *funny.* That was my first thought.' Others reacted differently to what seemed to be the end of Gladstone's political career. Lord Acton hated the idea 'because it makes Parnell king' which he thought was the worst of all possible outcomes. Certainly both the Conservatives and the Liberals needed the support of Parnell and his fellow MPs.

While ministers and secretaries scurried in and out of Downing Street, Mary worked in her tiny office on mountainous piles of papers, destroying confidential letters and creating order out of the rest. She described 22 June as the most extraordinary day; Sir Henry Ponsonby, the Queen's secretary, trotted between No. 10 Downing Street and Lord Salisbury's home in Arlington Street as conditions were negotiated between the incoming Tories and the outgoing Liberals. At first, Lord Salisbury refused what was on offer but by the evening, when Mary and Spencer dined with Arthur Balfour, he had decided 'in spite of all protestations' to take the highest office. Again the humour of it appealed to her; she thought they had gone too far 'in their arrangements and peerages to endure the ridicule of giving up'. Queen Victoria offered Mr Gladstone an earldom but he politely refused the honour, an action which only worsened relations between them.

Now it was time to pack their bags and move out of No. 10 Downing Street and into their new temporary home at No. 1 Richmond Terrace; there was no fun in this. Mary hated the house, and her bed was 'a fraud as it quivers with Underground trains'. She had to go back to Downing Street and would keep bumping into newcomers. She peeped in at Spencer's dismantled room and picked her last sweet rose in the garden. The Parliamentary session would run until the end of the year so the Conservatives could only act as caretakers until the next general election. Mary sought solace through sultry July in the garden of Richmond Terrace and she could often be found here taking tea, or talking with friends, or just quietly breathing the air until they could all gratefully escape at the end of term.

CHAPTER SEVENTEEN

Private and public worlds collide (1885)

*M*ary had learnt to deal with her father's various moods: from his intense earnestness when public affairs consumed him, to his gay boyish spirits at home. In Downing Street she had created a role for herself as the Prime Minister's special adviser, a role that has become of prime significance in modern times. In Victorian days it was not thought to be a scandal that members of the Prime Minister's own close family should hold influential positions in government, but it is worth noting that Mary was one of the first women to occupy such a position of privilege and power, and that she used it gently and discreetly; there is no evidence that she made enemies in high places, only grateful, life-long friends.

Hawarden had become her 'little green oasis in the wilderness' and the train journey to London provided 'a thinking carriage' before the full force of the political storms. Now the storms were past; her father had lost the premiership to Lord Salisbury who took over on 9 June 1885. His Budget had been unexpectedly defeated and he had lost the support of both Joseph Chamberlain and Sir Charles Dilke over his latest Irish measures. A general election could not be called immediately because the new electoral registers were not ready, so Lord Salisbury headed a minority government and began what would prove to be the shortest of his three premierships. Gladstone headed home to Hawarden, convincing himself that at the age of seventy-five, retirement was what he yearned for – but even now he left the door to politics ajar. He wrote to his brother Thomas, 'My profound desire is retirement, and nothing has prevented or will prevent my giving effect to that desire, unless there should appear to be something in which there may be a prospect of my doing what could not be as well done without me.'[1] Mary's life now centred on home, family and friends. Ten years had passed since her cousin May had died, 'ten whole quick years'. It was Alfred Lyttelton's approaching marriage to Laura Tennant that triggered thoughts of all that had happened since May's death. Mary would have liked it better if Laura had managed to bring Arthur Balfour to the matrimonial threshold because, as she told him, 'I often feel she is the one person who might have come nearest to what May was.' But Laura had decided that twenty-eight-year-old Alfred was all the things that she desired in a man; immensely charming, superbly athletic, an able barrister and a rising politician. More than this, she had seen in him the protector that her vulnerable inner self longed for. Through her sister Margot, she had invited him to her Scottish home and within a few weeks she was taken on a round of the Lyttelton relatives. She wrote to Spencer that she felt quite 'entered' in the Lyttelton inventory, having met five new relations in the space of a day 'and feel quite strong and well in spite of it. I think you are a divine family'; within a month she and Alfred were engaged.

Hard on the heels of this engagement came a wedding in the family. At last, forty-one-year-old Stephen, Rector of Hawarden, had met his true love, young Annie Wilson who was only nineteen. It was a whirlwind romance. 'Stephy has been going at it like a house on fire having only really known her during this one week,' was how Mary described it in her diary. After an earlier courtship had failed, his parents had almost given up on his finding another and they were delighted by Annie, an eminently suitable daughter of a Liverpool doctor. There was no reason to delay and the wedding was arranged for 29 January 1885 but only days beforehand, Mary's cousin Annie Gladstone died suddenly from blood poisoning. There was the most wretched confusion within the family, for Annie was a first cousin. The decision was made by Aunt Louisa, the bereaved mother, that the wedding should go ahead. It was 'an extraordinary mixture of death and life –

the two Annies, the white flowers for both (Constance and I were making the funeral cross and the bridal nosegay at the same moment), and as Maggie says: "Who shall say which is really happiest?"'

Maggie can be excused for such a gloomy reflection; she had suffered a most unhappy marriage and, after a year, had been deserted by her husband Sir Arthur Cowell-Stepney. She had fought for custody of her only child and her own family had turned against her. Right now she was being made wretched by her brother, the third Lord de Tabley, who was refusing to acknowledge her in public. When Mary tried to bring about a reconciliation, reminding him that he had promised always to protect and support his sister, he told her not to interfere in private family matters.

Home at Hawarden, contrary to the customary family pattern of children growing up and leaving home, the opposite was happening. William had brought his bride Gertrude into the family and now Stephen and his wife were about to start a new chapter at the Rectory. The village turned out with flags and cheers and a brass band to welcome the honeymooners and to escort their carriage home from the station. There was a tea party for the old folks and a ball for the young people. William and Gertrude now lived in their own home in the village; Mrs Gladstone had found it difficult to accept that anyone could look after her dearest son as well as she could and her daughter-in-law had not been happy at the Castle. Herbert, the youngest son, was still at home and Helen came home in between her Cambridge terms. Harry and Agnes had fled the nest; she was married with her own home and he was in business in Calcutta.

Stephen's new curate was finding his feet in the parish. While at Oxford, Harry Drew had declared that the last thing he would be was a parson; it was often the second son's destiny but his ambition was to be a barrister. Once he had gained his degree, there was a pressing need for him to earn some money so he took a post as tutor to the Duke of Rutland's son, accompanying him on an Italian tour. Shortly after they arrived in Florence his pupil fell ill and Harry nursed him through a month's sickness. Their money was running out and Harry sought advice from Lord Danvers and it was arranged that the tour should continue to Rome. His pupil did not regain his strength but gradually grew worse. In desperation and despair Harry made a pact with God that if He spared this boy's life, he would give his own life in His service.

The boy died; Harry returned to England, the only path that he could consider was into the priesthood. He took a year's theological study at Cuddesdon College, after which he was holidaying in North Wales when he heard of a vacancy in Hawarden parish. He had received a letter of congratulation from Mary's father when he gained his degree, but he had yet to meet any of the family. His year at Cuddesdon was in his favour as this was where Stephen had trained. He arrived at Hawarden in October 1883 to serve a year's probation before he was ordained priest. He was made welcome by Mrs Glad-stone and Mary was her usual warm, helpful self towards him. During the summer months of 1885 her diary entries hint of her happiness when they travel together from the village to the sophisticated intellectual climate of an Oxford clerical convention.

The family are not expecting a romance for Mary, she is approaching her thirty-eighth birthday and indispensable to her ageing parents. Her father is exhausted, and there is con-cern about him from the highest quarters. The Queen has asked for a report from Gladstone's doctor, Sir Andrew Clark, and is glad to hear that Mr Gladstone is in good health but appears grave and anxious. His voice has worn itself to a hoarse whisper and as soon as he is rested, a sea voyage is once again stated to be the cure.

In August 1885 Mary dutifully accompanied her parents on yet another sea trip. By kind invitation of Sir Thomas Brassey, Liberal MP and wealthy industrialist, they were bound for the Norwegian coast. Their luxurious yacht, powered by steam and sail, sped down the Thames and once they struck the open sea, everyone took to their cabins. Mary was abysmally sick. She sought comfort in a letter to Scott Holland whose sea legs were notoriously as weak as hers, and he hastened to send a cheery message to give her courage for the return journey.

> You did not even sink, or get drowned, or have any happy opportunity of escape ... I cannot tell you how I admire your courage. It represents to me one of the heroic feats, which are epic, historic, Biblical ... I hope the Ffiords (I have not ventured on throwing in a 'j' somewhere about this word to improve the local colour) are behaving with *some* decency.[2]

The scenery was spectacular and Mary had to admit that she was enjoying the holiday once they were cruising up and down the fiords, but her happiest moment was when they were back on dry land.

They landed at Fort George, took the train to Aberdeen and went on to Fasque where the family gathered to celebrate Sir Thomas and Lady Louisa Gladstone's golden wedding anniversary. Thomas and William Gladstone were now the only two surviving brothers, and the coolness that had existed between them after their father's death had long melted. For Mary, to be at Fasque was 'the very greatest delight in finding ourselves on an unwavering floor and in this great stillness, enjoying our food and our beds quite beyond words.' And once the celebrations were over, nothing could be sweeter than home 'to Harry and Herbert and Spencer, and mutton broth and tea. All well and comfortable, everything smelling so sweet and Hawarden-like and, best of all, great jabber.'

A general election lay ahead and the centre of political activity now moved from Downing Street to Hawarden. Numerous consultations were made by post and in person. Lord Richard Grosvenor, Chief Whip, came over from Eaton Hall, Chester. Lord Rosebery came to help put the finishing touches to the Party's manifesto; he had demonstrated his support after the fall of Khartoum and General Gordon's death, when the country was howling for Gladstone's blood. Hot on the heels of Lord Rosebery came Lord Wolverton, followed by Sir James Lacaita and Chamberlain, with his arms full of orchids. Mary called him 'our Joe' and sat next to him at dinner.

She warmed to his charm as they talked about everything under the sun but politics; Schlüter was suspicious of his easy manner, regarding him, Mary joked, as 'a kind of Robespierre'. It was a full house with a typical Gladstonian mix of all sorts of people. The Brassey family had been invited as an acknowledgement of their hospitality and Albert Lyttelton was newly back from five years in South Africa. Then the house emptied and at once refilled, with another mix of lords, politicians and family. Scott Holland breezed in for just a few hours and, after a couple of days, Alfred and Laura Lyttelton came to stay, as well as John Bright and Lord Dalhousie. Mary's father believed that all these meetings led to 'a healthy slow fermentation of many minds working towards the final product', his electoral address to be presented to the people of Midlothian.

Mary hardly had time to draw breath before she was off to Edinburgh for the Midlothian rally; this time with Maggie for company which made it all the more pleasurable. The same route, the same streets lined with the same eager crowds, the same tremendous swell of cheering, and yet the excitement was as great as if it were happening for the first time. At first she thought her father was in tremendous form, until Scott Holland's critical letter arrived. He told her that he sensed an aloofness and a disengagement in the elderly statesman, as though he were surveying the scene rather than a leader. She faced these criticisms squarely, telling herself that she did not want to drift into 'a fool's paradise'. It was true that her father soared above the practicalities, carried along on his lofty principles; she did not feel quite so confident of victory now. Herbert was campaigning for his own seat of Leeds and his father kept in touch by letter and, on the most vital issue of Ireland, outlined to him his scheme for Home Rule.

Mary was right to feel less confident of victory this time. Parnell had instructed all Irishmen to vote for the Tories, believing that they were offering more on Home Rule than the Liberals. However, the general election result was 251 votes for the Conservatives and 333 for the Liberals, the balance of power being held by the Irish Nationalists with 86 votes. The Conservatives would remain in power so long as they remained in Parnell's favour, a very uncomfortable state for everyone and one that could not last long.

In mid-December 1885, Mary went to Oxford to stay with Lavinia and Edward. She left her father at home preoccupied with tree-cutting and his thoughts on Irish Home Rule, isolated from the political manoeuvring that was going on at Westminster. On the day that she returned to Hawarden, her father drove to Eaton Hall where the Duke of Westminster was entertaining a house party. Arthur Balfour was among the guests and Mr Gladstone made a point of telling him that unless Home Rule was granted at once the Irish would resort to violence across the land. He indicated that he was willing to support Lord Salisbury in a cross-Party solution to the Irish problem.

Meanwhile Herbert took himself off to London, fervently believing that the only way forward for the country was with a Home Rule policy under a Liberal government led by his father. He organised with the newspapers what would today be called a leak. It became known as the 'Hawarden Kite' and in his book *After Thirty Years* he says, 'I was the bird and the flight was on my own initiative and sole responsibility.' He gives the explanation that, had he not acted, 'the movements against us would have taken definite shape'; there was a strong possibility that Chamberlain and Dilke would have broken away from Gladstone and formed their own party, taking many of the Liberals with them.

Not surprisingly, the newspapers manipulated the story so that Herbert's opinions were published as Gladstone's definite plans. Herbert's diary for 17 December reads 'Fat all in the fire. Standard publishes "Authentic plan" of Mr G and the evening papers and telegraph agencies go wild in the afternoon.' Mary's diary for the same day notes, 'Great hubbub all round and everywhere. General confusion, telegrams without end, copying long letters, and in the midst of it all he (Papa) despatched another "Dawn" article to *19th Century*. [The article was 'The Dawn of Creation and of Worship'] Wrote lengthily to Ld. Acton.' It was so like Gladstone that in the midst of general mayhem he could isolate himself and give his attention to something entirely different.

There was no question of taking Herbert to task, and in any case, the family suddenly found themselves taken completely by surprise from an entirely different quarter. While Herbert had been flying his kite, Harry Drew had been one of the god-parents at Stephen's baby daughter's christening, moving ever closer into the family fold.

Mary's home life revolved around Sunday-school teaching, helping at Mothers' Meetings, organ-playing, sick visiting; her friendship with the curate was a natural development of meeting at these functions, as well as at daily communion and weekly church services. Walks in the park with Harry's dog were a natural extension, with tea and muffins afterwards. And they were soon continuing in letters their discussions that had to be broken off when Mary returned to London. If anyone had asked her about her relationship with Mr Drew, she would have replied that they were just good friends.

But now Mr Drew declared his feelings for her, and Mary was overwhelmed by doubts and confusions. Had he made the same mistake as an earlier Hawarden curate, mistaking Mary's sympathetic and affectionate friendship for more? On 11 December she confided to her mother, 'I know that with him the flood gates are opened.' Could it be that this modest, handsome, devout young curate was strong enough to stand alongside her brothers and cousins and to follow in her father's heroic footsteps? At night she tossed and turned, and the nightmare did not dissolve by day. She escaped to Lavinia at Oxford, and a houseful that included Spencer and Scott Holland, and the nightmare went on. A raging toothache was accepted as accounting for her pale distracted face and loss of appetite.

For five days Mary was overcome by lassitude and nervous debility. She confided in her mother and turned to her for advice, as she had done eleven years ago when she had fallen in love with Arthur Balfour. On 15 December she wrote to tell her that, 'The nightmare which seemed to be wrapping its dark wings closer and closer round me is passing away just as you thought it would.' Her mother had the most marvellous ability to take to herself everyone's worries, burdens and secrets and to give loving, practical advice. Mary had inherited her mother's talent but now it was her turn to be advised and comforted. She described her worries as building to a climax on the morning that she was due to return to Hawarden and Mr Drew; at the last moment, these worries seemed to dissolve. If this were love, it was not at all what she had imagined. Her appetite returned and sleep was again possible.

Worldly considerations were not uppermost in her mind. She was waging a very private and personal struggle with herself. It had taken her many years, longer than most, to gain her self-confidence, to discover her true self and to be content with what she found. She was terrified that marriage would mean the loss of her hard-won independence; that life with her village curate would mean turning her back on the excitement of the outside world that she enjoyed and was a part of her. She had friends in many circles of London society. Would marriage to Mr Drew mean the loss of these friends? Once she had reached the calmer water of her decision she described this time as 'the great crisis of my life and it was too absorbing, too full of wonderings, misgivings, doubts, fears, hopes, to write about' – and, she could have added, to talk about.

On Christmas Day, Mary made up her mind to accept Harry Drew, 'it was too perfect a day to pass over and I kicked away the only barrier that remained and in the evening after dinner up in the schoolroom I was engaged to Mr Drew ... I sat up with Agnes and Helen talking it all over and trying to believe it was true.' Part of the remaining barrier may have been her parents' increasing dependence on her as the only daughter still at home; she had to resolve for herself whether her duty lay in her past life or in her future role as clerical wife. In a letter to Lord Acton she described her worries: 'I know that in outward things this marriage must separate me to a very great degree from those whose companionship and friendship I have delighted in. But it will not make any difference in inner thoughts and feelings, the links are too firm to be broken by outward changes.'[3] This worry of whether she would lose friends who were dear to her had been a major stumbling block; this is clear in her letter to Lord Rosebery written on 29 July:

> The person I am going to marry is a curate here, and it means a complete change of life to me. I do not shrink from this and I think I have realised in my soul all it means − But he is the first who has loved me whom I have loved, and so though he has none of the things which would recommend him to the world, and he is the most shy and humble and quiet and penniless, everything else must go to the winds ... I don't expect my friends to understand it. They will think it giving up *the* most interesting and unique kind of life in the world, for one which is quite the ordinary lot of mortals. I want you to send me your blessing and to try and sympathise with me a little, for your friendship has certainly been one of the best things in my past life.[4]

Harry Drew wrote to Mrs Gladstone to explain how events had led him to this moment; he knew it would be a great shock to her. He appealed to her tender and generous nature: 'I have always felt lonely in life, and have hungered for sympathy far beyond most men of my age perhaps.' He reminded her of the tragic death of his young pupil in Italy, that had revealed to him his destiny. 'And it seemed as if I was sent to Hawarden against my own will ... your daughter's sympathy and friendship gladdened my life more than I can say ... and now I know, as I never knew before, how she was growing into my heart and becoming everything to me.'[5]

His letter to Mr Gladstone was the customary one from a suitor, of how he hoped to support his daughter. All that he could expect from his own father was one-sixth of his estate, which only amounted to about £250, and an allowance for the next five years of £200 per year. He was aware of the insignificance of this settlement, but Mary's father was not concerned for her future financial status. He wrote in his diary, 'Everything substantial stands well except age: and that is not *too* much awry,' and to one of his colleagues on the matter of the forthcoming marriage he wrote, 'It is unadorned in the sense of worldly goods but it promises the most solid happiness.'

Of course, the first person to whom Mrs Gladstone poured out her feelings was Lucy, and she chose to dwell on her confidence in Mr Drew's integrity and Mary's with him. The difference of years between them, with Mary being ten years older, was 'a bore but then she is so very young of her age and he is not, even has many grey hairs.' She had to admit that his lack of money was a drawback but, ever practical, she pointed out that Mary would be unlikely to have more than two children so that they would be able to manage financially. It was already decided that they would live at the Castle but 'in a *corner* whilst we are away'.

It was evident to all that Mary was blissfully happy. She wrote to her friends with her startling news and they replied with their genuine support. Scott Holland was passionate in his prayer for their happiness. 'He has it in him, I know, to give you all that life is meant to bring you of intense and supreme loyalty. Let me thank God that you have found it, the good gift, and that it has been sent so strangely, found there at your feet, close at hand, in all quiet homely naturalness.'[6]

Mary had been prepared for a lack of understanding, but she explained to people that Harry Drew was the first man who had loved her and whom she had loved in return: 'he is most shy and humble and quiet and penniless, everything else must go to the winds.'[7] She described this letter as 'a goodbye letter'; she was saying farewell to all those who had been closest to her in her years as Mary Gladstone.

Lord Acton and Hallam Tennyson placed their faith in Mary's choice of husband, and Lord Granville wrote to Mrs Gladstone with his support: 'So remarkable a woman as Miss Gladstone is not likely to make a mistake on this point'; others, who knew her less well, were sceptical. Eddy Hamilton remarked that it was a very *small* marriage for her, while Loulou Harcourt noted that Harry Drew 'looks very ascetic. I wonder if he is so in his conduct! If he is I do not think he will satisfy Mary.'

Her two oldest friends were delightfully eccentric in their reactions to the news: fifty-three-year-old Burne-Jones wrote

to tell her that he liked curates much better than bishops, especially when they were perpetual curates, but on a serious note
he showed that he truly knew her. 'I am glad you will leave that
big world, it never was anything to you or yours,' he wrote.
John Ruskin, nearly sixty-eight and in a world of his own,
asked Mary if she knew that he hated girls marrying curates,
and did she think that she would get any credit in heaven for
being poor and living in a cottage? Scott Holland believed that
the old man was hurt by Mary's marriage, returning sadly to
the event many times over the next years.

Within the family, Lucy seems to have been the most startled
by Mary's sudden engagement and she wrote to sympathise
with Spencer for she felt that it must make an enormous difference to his relationship with Mary, 'a greater one than if she had
married into more of our own sort and condition, and someone
more her own age.' In her letter to Lavinia, she scathingly
refers to 'Mazy's great romance' and asks whether anyone
knows anything about Harry Drew. To Mrs Gladstone, she is
full of loving sympathy: 'My heart longs after you, for the
strangeness and emotion must be taking oceans out of you ...
Your being taken by surprise must make it all more overwhelming.' She fears that any marriage that might come
Mary's way 'at her advanced age' must be 'in some very sober
and prosaic form'. The thought of Mary taking delight in the
prospect of 'quiet poverty after all her full life of keenest and
most varied and exciting interest' could only mean love of the
strongest and deepest kind, and she is puzzled by the change in
Mary.[8] It is as though Lucy cannot bear to look upon Mary's
utter happiness from her own position of a lonely, loveless
widow. When her invitation to the wedding came, she was
unable to accept.

The person who was the most devastated by the news of
Mary's engagement was the one who had been her companion
and devoted maid for nineteen years. Auguste Schlüter just
could not believe it when Mary broke the news to her. 'Don't jest
with me on so serious a matter,' she cried, 'for such a thing
would be quite impossible.' Mary spent Christmas Day trying
to persuade Schlüter, who was cold with fear at the idea. Next

evening, at the family's traditional dance, when Schlüter saw Mr Drew, 'I felt like a tigress wishing to throw herself upon the enemy.'

Mary gave her one more day to get used to the idea and then insisted that she meet Mr Drew, but all his approaches to her were met by 'a fire of reproaches broken by big sobs'. The family were amazingly gentle towards their faithful servant who had entered so completely into their family, and Schlüter at last sadly came round to accept the loss of her dear lady. On the last day of the year, she wrote in penitence to 'Dear Reverend Sir', wishing them both a very happy New Year and asking God's blessing on their marriage. 'Do pray forgive me for my cruel behaviour to you last Monday,' she begged, 'a wound, when fresh, will have its time for bleeding, and mine felt very sore.' She had watched her beloved mistress and knew her to be happy and secure with a good man, and so 'I must learn to love you as much as I love her. I am a persevering scholar, and have good faith in passing my examination satisfactorily.'[9]

The engagement would be brief. A fortnight of letter-writing and saying goodbye to brothers Harry and Spencer, who were both leaving for India, left Mary drained and she spent a week being spoilt by William and Gertrude at their Hawarden home. The wedding was fixed for 2 February. Mary went to stay with Maggie at Wood End, Ascot, for a last time of peace before she was caught up in a mad whirl of shopping, pre-wedding partying, present-giving and political pandemonium. Her private and public worlds were once again hurled together, so that she never knew which was agitating her the more.

CHAPTER EIGHTEEN

A new life for Mary, but the old life refuses to go away (1886 — 91)

ary was not too absorbed in her own affairs to notice that the Queen's speech at the opening of the new Parliament was 'very vague' and the behaviour of the government 'most curious and ambiguous' but, of course, she is no longer quite so deeply involved. Her life has taken an unexpected turn; she is aware, she told Lord Acton, that her marriage will separate her 'to a very great degree from those whose companionship and friendship I have delighted in'. Burne-Jones had remarked to her that surely she knew how insignificant London society really was. 'It has a good side too; it's always wrong, and that is a clear and definite good.'

Lord Salisbury, with Parnell's backing, was holding the Conservatives in office although they were in the minority, and their plan was to split the Liberal vote. Once again, everything depended on the Irish question. On 26 January 1886, the leader of the House, Sir Michael Hicks-Beach, gave notice of the government's intention to introduce a new Coercion Bill. Gladstone declared to Sir William Harcourt that he was ready to bring down the government right away. '"What!" Sir William exclaimed, "Are you prepared to go forward without either Hartington or Chamberlain?" "Yes!" Gladstone retorted. "I am prepared to go forward without anybody!"'[1]; it was either a reckless gamble or an inspired move.

That night an amendment was put forward, regretting the omission from the Queen's Speech of measures to benefit rural labourers. It was commonly referred to as the 'three acres and a cow' amendment, and would have excited no one's attention if Gladstone had not stood up to give it his full support. Everyone in the House knew that they were voting on whether or not Gladstone, at the age of seventy-six, should be the next Prime Minister. The result was that the government was defeated by 331 votes to 252, with 76 Liberals either absent or abstaining. The Irish Nationalists voted with the Liberals, although a splinter group of Liberals led by Lord Hartington voted with the Tories, a sign that they were not prepared to join with their former leader in a Home Rule government.

Lord Salisbury resigned on 28 January and, shortly after midnight on Friday 29 January, Gladstone received a commission from the Queen 'to form a Govt. *unconditionally*'. Mary described these days as 'mad and extraordinary'. There was a perpetual stream of visitors, and she never knew whether they were coming with good wishes for her wedding, or promises of political support, or rumours of resignations. She declared that this last proved, 'all rumours turn out false'. Had she heard of the Queen's strong feelings which had been conveyed through her private secretary, Sir Henry Ponsonby, that 'She does not in the least care, but rather wishes it should be known that she has the greatest possible disinclination to take this half-crazy and really in many ways ridiculous old man – for the sake of the country.'[2] *Punch* carried a great cartoon showing 'the Grand Old Man' lecturing the raw newcomers of the House on keeping their own counsel and reserving their freedom until they could serve the public best.

Mary's last day as a Gladstone was her father's first day as Prime Minister for the third time. He was away all day at Osborne House on the Isle of Wight, and arrived back 'late for dinner, weary and harassed and having interviews most of the evening.' She added in her diary, a little too optimistically, that what had seemed like insurmountable difficulties were melting away and there were hopes of a strong Cabinet, even though Lord Hartington would play no role in it.

The Queen could not interfere with her Prime Minister's policies but she did raise many objections to members of the Cabinet who would be seeking to implement them. She stood firm against Dilke; his sensational divorce case placed him quite beyond the pale. She did not want Lord Granville back at the Foreign Office. Lord Rosebery was the Queen's favourite, and Lord Granville had to make do with the Colonial Office. Lord Harcourt was given the Exchequer and Chamberlain, who, Gladstone warned the Queen, had to be found a place somewhere, was eventually accommodated as President of the Local Government Board, a post that did not make him happy, so he only stayed there a month. John Morley was Irish Secretary, but responsibility for the Irish Home Rule Bill was the Prime Minister's.

Mary was glad that her 'private events should be so swamped by public'. She did not want any fuss, and she was kept busy making her bridesmaids' nosegays, with snowdrops sent from the Tennyson gardens at Farringford and orange blossom from Lord Acton. Her last act before retiring to bed on the eve of her wedding was to give herself a large dose of bromide, a favourite Victorian cure for settling stomach and nerves, and inducing sleep.

By marrying at St Margaret's, Westminster, in the presence of the Prince and Princess of Wales, and in a plain white muslin bridal gown, Mary once again demonstrates her individuality. It is her public statement that she does not intend to say goodbye to the 'me-in-the-world' part of her old life, but that she will go forward into her new life on her terms. She could have married her Hawarden curate at their village church, which would have been a complete renunciation of London sophistications. Instead she chose a London church that had family connections, for her ancestor Sir John Glynne (who had bought Hawarden Castle in 1653) was buried beneath the altar. He had risen to the post of Lord Chief Justice under Cromwell and had the good sense to change sides on the return of King Charles II, who gave him a knighthood.

Mary's wedding day on 2 February 1886 was as she wanted it, a blend of the simple and the sophisticated, intimate and public; a kernel of what her whole life had been. The day began with devotion at St Paul's. She drove with Helen to the cathedral for the feast of the Celebration of the Purification of the

Blessed Virgin Mary. Inside the small chapel she met Harry, Stephen and a handful of cousins and closest friends. After the service which, she felt, gave her 'an astonishing calmness which saturated me all day', she and Harry took the horse-bus home to Harley Street for a breakfast of bacon and coffee. It could have been any normal Sunday. Only then did she don her white muslin gown, and with her six little bridesmaids similarly attired, and carrying snowdrop nosegays, she walked down the aisle on her father's arm. The marriage ceremony was conducted by her brother Stephen. All her nearest and dearest were there, except Spencer and her brother Harry, who were both in India, and Scott Holland, who was at a niece's sickbed. On the wedding certificate, her father gave his profession as Prime Minister, and signed witnesses included the Prince and Princess of Wales, Lord Rosebery and Mr Balfour.

It was all over so quickly. There was no formal wedding break-fast; instead they had soup and chicken at Lucy's London home in Carlton House Terrace, a few quiet moments back at Harley Street with her mother while she took off her bridal gown, and then the newly-weds were off on their simple, quiet honeymoon to a house near Ashridge in Hertfordshire, which had been lent to them by Lady Brownlow. Waiting for them was 'the snuggest and best' tea, warming fires, books and flowers. It all felt so amazingly natural, Mary thought, 'to feel I was I when I thought I was going to be somebody else'. Two weeks later they were back in the family fold, meeting family in Downing Street where Mary felt that everything was absolutely unchanged, even finding 'a box of oat cake in the corner of the dining room where I had left it in Jan.' This is how her life would be for the next forty years; a blending of the old with the new.

Harry Drew was all that the Gladstone family could ever have hoped for in a husband for Mary. They could not fail to give their support and blessing to the marriage, for there was no other man who would have entered their lives so effortlessly. They did not lose a daughter, but gained another son. He moved into Hawarden Castle as a kind of domestic chaplain and caretaker, and allowed Mary space to be herself. Her life in politics for the past ten years had been nearer to a religious passion than a worldly involvement; she had believed that her father was answering the Almighty's call to duty. Now she looked forward to her own call as a clergyman's wife with all the sacrifices that would involve, sharing the burdens, as she told her mother, 'of sickness and suffering, Sin and Death and every form of sorrow and poverty.'

This would be no mean and dreary task; Harry Drew was a strong, handsome man with a fun-loving nature like Mary's own. She soon discovered that he was 'the most wonderful person for fitting in to all my nooks and crannies and yet at the same time keeping his own individuality, letting me propose and plan and initiate and yet like a firm rock for me to lean on.' Of course there were times when her loyalties were finely stretched, but there was an openness and honesty between them that made for serenity. She had long been strong enough to stand up to her mother's demands and could deal with her thus: 'You may imagine how divided I feel, always one string pulling me towards you and the other towards Harry, but as you will have Gerty and Will as well as Lucy, I feel how well off you are next week.' Luckily for Mary, there were brothers- and sisters-in-law within arms' length and cousins within call.

Even while home at Hawarden, Mary was still preoccupied with Westminster politics, and kept abreast of the news on the approaching Irish Home Rule Bill which she knew was her father's guiding star. Her diary for 3 April reads, 'The plot thickens. The Scotch attitude extremely fishy. Half the world ag[ainst] Home Rule and the other half ag[ainst] Land Purchase.' A few days later she is in London to hear her father move the first reading of the Home Rule Bill, a day described by Eddy Hamilton as 'indeed a notable day – the most notable day probably in the annals of the present Houses of Parliament.' All three Gladstone sisters, Agnes, Mary and Helen, accompanied Mama, and even Lucy came, her first visit to the House since her husband's assassination almost exactly four years ago;

The rain came down in torrents, but above the storm and above the roar of London thrilled the cheers, all the way fr[om] D. St we heard them, and we stared and stared as if we had never seen him before, or as if he wd. look quite different, and then we flew up the 200 steps to the gallery and saw the splendid reception there. The starting to their feet of the MPs, the wonderful cheers. Every spot was covered. The floor had seats up to the table like the free seats in a church – the air tingled with excitement and emotion, and when he began his speech we wondered to see that it was really the same familiar face – familiar voice. For 3 hours and a half he spoke – the most quiet earnest pleading, explaining, analysing, showing a mastery of detail and a grip and grasp such as has never been surpassed. Not a sound was heard, not a cough even, only cheers breaking out here and there – a tremendous feat at his age. His voice never failed – we cd. not judge of the effect yet, only that deep and anxious attention and interest were shown throughout and the end was grandly cheered. I think really the scheme goes further than people thought. It is astonishing in its faith and courage.[3]

While Mary's father was fighting for his political life, tragedy struck down that golden couple, Alfred and Laura Lyttelton. In April, a year after their marriage, Mary heard the good news of the safe arrival of a baby boy. Alfred wrote, 'a fine son – a nine-pounder is the result of an awful night's anxiety. We had to have Matthews-Duncan (one of the leading obstetricians of the day) to help, for hardly anyone could possibly have had a worse time.'[4] His letter reveals all the surging emotions of pride, joy and relief of a loving husband who has just become a father. Laura had never been strong, and throughout her pregnancy she had feared for her life; her premonition, sadly, came true. Within a week of her baby's birth, she was dead. Alfred was completely shattered, and their friends were desolate. Mary wrote to tell Henry in India about the funeral: 'It seemed too much to bear, the little white bride inside the coffin, and all the broken hearts around'. Two years later, when Alfred's son died of

tubercular meningitis, she could not help but wonder what
all the pain had been for.

Mary herself was pregnant after just two months of marriage. She was thirty-eight, and there were many who were
anxious for her. She wisely decided not to risk the excitement
of the House of Commons in June 1886, when the Irish Home
Rule Bill received its second reading. Harry was sent as her
deputy, and he faithfully sent back a detailed, pencilled report
of events as they unfolded before him. He sat next to Stephen
Gladstone in the best seats and they watched the MPs file into
the debating chamber. However, the doorkeeper had warned
him that writing was forbidden, so it had to be done by stealth
while Stephen kept a watchful eye. His brevity added to the
drama: '4.30 House filling quickly ... 4.45 The P.M. just
arrived. Great cheering. House full, nearly. Bright, Chamberlain, Caine and Rylands side by side ... 6.40 Parnell up. Very
quiet and white. He spoke so quietly and calmly and effectively
... He says you must pass the Bill or you will have to coerce as
you never did before ...'.[5]

At 11.25 p.m. Gladstone took the floor to give the last of his
five speeches on the Irish Bill. He wore a white carnation in his
lapel which, members noticed, reflected the pallor of his face.
He opened his speech with reason and persuasion, his eloquence strengthening with his fervour. He mocked his erstwhile colleague Joe Chamberlain, describing his arguments as
'creations of the vivid imagination, born of the hour and per-
ishing with the hour'. He ended with a plea on behalf of
Ireland, standing 'at your bar, expectant, hopeful, almost sup-
pliant ... Think, I beseech you; think well, think wisely, think,
not for the moment, but for the years that are to come, before
you reject this bill.'[6]

The bill was open to committee, discussion and amendment,
but its basis must remain the establishment in Ireland of a
domestic legislature to deal with Irish home affairs. All matters
that could not be dealt with were specified, such as defence
and foreign affairs, but there were so many imponderables, so
many fears from too many quarters, and general unease that
made the bill's defeat seem inevitable; the only question was

the scale of defeat. Harry feverishly scribbled to Mary that it was 'quite splendid. I shall never forget it. Division for 311. Against 341. Lost by 30. A fearful row in the lobby. Goodnight darling.'

Parliament was dissolved. Gladstone's third term as Prime Minister had lasted only five months. The country must endure another bout of electioneering. Mary, pregnant as she was, jumped on the family bandwagon to Manchester, with her husband to support her. She found the intense summer heat in the Free Trade Hall quite frightening. There were no windows and every ventilation shaft had a coat stuffed in it and a man sitting on top. 'It seemed impossible to breathe,' she wrote in her diary, and added, her sense of humour not deserting her, 'as hot as the hottest hot-house, only human instead of grape atmosphere.' Then it was on to Salford and Liverpool for more tub-thumping.

She sensed that despite her father's rousing speeches and the madly cheering crowds, it was not going well for them. Lord Randolph Churchill's description of Gladstone as an ambitious old man in a hurry who had torn his party asunder for his own ends was just the slogan that the Tories welcomed, and it made its impact on the electorate.

It was July, and while waiting for the results, her parents stayed at home in Hawarden's cool fresh air while she and Harry went visiting friends and family. With no secretaries to lay a restraining hand, the ex-P.M. sent off a volley of wild and indiscreet letters and telegrams to candidates, which were published in the Press. The Queen thought that he was quite off his head and was inciting revolution. The Duke of Westminster was so appalled by his behaviour that he removed from his walls Millais' portrait of the erstwhile statesman and sold it to Sir Charles Tennant, who later presented it to the National Gallery, where it still hangs.

Even Mary thought that her father had gone too far, and had given a 'mistaken impression as to his condition of mind, and that he soon realised it was a mistake'. When they all met up in London, he was in high, carefree spirits and greeted Herbert, 'Well ... my dear boy, we *have* had a drubbing and no mistake.'

Mary described him as 'like a conquering hero, not a bit cast down', although the election result was the Conservative Party 316 with 78 votes for the Liberal Unionists, 191 for the Gladtonian Liberals and 85 for the Irish Nationals. The ageing politician had divided his party in pursuit of what he believed to be an honourable cause, which he alone must champion.

On 30 July 1886, he travelled to Osborne House to offer his resignation to the Queen, who accepted with no word of regret or thanks for his service, only an ungracious comment that the timing might inconvenience Lord Salisbury by shortening his time in France. This was probably a barbed comment on Gladstone's electioneering which she had thought most undignified for a Prime Minister. She could not resist following this up with a letter informing him that she had never liked his Irish policy, that it had been bound to fail and that now she hoped he would be silent on this matter for her peace of mind and the sake of the country.

Mr Gladstone came home to Hawarden, to the tranquillity of his library, his Temple of Peace. Now he had time for his beloved Homer, every reading 'richer and more glorious than before'. But, first, he desperately needed a holiday, and Lord Acton was ready, with an invitation to Tegernsee. This time he had his daughter Helen to keep an eye on him, but she was the first to admit that 'Mary is Mary and I can't expect to replace her in anything like a full measure.'

Mrs Gladstone stayed at home to be near Mary who was four months pregnant and not well. She had helped in the clearing out of Downing Street on the last day of July, and then gone with the family to spend the weekend at Coombe Wood, Lord Wolverton's country home. She travelled back to London in Lucy's Victoria, a four-wheeled carriage for two with a collapsible hood, so that she could enjoy the fresh air of Wimbledon Common. She had tea with Maggie and dinner with Lord Acton, not wanting to disappoint her friends, before taking the train back to Hawarden with the possessions cleared out of Downing Street. Straightaway she plunged into home responsibilities, church duties, mothers' meetings and parish visiting, until she was quite exhausted.

The fourth and fifth months of pregnancy were considered the most risky, and it was estimated by one Victorian doctor that eight out of every ten women miscarried at least once. Maggie wrote urging her to rest, 'I do hope you are staying quite in bed or at least on a couch till the next month is over' but the warning came too late. Mary was experiencing pain, and a miscarriage was feared. Mary's doctor ordered her to bed for a week; the pain grew steadily worse and her temperature rose. A nurse was called in from Chester to help Schlüter, who was taking care of her 'beloved Lady'. A miscarriage could not be avoided, and on the first of September 'a wee boy was born dead' Schlüter sorrowfully wrote in her diary. 'Lady Grosvenor and Lady Stepney both saw the sad little one before his burial.'

Despite being in the care of two doctors, Mary's terrible pain and sickness continued, and throughout September, she was fighting for her life. Harry wrote down her last wishes as she remembered everyone, her brothers and sisters, her nieces and nephews, friends near and far; for 'dearest Papa' to whom 'I would leave everything I have if it were to shew in any way what I owe him' and for her old governess Miss Syfret 'the armchair Stephy gave me with my love and my belief that I wasn't such a little curmudgeon she took me for'. Faithful Schlüter never left her side, reporting every small turn in her mistress' condition: '1 Oct. My beloved Lady keeps very ill ... agonising pains have almost beaten her ... my darling Lady is a wee bit more comfy, as they have given her morphia. Oh may God help her! My eyes are only satisfied when feeding on her face. 6 p.m. Doctors all here. London doctor gives hope and stays all night. They have decided to operate, and she is now under chloroform.'[7]

Sir Andrew Clark was the London doctor who informed Harry that his wife was suffering from inflammation in tissues around the womb. He added his medications to those of the other doctors. Schlüter wrote sceptically, 'Sir A. Clark has left again and we are as wise as before. All he says is that it will take time. What do they call long? Oh, how frail is the eye of man.'

It was long before the days of antibiotics, and Victorian women were most vulnerable to infection during childbirth.

Mary was lucky to survive; she slowly regained her strength until on her thirty-ninth birthday, the nurse was dispensed with and Schlüter was given sole charge, but it was not until Christmas Day that she was carried downstairs for the first time. Scott Holland wrote with his usual blend of affection and humour. 'How are you? ... I hear dim rumours of movements that begin – voyages across rooms, grand journeys round the world from sofa to sofa, Cook's Tours down the Grand Passage ... So trying, these long days of dragging recovery', and when she was strong enough to write, his immediate response to her was, 'Your letter was delicious to my heart: if I knew where its cockles were, I should certainly have demanded their being warmed.'

January 1887 was spent convalescing at Holker Hall with Lucy and Maggie for company, and Schlüter to look after her needs. By February she was judged strong enough to take the sea air at Penmaenmawr, where so many happy family holidays had been spent. And so her gradual return to health continued, with Schlüter gradually changing her role from nurse to maid to housekeeper. Mary slowly picked up the threads of her old life, dividing her time between Hawarden and London, while Harry carried on as curate to Stephen at the rectory.

Gladstone was no longer an old man in a hurry, but was content to wait for the tide that was turning away from the Tory government. As always, Irish matters were uppermost; Arthur Balfour was now Secretary of State for Ireland and was showing an iron hand. His nickname of 'Clara' soon gave way to 'Bloody Balfour' as he enforced the new Coercion Bill. In the House of Commons he emerged from his chrysalis of hesitance and diffidence to show himself as a formidable figure. Gladstone did not like the new man. 'I think I loved him better than any young man I ever knew,' he wrote to Margot Tennant, 'but he is changed now.'[8]

Parnell was once again in the headlines. A Special Commission had been set up to inquire into the authenticity of letters alleged to have been written by him, and into the truth of charges made by *The Times*. It sat for a year and a half, and resulted in the suicide of a shady journalist, the withdrawal of the newspaper charges and the elevation of the Irish leader to popular hero. Mary went with her mother to the Commission hearing in May, and was completely won over by Parnell's behaviour before the judges. 'He really exhibited all the fruits of the Spirit, love, peace, patience, gentleness, forbearance, long-suffering, meekness,' she wrote in her diary. 'His personality takes hold of one, the refined, delicate face, illuminating smile, fire-darting eyes, slight tall figure.'

When Parnell returned to the House of Commons after his court victory, he was given a standing ovation by the Liberal and Irish benches. Gladstone was ready to mend bridges; he invited him to Hawarden and the two men spent hours closeted in the Temple of Peace. Mary sat next to Parnell at dinner and thought that he looked more ill than anyone she had ever seen 'off a deathbed', but when he turned his gaze upon her his eyes looked 'bang through, not at' her. At the end of his visit she summed him up as 'a most mysterious man of compelling power' although she could not quite decide where that power lay, for he had a low, quiet voice and gentle manners. Almost exactly a year later, when the scandal broke over the O'Shea–Parnell divorce suit and everyone knew of his long-term affair with Mrs O'Shea, she was beside herself with anger over his duplicity, and grief at his wasted talent. She wrote to Lavinia, 'Of course, you never believed in Parnell, so it's no blow to you. If only he had fought O'Shea and gone off with Mrs and owned it to everybody, I wd. not half mind.' Parnell and Mrs O'Shea did not offer any defence in the divorce case, and Mary saw this in his favour. As she wrote to Lavinia, 'The only one ray of light is his refusing to publicly perjure himself, as all our English *gentlemen* think it right and honourable to do in these matters.' Her father would not act as Parnell's judge, but public opinion and that of his colleagues forced him to refuse to act with Parnell as leader of the Irish MPs and on this Mary was agreed, 'for no one with soiled hands ought to lead or can lead a noble cause.'

The twenty-ninth December 1889 was Gladstone's eightieth birthday, but he was in no way ready for a place in the shade. Margot Tennant, described by Mary as 'a madcap, a dare-devil, impetuous, impatient, fearless, generous, with much wit and little wisdom, quick in insight, rapid in repartee,' came to pay them all a visit. Gladstone was so captivated by her youthful vivaciousness that, as soon as she had left, he dashed off a gallant compliment to her in verse that began,

> When Parliament ceases and comes the recess,
> And we seek in the country rest after distress,
> As a rule upon visitors place an embargo,
> But make an exception in favour of Margot.

> For she brings such a treasure of movement and strife,
> Fun, spirit and stir, to folk weary with strife.
> Though young and though fair, who can hold such a cargo
> Of all the good qualities going as Margot?[9]

She was most moved by his admiration, and replied,

> Very dear and Honoured Gentleman. At first I thought your poem must have been a joke, written by someone who knew of my feelings for you and my visit to Hawarden ... It has had the intoxicating effect of turning my head with pleasure, if I began I should never cease thanking you ... It is impossible to believe that you will be eighty tomorrow, but I like to think of it, for it gives most people the opportunity of seeing how life should be lived without being spent ... Yours, Margot.[10]

Mary's father decided it was time to start work on a project which had occupied his thoughts for many years; that of building a new library where his books could be shelved and catalogued properly. They had already taken over the passage and the billiard room, and Mary compared them with Browning's rats,

> Great books, small books, lean books, brawny books,
> Brown books, black books, grey books, tawny books,
> Grave old plodders, gay young friskers,
> Fathers, mothers, uncles, cousins,
> Families by tens and dozens.[11]

Life would go on in the same comfortable grooves and at first everything seemed to continue as it had always done. A branch railway line was opened at Hawarden for the ex-P.M.'s convenience, and for the many VIPs who came calling. It helped very much that rich friends put their London homes at her father's disposal. Dollis Hill, owned by Lord Aberdeen, was an attractive country house set in acres of farmland within pleasant carriage-driving distance of London. Mr Rendel, related by marriage after his daughter Maud married Henry Gladstone, was most generous in offering his city home at No. 1 Carlton Gardens, his country mansion in Surrey and his chateau in Cannes, the last enjoyed by many of the Gladstone family. Mary was there for the Christmas of 1888 and into the new year with parents who were 'childishly happy'. She was having 'a most delicious time' and, when Harry joined them after his Christmas duties, she was able once again to enjoy the best of all worlds.

But, as happens in families, the framework of relationships and dependencies was shifting. In January 1890, at the age of thirty-eight, Henry Gladstone married Maud Rendel. In July 1891 William Gladstone, aged fifty-one, died of a brain tumour. A last desperate attempt was made to save his life by surgery, and Mrs Gladstone travelled to London to be at her first and dearest son's bedside. It was Mary who gave her father the dreaded news that the operation had not been a success. Her diary makes sad reading: 'At 6 (in the morning) I went in to Papa and told him gradually of the alarming news, tho' keeping the worst from him till we were within half an hour of London. He was terribly shocked and broken down, and at Liverpool Street the little note from Helen reached us telling us of the end at 5.30.' They were too late to say goodbye, but were comforted by knowing that Stephen had been with him for the last prayers.

'These sad, sad days crept quietly on,' wrote Mary. Her father found comfort in *Pilgrim's Progress*, which he read through on the day that William died; her mother sought relief in practicalities. Of all her losses, this was the most difficult, and came at a time when her age made her less resilient to bear it. Never again could she look upon his photographs; she hid them away in a drawer in her room.

There was, however, one blessing that brought great happiness to Mary and husband Harry, and comfort and joy to Mary's ageing parents, changing the family network of relationships in the happiest of ways; such good news deserves to be told in a new chapter.

CHAPTER NINETEEN

'As much Mr Gladstone's daughter as ever' (1890—3)

When Mary became pregnant again in the summer of 1889 she followed her doctor's advice to lead a very quiet life and to rest during the day on a sofa. Miscarriage in the fourth month of pregnancy was, sadly, a common danger to Victorian women and even after she had passed this date, Mary did not feel safe. She stayed at Hawarden, joining in family life and, as the months progressed, even taking part in entertaining guests; in December, when she was six months pregnant, she was dinner partner of Parnell who was at the Castle for long talks with her father, and she shared in the family celebrations for her father's eightieth birthday.

In February 1890 she travelled to London, anxious not to miss her brother Henry's marriage to Maud Rendel, and she stayed there for the last weeks of her pregnancy. She told Lavinia that she found London's social scene 'a perfect God-send' and plays and people 'the greatest boon'. She believed that all would be according to God's will. Harry had of course returned to his clerical duties; faithful Schlüter had been most unhappy to leave her mistress, 'for I may never see her again'; a thought she could confide only to her diary. Three weeks later she writes, 'Mrs Drew sends me bits of news nearly every day. We are anxiously awaiting the arrival of the stork.'

On 11 March 1890 Mary, aged forty-two, gave birth to her only child. As soon as Harry heard the longed-for news, he hurried from Hawarden to be with her. She recovered quickly and was soon writing to her friends to give them the glad news of the safe arrival of Dorothy Mary Catherine, known to everyone as Dossie, a baby who was all the more precious for being long-awaited. When she took her treasure home to Hawarden, Mary was sure that all the Hawarden folk were sharing in her joy. 'All the women come out of their cottages as she passes up the village to get a peep at her,' she wrote to her father.

Burne-Jones wrote with affection and in capital letters:

DEAR MRS DREW – WHAT GOOD NEWS YOU HAVE SENT. BUT HOW ON EARTH YOU HAD THE POWER TO WRITE LETTERS PASSES MY UNDERSTANDING. I AM WRITING, YOU SEE, IN BIG LETTERS SO THAT YOUR EYES MAY NOT BE TIRED AND I WILL TRY AND FIND SOME COLOUR TO AMUSE YOU, THOUGH THE STUDIO IS SPECIALLY EMPTY NOW. I AM SO GLAD, AND THESE ARE NICE DAYS TO BE BORN IN – BLUE AND BRIGHT – THE DAMSEL WILL THINK THE WORLD IS A BONNY PLACE IN SPITE OF ALL THE BAD THINGS SHE HAS HEARD OF IT. ARE YOU GLAD IT'S A DAMSEL?[1]

Schlüter was overjoyed for her beloved mistress, and wrote in her diary on Easter Sunday, 6 April, 'The baby has ten god-parents. She ought to be very good.' One very special one was Henry Scott Holland who wrote that, 'it will be the most delicious task that I could possibly be given – only that it will be no task at all; for I shall only have to watch at work one whom I would rather study in the character of a mother than anyone in the world, I think.' He sent a present of Egyptian flannel which he found 'close to the very bulrushes in which the tiny baby Moses was taken'. He wrote, 'It is soft and warm, and may carry with it, folded round the little white body, all the wisdom of the Egyptians'; and within the flannel he enclosed a little blue mummy relic from the tombs at Thebes, 'so old that even if she sucks it, I don't think the blue will come off.'[2]

It was typical of Mary that she should worry about whether she could ask Lord Rosebery to be a godfather and decide that she should not, for fear it would bore him, only to impetuously change her mind when they were gathered for the christening.

And it was just as typical that afterwards she should write him a long letter of explanation:

> Then when I saw you actually in Church and thought how much you represented to me of friendship and affection, of a time in my life full of deep interest when I seemed to be allowed to know you in a deeper, more real sense than almost anybody, I could not resist just asking you. And so I bore you with this long explanation because otherwise you would think it was an afterthought born in the Church. So I shan't be able to help counting you as one, because of your goodness and kind interest in being present.[3]

The arrival of a baby was bound to bring changes at the Castle; perhaps the person most affected and least noticed was Auguste Schlüter. A new young nurse was engaged, and Schlüter reluctantly took on more housekeeping duties. A new cook and a new butler joined the staff, and Schlüter felt like 'a fish out of water'. She wrote in her diary, 'Cook seems nice, but the butler I do not approve of. Our Castle is full of company, mostly family – Lytteltons, Talbots and Wickhams.' She began to feel that she could no longer remain at Hawarden, although everyone said that they wished her to stay; she felt that there was no room for her any longer here 'after twenty-two years, a long time, yet passed like a dream. I am very busy. I love to nurse the wee baby; she is very good.'

It was decided that Schlüter would leave in October, after Mr and Mrs Gladstone had left for another Midlothian campaign. She was relieved by this, for she knew that it would be very hard to say goodbye to them. Somehow another few weeks went by, and it was November before she had tidied up the remnants of her life at Hawarden and goodbyes were said. 'My darling Lady, Mrs Drew, tried her best to make me feel brave, and promised me I should never want; she had also collected a little money for me to start with – such a blessing.' She wrote this remembrance in her diary after she had returned home to Hamburg to be with her aged mother. Her last letter to Mary, twenty-seven years later and dated 20 March 1917, ends, 'I want you to know once more how you have cheered and brightened my life, and once more I want to thank you, but if anyone has loved you, it was Your humble servant SCHLUT.'

Mary was conventionally Victorian in her opinions on birth control; she was strongly against it, believing it 'a sin against nature as well as against God'. She wanted to borrow her father's copy of *Ethics of Marriage*, a sternly moral book published in Boston in 1888. The author HS Pomeroy had sent Mr Gladstone a signed copy with his compliments. In his book, the author speaks out clearly and unequivocally against 'the prevention or destruction of unborn human life', described as '*the* American sin', spelling out the dangers of childbearing, the dangers of abortions, and reminding readers that all married couples have a duty to become parents. Advice is given on pregnancy, with the reassurance that 'Nature is infinitely wise'. Mary hoped her father would not think it 'an unfitting book to lend'. She felt the need to be better informed because, she told him, 'As a clergyman's wife I have been a good deal consulted and have found myself almost alone amongst my friends and contemporaries in the line I have taken.'

She knew that most of her friends did not agree with her and were limiting the numbers of their children to a handful. She told her father that among those in the peerages married in the last fifteen years, 'the children of the large majority are under five in number and it is spreading even among the clergy and from them to the poorer classes.' She thought that perhaps he was unaware 'of the great battle we of this generation have to fight on behalf of morality in marriage'. She did not want to discuss the subject with her mother 'because when I did, she in her innocence, thought by ignoring it, the evil would cease to exist'.[4]

The suffering and death in childbirth which was all around her, and which had been experienced by members of her own family and her closest friends did not weaken her resolve. 'Had to send for Dr Burlingham as there was a prospect of little no. 2 child which came to an end today,' she wrote in her diary on 7 December 1891. She was forty-four; it was her second miscarriage, and there would be a third in seventeen months.

Her second miscarriage did not make her seriously ill but did leave her low in spirits. She was confined to bed for only a week but, in her weakened state, she developed an eye infection that left her eyes bloodshot and sore. The treatment prescribed was a blindfold in bed, a great nuisance, and the tiresome condition lingered for months. Feeling low and depressed, she confided in Scott Holland who responded in his usual warm and witty way. He compared her tunnel of unhappiness to the Channel Tunnel which Sir Edward Watkin, the railway promoter, had tried unsuccessfully to build from Dover to Calais. He hoped that her unhappiness would not all be underground but would be rather like 'a sort of Ealing and Acton District Railway that flashes out into larger and larger openings.'

Now that Mary had a child and husband, she could not be constantly at her parents' beck and call. Helen was asked to take a larger share of the burden of parent-minding, and this meant making sacrifices in her career. In 1886, when Mary had married, Helen had turned down the headship of Holloway College in London, after much searching of her conscience. It was not just a question of family commitments that she weighed in the balance, but the knowledge that her heart lay at Newnham where she felt that she could do her best work for higher education.

In a joint letter to Mary, Stephen, her brother-in-law Edward Wickham, Lucy and Lavinia's husband Edward Talbot, Helen gave her views on the family situation and asked for theirs, adding, 'I am not of any immense use to my mother at any time but at least I am available.' Mrs Gladstone had never appreciated having a career-minded daughter. In her opinion, it was an unnatural state of affairs, and quite beyond her comprehension why any young lady should not seek the security and status that a husband could offer. Why, it was common knowledge that gentlemen did not look for intelligence or learning in their wives! Helen had hoped that meeting her students might help to change her mother's attitude to young women at universities. By dining with them and talking to them in her room, she hoped that she might see them as 'nice womanly girls', but Mrs Gladstone's prejudices were deep-set and shared by most of her generation.

Helen made it known among her Cambridge colleagues that she was not available to be considered for the Newnham head-ship, but she did stay on at the college until 1896. She did not feel that she would ever be as capable as Mary at organising her father, but felt duty-bound to serve her turn. The two sisters were always supportive of each other, whether in praise or commiseration. When Helen's year of students did particularly well, Mary crowed, 'Out of 45 she has 12 firsts, 20 seconds and 13 thirds', and when Helen found the strain with father 'ghastly horrible', Mary was quick to sympathise.

Mary was faced with the worrisome task of organising suffi-cient family backup for their aged parents who, at times, were still as 'frisky as three-year-olds'. She drew up a rota of helpers between them all, telling her brother Henry, 'I can be with them the ten days of the Lent term during which Helen must be at Cambridge, and Helen will then stay with them after Easter. Then I take the Whitsuntide and after Whit, Harry and I have our holiday and can be with them.'[5] She thought that it was best not to ask her two sisters-in-law to help; as she explained, 'you know how it takes a lifetime to learn how to live with her [Mrs Gladstone], and is really impossible for daugh-ters-in-law unless they utterly give up their own wills which is impossible and would not be right.' Agnes was the only one who, as wife of the headmaster of Wellington College, had a status and life quite independent of the family.

Mary had been the daughter with robust common-sense, able to cope with the male power and intrigue of Westminster. During the years that she had her tiny office in Downing Street, she had been respected for her strong opinions and appreciated for her sympathetic ear. There are numerous examples of men seeking Gladstone's presence, finding Mary's company and valuing it for a lifetime. Arthur Gordon, fourth son of Lord Aberdeen and briefly Gladstone's secretary during his time as High Commissioner for the Ionian Islands in 1858 when he had fancied himself in love with Agnes, went on to be Mary's good friend. He progressed to the title of Lord Stanmore and Governor of New Zealand and continued to appreciate letters from Mary, even when they did not agree. There is a letter to her after her marriage in 1889 when he tells her, 'I like what you say of Tolstoi. The remark you make as to the source of the power of his analysis of character is, I think, both original and true.' But on the equality of the sexes, he cannot accept that women's bodies are equal to men's, even if their minds are: 'If women took on men's role, they will be coarse, hard, selfish like men and even more unscrupulous.'[6]

Mary could be fierce when she was confident that right was on her side. She wrote to Arthur Balfour when he was Chief Secretary for Ireland, to ask his opinion on certain lectures of which she sent him copies. Balfour sat on the papers for months until she sent a telegram: 'Murder. Where are the papers?' By return came an apology with the papers, 'It is melancholy indeed to find that, with advancing years and increasing responsibilities, I see no improvement in my inveterate habit of invariably postponing from today everything which by any possibility can be done tomorrow.'[7]

Burne-Jones remained a true friend, not afraid to speak freely to her even when, 'You won't like me for saying that if I were an Irishman I would stand by Parnell through thick and thin – but I would. And a thing to my mind far more calamitous than the loss of Home Rule is the aspect of English hypocrisy right and left, and the tone and spirit of English journalism – Ah!' He was ever, he reminded her 'your old affectionate friend'. He welcomed three-year-old Dossie to his garden studio: such a 'tornado of energy, barefoot and wildly curly' was how he described her. When Dossie was an old lady, she looked back to these days and recalled the artist's kindness to her and how fascinated she had been by the mice running round the water pipes in his studio.

In August 1892, against all the odds, Gladstone (at the age of eighty-two) was re-elected MP for the twenty-sixth time and Prime Minister for the fourth time, but before he could take up his duties in Downing Street there was the small matter of the Hawarden village fete to attend. Thirty-two special trains were laid on and people poured into Hawarden Park, all with the aim of spying 'the Great People'. The weather was perfect, 'the P.M. meek as a lamb led out into a flower garden whenever Herbert ordered it,' Mary wrote in her diary. She had helped to lay out her parents' golden wedding anniversary presents which proved an overwhelming success, 'over 6000 people saw them, in at oak door, out by porch.' On duty from morning to night, she declared that the more she had to do, the less tired she became, and it was all worthwhile, for they raised nearly £1200 for the rebuilding of the Mechanics Institute in the village.

Many miles away in the nation's capital, the Queen was appalled by the election result. 'The idea of a deluded excited man of eighty-two trying to govern England and her vast Empire with the miserable democrats under him is quite ludicrous. It is like a bad joke,' she wrote to her secretary. Lord Salisbury thought that Gladstone had 'entirely outlived his judgment'.

It would seem that Mary's father was well aware of his failing faculties; he told his private secretary Sir Algernon West, 'You have attached yourself to a corpse, and for so short a time.' Eddy Hamilton, who had handed over secretarial duties, criticised Mrs Gladstone and Helen for their too obvious presence, 'waylaying everybody, and scheming this and scheming that'. Sir Algernon was equally at odds with some family members whose interference he resented. Mary's presence was missed; she would have known how to handle disgruntled secretaries and politicians like Lord Rosebery who found himself becoming irritated by interfering family. Rosebery had very reluctantly accepted the position of Foreign Secretary and in Roy Jenkins' judgement made a poor job of it; 'By September he had got the government in its first but considerable mess with his unilateral and jingoist handling of Uganda which, Rosebery, against the views of Gladstone, Harcourt and most of the rest of the Cabinet, was determined to turn into a permanent British possession.'[8]

It was not only family who were accused of interfering. John Morley, who became Secretary for Ireland, regarded Lord Acton as a meddler and intruder and would not hear of having him in the Cabinet. Lord Acton had to be content with a position in the Royal Household which he accepted because, as he explained to Mary, he needed the money. He was bitter over what he saw as Morley's excessive importance, criticising him to Mary as 'at bottom, a fanatic'. If he could not deal directly with Gladstone, his way barred by other ambitious politicians, he could still reach Mary directly. He told his daughter, 'I have had to resume the old correspondence with Mrs Drew. It is a way of conveying some things I cannot say right off. She was nicer than ever.'[9] Even though Mary was not at Downing Street as she had been in her father's second administration, she was still active from Hawarden by correspondence. She remained, as Frances Horner put it, 'as much Mr Gladstone's daughter and as little the Rev. H Drew's wife as ever.' She never wavered in her belief that her father's cause was 'the only one that is right and wise'.

After Tennyson's death in 1892, there was a vacancy for the office of Poet Laureate. Mary put forward to George Wyndham the name of Ruskin, although he could not strictly be regarded as a poet, and Wyndham replied that 'the precedent might prove embarrassing' although he regarded her idea as 'most ingenious and attractive'. He preferred Swinburne, and sent Mary a copy of his poems, but her father's opinion on Swinburne, related to Lord Acton, was that his poems were 'bad and horrible' and that he could not possibly tread in the hallowed footsteps of Wordsworth and Tennyson. Other names were canvassed but found wanting, and the post took four years to fill. In August 1892, Burne-Jones requested that Mary put forward Poynter as the new Director of the National Gallery when a vacancy arose, and he became Director in 1894.

Fourth-time Prime Minister Gladstone was not having a happy time with the Queen; he thought that her mind had slowed and her judgement was unreliable. After visiting Osborne, he told Sir Algernon West that 'the interview had been as dismal as that which might have taken place between Marie Antoinette and her executioner.' He wrote in his diary that at the main interview the Queen 'was certainly polite, in nothing helpful' and a year later he described their meetings as 'a sham'. The Queen was equally harsh in her first impressions. She was quite shocked by the physical changes in her Prime Minister, noting that his face was 'shrunk, deadly pale, with a weird look in his eyes, a feeble expression about the mouth, and the voice altered.'

The Liberals had won only a small majority over the Conservatives and the Irish Home Rulers held the balance of power. It promised to be a demanding Parliament, which would tax the powers of a much younger man. As it was, Gladstone was having to fight increasing deafness and such poor eyesight that within eighteen months he admitted that he was living in a perpetual fog. In the electioneering campaign, he had been hit in the face by a hard-baked gingerbread that had been flung with such force by an irate woman that he had spent four days in bed, and the eyesight of his good eye had been seriously impaired. Eventually he tried spectacles; his first attempt Mary described as 'failure, speechless disappointment', but he persevered. They were not the neat pince-nez that he had often worn for reading, but what his colleague John Morley called 'monstrous spectacles'.

The formation of the Cabinet proved the most difficult of any he had undertaken. There was frenzied activity at Hawarden while the final positions were being juggled. Mary described home as 'like Clapham Junction, all going different ways, and such interviews taking place, each running after the other with proof sheets.' Once the political machine was up and running, her father could divert some of his energies from public affairs to literary pursuits. He was working on a new translation of the *Odes of Horace* which he was loath to interrupt.

Mary accompanied her parents to Oxford in October. There is no mention of Dossie, but it is quite likely that she was with them, for Maggie turned up with her daughter Alcy. Mr Gladstone had been invited to give the first Romanes lecture on his chosen subject of mediaeval universities. Mary described in her diary the scene outside the Sheldonian Theatre when the doorkey could not be found, 'the youths in a fever of excitement leaping up the railings, tearing their clothes to shreds. Then when the gate was broken open a fearful crush on the stairs, many fainting.' Wearing his scarlet robes, Gladstone was received with loud cheers and his lecture went splendidly. 'He braced himself up at the finish for the great peroration; his voice vibrating with emotion, the last words remaining unspoken, he bowed his head in a storm of enthusiasm.' It was, she thought, one of the most moving occasions of her life.

On 27 October 1892, the first Cabinet meeting was held at No. 10 Downing Street. A way round Gladstone's increasing deafness and blindness was found by using the P.M.'s room and, at his suggestion, he sat at his writing table with Lord Rosebery at his side while the others sat closely round.

In the House of Commons, once more Gladstone was trying to push through an Irish Home Rule Bill. It was to be his last great statute, and he was tireless in his efforts. Mary was in the House in February to hear his last great oration on the motion to bring in the first reading of the Government of Ireland Bill. He spoke for two and a half hours. After his ordeal he wrote in his diary that he had slept little the previous night, and heard the chime of every hour. Seven weeks later, the second reading was debated and eventually carried after nine gruelling nights. There is a family story that Mary took her daughter to see the final performance and Dossie thought her grandfather was doing his exercises, what she called 'nastics'.

In May 1893, Mary suffered yet another miscarriage; this was to be her last attempt to add to her little family. During the stiflingly hot summer days the Irish bill was fought through one division after another. Lord Randolph Churchill openly admired the Prime Minister's refusal to admit defeat, as time and time again he rose to his feet to speak on numerous amendments; eventually the third reading was passed by 307 votes to 267. Gladstone's reaction was 'This is a great step. Thanks be to God.' The fate of the bill now rested with the Lords where, on 8 September, Lord Salisbury damned the Bill with these words, 'If you allow this atrocious, this mean, this treacherous revolution to pass, you will be untrue to the duty which has descended to you from a splendid ancestry; you will be untrue to your highest traditions; you will be untrue to the trust that has been bequeathed to you from the past; you will be untrue to the Empire of England'; it was thrown out by 419 votes to 41, an utter rejection that seems to have been accepted without comment by Mary, her father, or any member of the family. At the same time, other family problems were coming to a head at Hawarden, with Mary as ever trying to organise the best of all possible worlds for everyone.

CHAPTER TWENTY

A calling home (1893)

$\mathscr{A}$ ll Mary's diplomacy and organising talents, finely tuned during her time in Downing Street politics, were being called upon. She and Harry had been living with her parents for seven years; a strain under any circumstances. The time has come for change. Harry felt strongly that he needed to gain experience elsewhere and cannot be promoted from the curate's post at Hawarden. Mary took on the role of negotiator and facilitator.

In May 1893 she wrote to her father that Harry had visited Nuneaton where there was a vacancy for a rector, and he was excited by the possibilities. Nothing came of this, but there were other plans afoot. Stephen Gladstone was equally unsettled; he felt increasingly unsure that he was suitable as rector of Hawarden and his confidence was undermined by the knowledge that the position had come to him through a family connection. Likewise, Harry Drew was feeling the burden of Gladstone influence and patronage.

Mr Gladstone sensed that he might have a brilliant solution to lay before his son and son-in-law. For a number of years he had been intent on building a home for his vast library of books, which numbered almost 30 000 volumes by this time. Already a temporary iron building had been built near the parish church, and slowly and laboriously the books had been carted from the Temple of Peace, stacked on the floor of their new home until Mr Gladstone could sift and shelve them. After all, 'What man who really loves his books,' he asked, 'delegates to any other human being, as long as there is breath in his body, the office of introducing them into their homes?' Now he was looking for the best way to catalogue them, and then to build a place of study and research for students of theology, along with a hostel where they could lodge at little cost. His aim was to bring together 'readers who had no books and books who had no readers'. He was sympathetic to Stephen's need of a break from parish responsibilities, and suggested that he could set his library on organised lines, open up the institution and become the first head of St Deiniol's Trust. That would leave the rectory free for his son-in-law. Of course, the sub-plot was that Mr and Mrs Gladstone would continue to use Mary and Harry, Stephen and Annie to attend to their daily requirements, sort out household problems and keep financial arrangements in order. The suggestion was favourable to neither Stephen nor Harry. It was a well known fact within the family that no one could meet the parents' needs as effortlessly as Mary, and Mrs Gladstone had never been an easy mother-in-law, too doting on her sons to fully appreciate their wives' merits. Now Stephen chose to interpret the offer as a slight upon his wife Annie, and Mary was forced to explain what might have seemed to be ingratitude on Harry's part: 'it gave him the feeling that it was mostly for my sake, and because he is my husband – and no man of strong individuality can like this.'[1] Harry made it clear that he was not willing to step into Stephen's shoes just because they were convenient.

Such ruffling of sensitivities can occur in the best of families. The ageing parents could not appreciate the depth of frustration in both men that led to Stephen having a complete breakdown and having to take six months' rest away from the parish and Harry suffering from fatigue and restlessness.

In desperation, Mary turned to Scott Holland, whose religious commitment was passionately bound up with the anxieties and aspirations of the labouring poor, and asked his advice about the idea of Harry taking a six-month term of duty in a South African church. His reply was wholeheartedly enthusiastic. 'The experience of just touching the Colonies is becoming more vitally precious every day.' Even six months he thought 'would give new eyes – new mind – new sensitiveness – new range – new judgement. It is wonderful.' In his opinion 'it would be pure unmitigated gain.'

Just before Christmas 1893, personal problems were pushed aside by the disappearance of Mr Gladstone's valet. Zadok Outrem had been missing for twelve days before his body was fished out of the Thames on 14 December. Zadok had been with the family for twenty-five years and had worked his way up from footman to personal valet. For the past twelve years he had been indispensable, travelling with his master up and down the country and on trips abroad. The family had been worried for some time by his heavy drinking and had tried to help him by arranging treatment which he promised to undergo. This had been in October; life had obviously become unbearable for Zadok, and he took what seemed to him the only way out. 'Poor, poor Zadok,' Mary wrote in her diary.

On 27 December Mr Gladstone spent his eighty-fourth birthday at his desk in Downing Street. The Cabinet was struggling to find common ground over the Naval Estimates, and discussions dragged interminably on. He was out of step with practically all his colleagues over the cuts he wanted to make. He regarded their scheme as 'mad and drunk', 'the most wanton contribution ... to accursed militarism'. He told his secretary that the prosposed increase 'would end in a race towards bankruptcy by all the powers of Europe' as they raced into armed rival camps. He convinced none of his Cabinet. His hearing and eyesight were poor, yet he had not felt that his failing faculties gave enough reason to cause what he thought would be a major upheaval to his colleagues; but here was the chance that he had been seeking, to resign on a 'rational, sufficient and ready to hand' cause. He placed before them his offer of resignation and looked forward to rest and renewal once more in the south of France.

Meanwhile, at Hawarden, Harry had resigned from his curacy and, on 13 January, he left Southampton for South Africa with the Reverend JW Williams, later Bishop of St John's, Kaffraria and a young layman, Campbell Crum, later Vicar of Mentmore. The same day, Mary once again shepherded her parents abroad, this time with three-year-old Dossie's help. They headed for Biarritz, as guests of Mr George Armitstead, wealthy Liberal MP and financier. Lord Acton went along with them. Mary had said goodbye to Harry with an aching heart, her comfort being that it was a wonderful experience for him, and meanwhile, as Scott Holland said, she 'could help the parent-birds through the Session'.

Gladstone ordered that there should be no Cabinets held in his absence. He left behind rumours circulating on his imminent resignation. His secretary, Sir Algernon West, shuttled back and forth over the Channel and put out a statement that the condition of the Prime Minister's sight and hearing 'made relief from public cares desirable'.

Lord Acton was on hand to persuade the Prime Minister against resigning over the Naval Estimates. Herbert sided with the Cabinet, and Mary tried to put Herbert's views before her father, but she was overruled. She put her thoughts into a letter; while it caused her 'acute pain' to differ from him, it had to be said that they all agreed with Lord Acton. In her heart she knew that her father needed a constant challenge to fuel his fading energies, and retirement would be a severe shock to his mind and body. She was also concerned for her mother, knowing how she loved 'being inside the mainspring of history, and all the stir and stress and throb of the machine is life and breath to her'.

When they returned to London on 10 February 1894, Mary was back in the midst of Downing Street politics as if she had never left. She desperately tried to reassure everyone that her father was in the best of health. An operation to remove a cataract was imminent. At the first Cabinet meeting, everyone expected a declaration from the Prime Minister on his future purpose, but it did not come. Instead he threatened to go to the country over the Lords' dismissal of his Home Rule Bill. He talked of a 'Peers versus the People' rallying cry. Of course, his colleagues would have none of it, and it seems to have been more of a mischievous tactic to cause confusion than any serious intent; or was it a last forlorn gesture against the inevitably closing door?

By the first of March, Gladstone was prepared for retirement. His last Cabinet meeting was short and smooth and ended with a quiet 'God bless you all'; private friendships would outlast public differences. He alerted the Queen's secretary, Sir Henry Ponsonby, to prepare the Queen for his retirement. Mary was in Downing Street for his final days and dined one evening with Arthur Balfour who was now the leader of the Opposition in Parliament; she commented astutely in her diary, 'A Conservative believes in a real past, a radical in an imaginary future.' She was in the House of Commons to hear her father's last speech, which was received with vehement applause and cheers.

The next morning, there was time for a little verse translation of some of Horace's *Odes* before the last drive to Windsor, his wife by his side. He was not a bit downhearted although he was deadly tired. Mary thought that at a dinner party a few nights later he behaved 'like a boy out of school'.

The last meeting with the Queen was a most unsatisfactory affair, and many have commented on the absence of gratitude and praise in Her Majesty's last letter. She did not thank him for his years of service nor seek his advice on his successor; she had decided to send for Lord Rosebery. Gladstone felt that he was dismissed as one would a tradesman, and it rankled. It was as though she were glad to be rid of him, rather as he had felt about a Sicilian mule: 'I could not get up the smallest shred of feeling for the brute, I could neither love nor like it.'[2] On reflection, Herbert thought that the change in relations between his father and the Queen could be traced back to 1876, from the time of the Eastern Question, and he believed that she had interpreted Mr Gladstone's policy as a vindictive and personal attack on her favourite, Lord Beaconsfield. When he was sworn in as a Privy Councillor in 1894, he noticed that a portrait of Disraeli hung above the doorway of the small room used by the Queen for audiences and councils: he was still a favourite thirteen years after his death.

Burne-Jones' reaction to Gladstone's final exit from Parliament must have been echoed by many. 'How dull it will be. Who cares who is made chief minister or not? Nobody else will fill the stage as he has done.' Mary wrote to Lavinia that it had been a unique time; it felt to her like death with all the honour and glory and none of the terror, 'the flowers without the funeral'. Her father headed home to Hawarden, to what he called 'a free place on the breezy common of humanity'.

Harry's six months in South Africa had given him a kaleidoscope of experiences; he had visited Robben Island which held 'a hundred convicts, three hundred lunatics and five hundred lepers, all shades of colour including white.' He had been appointed to serve in St Saviour's in Cape Town and had taught in the Mission School. He had been forced to spend time in hospital with a severe chest infection and, while recuperating in Kimberley, had seen conditions in the mines. He had travelled into Zululand, talked with the Basuti chief and been present at the ordination of the first native priest. His journey home aboard the *S.S. Dunnottar Castle* had almost ended in disaster. As they rounded the Eddystone Lighthouse in thick fog at 4.30 a.m. on 24 August, Harry 'noticed the engines had stopped, and immediately our foghorn sounded grimly every half-minute or so'. Suddenly the engine started again and almost immediately he felt a jolt followed by a quivering of the whole ship. On deck he found that lifeboats were being lowered, the crew cool and collected and stewards serving cups of tea as if nothing had happened. The fog thinned slightly; Harry went forward 'and there stood the great grim lighthouse towering over us straight in front, the stump of Smeaton's tower on our left, and a great jagged mass of rock above water on our right. I could throw a stone easily against either, they could not have been more than thirty yards off. We could see and talk to the lighthouse men through the mist as they stood on the balcony running their lantern.' The tide was rising and the bows of the ship were soon floating again. Engines were immediately reversed and 'amid loud cheers and much excitement' they glided slowly back off the reef into deep water, seemingly undamaged. The pilot boarded and an hour later they anchored inside the breakwater; breakfast was served, luggage taken off by tender and at last the ship made for the Plymouth dock to much cheering and shouts for the captain who, Harry thought, was touched by the spontaneous outburst.[3]

Home again at Hawarden, the dilemma of what to do about Harry and Stephen surfaced again. Mary told her father that

Harry should not be approached until he and Stephen had agreed on a definite proposal. She had to tread very delicately between all parties. She wrote to her father to explain that last year 'everything was done first in the form of hints and gradually of conditional and rather uncertain proposals through me', which gave Harry the feeling that all was being arranged because he was her husband, and this had caused a great deal of trouble and anxiety.

By the end of of September it had been decided that Harry should become the Warden of St Deiniol's Library and Hostel, with a salary of £200 for the first six months. Mary wrote to Herbert that he was 'full of hopes & spirits & bristles with ideas and plans'; all this was delightful but she could not help feeling that their gain had been to the disadvantage of Stephen, who was tied by family duties in a job that had become a burden to him, and where he was destined to remain until after his father's death.

In the final scenes in Downing Street in spring 1894 Mary played hostess to her father's friends and colleagues, three-year-old Dossie wandering in and out of the rooms 'singing Alleluia' with her nurse in tow. Harry had to be in Hawarden; as Mary explained to Lavinia, 'I am sure he feels now that in a time of such anxiety and strain I really was wanted more than usual.' Lord Rosebery had taken over as Prime Minister, Mary's long friendship blinding her to his faults. She had complete confidence in his abilities, 'Difficulty is his great opportunity. And he will (as I fully believe) rise to it.' She had stayed to give her support to his first meeting with the Foreign Office Liberal members; his short speech nervously made, she thought, was well received but 'lacking in thrill'. Others were not as confident as Mary and the government limped along; 'What a pricked bubble the Rosebery is!' Chamberlain observed a year later.[4]

She was at her parents' side during her father's cataract operation in May 1894. Once again they were enjoying Lord Aberdeen's hospitality, staying at Dollis Hill, his villa near Hampstead where the operation was performed by Mr Nettleship, the leading eye surgeon from St Thomas' Hospital. Mary gives the details in her diary: 'Father had cocaine drops in his eye and was totally unagitated; it only lasted a moment and was perfectly done.' She waited with her mother in the next room 'with door open, I watching Nurse Pitts who had front place for watching him'. Afterwards it was Mary's job to let family, friends and the general public know how the ex-Prime Minister was faring and, as soon as her father was well enough, the Duke of York and the Prince of Wales called to pay their respects; even Mr Roosevelt, later President of America, was anxious for news when she sat next to him at dinner soon after.

Home again at Hawarden, her father's eighty-fifth birthday was marked by an Armenian deputation who came to present a chalice to Hawarden Church, an act of appreciation for his passionate support of their cause, support that lost none of its passion over the last years of his retirement. The next summer brought another general election and the Liberals were routed. The Conservatives–Unionists bounced back into power with a massive majority and with their victory ended Britain's isolation from foreign affairs; they would remain in government into the twentieth century. Lord Rosebery did not last long as leader of the Liberals; in October 1896 he wrote to tell Mr Gladstone of his resignation from a position that he had never felt confident in holding. The final straw for him was the ex-Prime Minister taking up yet again the Armenian cause.

Just before the election, Mary left her husband and Dossie at home while, with Herbert's help, she shepherded her parents to Hamburg and Copenhagen, guests once again of Sir Donald Currie on board the *Tantallon Castle*. She enjoyed the sight of the fine cathedral at Hamburg but not the huge banquet given in their honour that lasted for four hours. 'I never saw such gluttons as they all are,' she wrote in her diary. They returned hospitality on board their ship and entertained the King and Queen of Denmark and their family. Mary now refers to her father simply as 'X'; 'The X proposed HM of Denmark's health and all stood during his speech.' The ship was left open to all visitors with no thought of the need of security; Mary thought that 15 000 people came aboard, 'many eyes peeped through our portholes, our cabins being pressed up against the shore.'

Their destination was Kiel for the formal opening of the Kiel Canal as the German Emperor and Empress sailed through to a royal salute of guns only matched by the thundering skies. It was a bizarrely theatrical event as the day veered from moments of danger when an Italian boat ran into the side of them to the comic delay of the Duke of Coburg's ship, which had got stuck in the canal for hours. Throughout the day there were magnificent thunderstorms interspersed by brilliant sunshine that quite overpowered the illuminations and flags of the ships drawn up like huge beached whales to be inspected by the Emperor, Kaiser Wilhelm II, in his yacht the *Hohenzollern*. Mary's father saw beyond the celebrations and remarked to those nearby, 'This means war', but he was no longer at the political helm and, when they returned to London, there was a different set of officials in power. Their London base, lent to them by the ever hospitable Mr (later Lord) Armitstead, was No. 1 Carlton Gardens; Mary slept at Lucy's home and perhaps it was here that she was reunited with Dossie who must have been as used to her mother's absence as Mary had been to the absence of her mother a generation earlier.

At dinner in Downing Street, Mary found it all so familiar that it was difficult to realise all had changed. The new occupant would be Arthur Balfour and over an afternoon's visit from his sister Alice they 'settled all the Downing St rooms'. There was one more important engagement, a visit to Marlborough House to call on Princess Victoria and her baby son, 'an immense boy of fourteen months'. Dossie was already well versed in how to meet important people and she followed her Mama's example and kissed the royal babe's hand.

Back home at Hawarden there were summer days of tennis and bicycling; Mary sent her old friend Scott Holland a photograph of them all on bicycles. 'Dossie on wheels is delightful,' he wrote, 'Like a summer insect, fluttery and wispish, and quaint and winning – just the thing a salmon would rise at, hovering over a sunny pool – I am that salmon, in a long black coat, rising at the Fairy Fly'.[5] But there was no escape from Mary's duties as daughter-at-home, as a constant stream of important visitors poured in. One weekend it was the Rothschilds, two weeks later the Chinese statesman Li Hung Chang came calling; his visit necessitated a garden party to accommodate the crowds who wanted to meet him.

None caused more confusion than the Archbishop of Canterbury. It was the Sunday after Trinity, and in church Mary noticed that the Archbishop seemed to be sinking in his seat. He was carried unconscious to the Rectory where he lay on the library sofa and died. Stephen announced the news of his death to the congregation while Mary spent the day with the widowed Mrs Benson. There were many arrangements to be made before his coffin was taken to the local railway station three days later. First went Harry with the great cross he had borrowed from Chester Cathedral. The Bishop of St Asaph led the white-robed choir and clergy in prayers and hymns along the way. On the platform the *Nunc Dimittis* was sung, and while the coffin was being placed in the carriage Harry held his Cross steadily uplifted in front of it, and the Bishop pronounced the Blessing. She could not help feeling that it was 'quite overwhelming when one thought of him and her arriving only last Saturday in unsuspecting health, at this very platform.'[6]

Two weeks earlier, there had been another of those tumultuous times when lives change irrevocably; it was 24 September 1896 and the occasion was her father's final public speech. The oddly chosen venue was Hengler's Circus, to which the family drove through Liverpool's crowded streets in carriages lent by Lord Derby. For an hour and twenty minutes Mr Gladstone denounced the Sultan of Turkey as an assassin and demanded that the Turkish ambassador be given his passport. Thunderous applause echoed to his words which Mary described as 'not of the burning eloquence sort but full of reserve, dignity and strength, careful beyond measure, and yet shadowing forth a policy as wise as it would be effective.' To the end she remained a devoted disciple and her lasting memory was of his white-haired figure, like an Old Testament prophet, receiving the homage of the people.

Before the family went off to Cannes in January 1897, Mr Gladstone went out of his way to help his son-in-law. Harry Drew would have been a good choice for vicar of Buckley Parish on his own merits. No doubt urged on by his wife, Mr Gladstone had taken the trouble to point out to the Bishop of St Asaph his son-in-law's exceptional qualities, not forgetting to add how important it was for 'my wife in particular, that such employment should be so near as not to remove our daughter, his wife, beyond the circle of constant domestic intercourse.' Having paved the way for Harry's promotion, the family left for the Riviera and it was here that two important letters reached them offering Harry a choice of appointments. The Buckley living was accepted over one offered by the Keble trustees of St Albans church in Birmingham.

The kind of luggage that Mary took with her on these trips can be appreciated from the list inside her new diary headed 'Hints for Riviera Hotel Life'. It lists:

Etna [for heating water by spirit burner]
Cups, plates, spoon, knife and fork
A lb. of tea
Two lbs. of candles
Potted ham and potted meat
Sunday skirt and blouse and bonnet to match
Smart blouse for table d'hôte
Two common skirts and blouses for walking or bicycling
1 jacket to match for easy taking off, walking or bicycling
1 fur cape or cloak
1 straw hat (white) for Sun
Reading candle
Mackintosh
[The last two items are added in pencil]

Here too at Cannes was Queen Victoria, resting in preparation for her Diamond Jubilee. It was arranged between Mary and Princess Louise that, as Mary put it, 'our Grand Old People should meet'. At first her father was unwilling to cooperate and declared he would not visit the Queen unless she sent for him but, when a note arrived for him personally from Princess

Louise, he submitted. At the arranged meeting the Queen graciously shook his hand, a gesture he had never received from her before. The Queen went so far as to invite Mary to bring Dossie to Windsor and it was a happy group that left Cannes station for the homeward journey.

And so it was that on 5 May 1897 Mary travelled up to London with six-year-old Dossie. They were made welcome at Kensington Palace by Lord Lorne and Princess Louise and next day travelled to Windsor. A lady-in-waiting asked Dossie if she had ever seen the Queen and was much amused by the reply, 'Oh yes, but she hasn't seen me.' When that moment came, in white silk dress with yellow sash Dossie was 'like a gleam of sunshine'. And the good relationship with royalty continued a few days later at Hawarden when the Prince and Princess of Wales drove over from Eaton with the Duke of Westminster. 'The bands played and the sun peeped forth and the orphans cheered and the old women waved, and they all went off in a flourish,' wrote Mary in her diary.

Now the challenge of their new parish lay ahead. Mary described Harry as 'happy as a king in his work' although it was difficult living in two places at once. The builders were dragging their heels over starting work on making the Vicarage habitable, and it took until mid-November before Mary could write in her diary, 'Harry and I slept for first time at the Vicarage. Wildly exciting and all so pretty, dainty and cosy, *a huge success.*'

Buckley was a poor rough village of coal miners, steel and brick workers and farm labourers, all living poorly on the bleak hills that rose behind Hawarden. Their schools were tumbling down, their church was neglected, their vicarage was in need of modernising. Harry Drew was a modest man, with no affectations and with tireless enthusiasm. In his first parish magazine, he listed his priorities to be the enlargement of the day schools, the improvement of the churchyard and the erection of a flag on the church tower. There was no street lighting in Buckley, and he made himself responsible for almost a mile of road to be lighted until the new urban council took it over.

No one could imagine Hawarden Castle without Mary's presence. It had been the home that held her heart for all of her fifty years, and she had continued to live here for her eleven married years. Her father was now eighty-eight and her mother nearly eighty-six. Little curly-haired Dossie had danced into her grandparents' hearts and was the sunshine of their twilight years. Buckley Vicarage was only a few miles away and on New Year's Day 1898, a private telephone link was installed between castle and vicarage, so that everyone could be in touch instantly. Mrs Gladstone was still able to consult her daughter on what she should give her husband for breakfast.

Mary did not accompany her parents on their last winter in Cannes. Helen had taken over more of the daughterly duties since leaving her Newnham College post in November 1896. It had been a painful decision for her and she had written to her father that she had not made the move 'lightly or easily'; she was well aware of all that Mary had endured and achieved in her years as parental assistant and she knew that her character was less resilient; she would have to 'set one's teeth and go on from day to day'. It was a task that she only relinquished after their deaths when she took the job of warden of the Women's University Settlement in Southwark.

And so the two unmarried children, forty-eight-year-old Helen and forty-four-year-old Herbert, were in attendance for almost three months in Cannes until February when the weary band returned to Bournemouth. They were welcomed back by Mary and Harry along with cousin Lucy but they did not stay; and there was little time left. Mr Gladstone had cancer, and on 22 March he came home to Hawarden. Mary described the day: 'After luncheon I went to the Castle and arranged flowers. They arrived at 7.30, the journey wonderfully accomplished. It was a blessed moment to see him *come home* – even though it was to die. It was most piteous, he quite under the morphia influence, she all innocent of the tragedy.'[6]

The end came on Ascension Day, 19 May 1898. All the family were gathered at Hawarden. Mary had kept informed all those who could not be near. Alfred Lyttelton wrote to thank her, 'for

233

telling me and letting me be with you in heart where I have been with you always and you with me in all the great sorrows of life.'

Then came the avalanche of letters and telegrams, and reporters camping outside in torrential rain. Tributes poured in from all corners of society, heads of state, ambassadors, mayors, bishops and cardinals. The House of Commons adjourned and the next day Lord Salisbury in the Lords and Mr Balfour in the Commons proposed a State funeral, with burial in Westminster Abbey.

On 25 May, Hawarden workmen, colliers and farm labourers, estate tenants and villagers pulled the hand bier from castle to church where thousands of ordinary people came to say goodbye. Gladstone's last journey had begun. A special train took the plain oak coffin from Hawarden to London for the lying-in-state in Westminster Hall, and as the train passed through the major stations crowds stood silent and with bowed heads – how different it had been on those triumphant Midlothian campaigns.

The State funeral took place in Westminster Abbey; the pall-bearers included old friends and politicians, dukes and earls, the Prince of Wales and the Duke of York. It was a great Victorian pageant, but it was also a family affair. Mrs Gladstone's four grandchildren were near her to comfort and be comforted. Some of the family disliked the position of the grave in the open gangway of the North Transept but Scott Holland assured Mary that it was right that her father should lie 'in the thick of the throng. Ever the feet pass over him – the tramp of the multitudes. All the great ones who lie there are become the property of the people'.[7] He was sure that Mary would not wish his body to be anywhere other than in 'the great Church of the Nation'.

In Hawarden Church, just a week after the funeral, Burne-Jones finally completed a new West Window. It was two years in the making, and was the artist's last work, for he died a week later. It is a thanksgiving from all the Gladstone children for their parents' long and loving lives. The subject is the Nativity, and Mother and Child are the last image visible in the church as the last rays of evening light fade. Six more windows of Burne-Jones' designs were added later so that Hawarden Church is a glorious memorial of Pre-Raphaelite colours.

Mary found that first Christmas without her father especially hard. On her father's birthday, she wrote in her diary, 'What a contrast this day to former years – empty post, silent bells', and on New Year's Eve, 'Heard the bell tolling it out and then – fell asleep. I grudged the hours as they went, the last that we can say, "This year Father did so and so".'

Postscript (1898 – 1928)

*B*uckley parish, 'with its masses of poverty and ignorance and sin was at first a fearful effort. I hated it, but have blessed it since, and I do bless it. It is a thirsty land and we can have the joy of watering and refreshing it a little'.[1] Mary described it thus to Lord Rosebery in August 1898. In the seven years that she and Harry were there they were responsible for a new mission chapel, a new Sunday school and a restored mission room, a free library, a parish room, a recreation ground and an ambulance. St Matthew's Church in Buckley was transformed into a holy and beautiful place.

The chancel, in memory of Mr Gladstone, was the first step in the restoration work and on 21 September 1900, the foundation stone was laid by Helen, Mary and Dossie, now ten years old, replacing the original foundation stone which had been laid in 1821 by Stephen and Henry Glynne. The restoration of the church tower followed, with a baptistery as a memorial to Mrs Gladstone who had died on 14 June 1900 at Hawarden, the home where she had been born, from where she married and where she had lived with her husband for almost sixty happy years. In her last two years of loneliness, her mind lived increasingly in the past, in crystal-clear precious memories; Stephen brought his wife and family back to live at the castle and Mary was a daily visitor, bicycling over from Buckley, often with Dossie.

Catherine Gladstone was buried at Westminster Abbey alongside her husband, and as at his funeral service there was the same music and the same mourners of family, friends and people from all walks of life. Later, Mary said of her parents, 'Without her, it is likely that he would still have made an indelible mark on history, but much of the lighter side, the charm, the fun, would have been lost. Without him, her life would have lacked public importance and interest, but in whatever circumstances or conditions she had been born, she would have stirred the waters'.[2]

The fine stained-glass windows of Buckley Church are by Henry Holiday. To the side of the tower is a porch in memory of John Ruskin. As a final touch, a peal of eight bells, the clock and chimes were given. A new organ was installed at Easter 1903. The outer stonework was cleaned and refaced and a new nave was added. Much of this restoration was made possible through the generosity and dedication of the Gladstone and Glynne families; parishioners also contributed in memory of loved ones.

Over the years Harry had many offers of promotion, all of which he turned down. Both Mary and Harry knew that they had found the home that was exactly right for them; he explained to the Bishop of St Asaph in 1903 when he was declining livings in Birmingham and Plymouth, 'Surely it was no mere chance which sent us to Buckley just at the moment when the poor neglected place was for the first time given an articulate voice by means of the establishment of a local authority which could in some way atone for the grievous neglect of the past.' He went on to say how hard it had been to minister at first in a church 'mean and miserable in its construction and appointments, and not free and open to all alike' and what joy he would feel in the afterlife to know that they had 'beautified it from end to end, and made it all it could become to every one alike.' He had no desire to leave Buckley, for there was still work to be done. Later in 1903 he fought hard against the secularisation of state education and wrote forcefully to his Bishop, 'to go back to the miserable policy of offering us facilities *out of* school hours for denominational teaching at our own expense, while they propose to provide *un*denominational teaching *in* school hours and at the ratepayers' expense, is gross injustice.' His fight led him into local politics and he became a local councillor, described by one of the villagers as 'a Council in himself'.[3]

It was only with extreme reluctance that he allowed himself to be persuaded in 1905 to take over as Rector of Hawarden when Stephen Gladstone moved on to Lincolnshire, to an undemanding living as rector of Barrowby. Stephen had at last been freed from parental obligation, but it took him four years to take this step into an uncertain future until the decision was forced upon him; he could no longer manage the parish, which had seen a large influx of labourers for the iron and steel works, the brickworks and the shipyards that were mushrooming along the Dee estuary. Hawarden was now a much smaller benefice; at one time, the parish had been one of the richest in Wales and the rectorship was what was known as an ecclesiastical peculiar, independent of the authority of the bishop of St Asaph, with its own yearly court that proved wills, granted marriage licences and dealt with minor misdemeanours. Now the rector's annual stipend was a meagre £500–£600 compared to £3000 in 1874, and even this dwindled over the years. Mary was furious that her brother had left 'at the moment when its difficulties are at its thorniest, its income at its poorest, and its clerical staff at its feeblest.[4] Moreover, the fine eighteenth-century Rectory set in four acres of landscaped beauty had been left to rot. 'The rats have done mischief in the rectory drains' and there were many discussions within the family of an alternative home, but it did not cease to be the Rectory until 1925, long after they had left.

Harry Drew's last service at Buckley was on 15 January 1905. He wrote in his journal, 'A wonderful congregation in the evening, some standing, many unable to get in, every available bench and chair from Vicarage raked up; splendid hymn singing; a blessed and inspiring day.' On Easter Monday 1910, he walked in his garden with Herbert Gladstone who was staying at the Castle, before leaving to take up his post as the first Governor-General and High Commissioner of the Union of South Africa, an appointment that came to him after five years as Home Secretary in Asquith's government. After tea Harry went bicycling on a pastoral visit. That evening, he was suddenly seized by terrible internal pain. After a night of suffering, Mary was told that her husband would not last the day without an operation, but that this was almost always hopeless. She prepared to meet her greatest challenge. 'I had to give him up then to God, as he did himself when I went in to tell him.' He died in the early evening. Alfred Lyttelton wrote of Harry Drew, 'He seemed to me a perfect comrade and counsellor. Of how few can one say in the world that they never jarred us, or wounded us, or contributed one fraction to our baser part?'

Mary then faced the agony of widowhood. She wrote to Lavinia that people told her how brave and good she was. 'But you can't kick and scream! And if one doesn't do that sort of thing, they imagine one is all right, instead of being filled with wild rebellion. Every now and then, "I can't bear it, I won't bear it." But after all the most rebellious of us has to bear it.'[5]

Scott Holland had once advised her that, after a death, one must let the days pass, without inquiry, so that the quiet passage of time may heal. This is what she did. After the funeral, she went first to Helen's home in the village, 'The Sundial' in Tinker's Lane. Then she sought peace at Windsor, in the Clewer House of Mercy, which had been one of her mother's first charitable concerns over fifty years ago. She was sixty-two, and had to reshape her life into a solitary one; she confessed to Lavinia that she had once been able to write such beautiful letters to troubled and grieving people but it was only because she had never experienced the searching depth of sorrow. Within a year she was severely tested by the engagement of Dossie, who was barely twenty-one, to Captain Frances Parrish of the 60th Rifles. He was on the staff of Government House where Dossie was visiting her Uncle Herbert. Mary was devastated by the sudden engagement and wailed to her old friend Maggie that her future son-in-law 'was not quite big enough, out of the way enough', and once the bloom rubbed off, she feared that Dossie might see him as she did, as 'a commonplace very plain young man'. Long ago, Mrs Gladstone had been more charitable over Mary's shock engagement announcement, and Maggie's reply that the only fairy princes are in fairy stories were wise words.

For a while, homeless and rootless, Mary drifted between friends and relations until she settled on a London home where she was much in demand for social and political occasions. There were luncheons with the Asquiths at No. 10 Downing

Street, tea with Mrs Lloyd George, tête-à-têtes with Lord Rosebery. She made two trips to South Africa to stay with Herbert in Government House, Pretoria, and she was there when she heard of Spencer's death: 'Spencer, since 1875 the nearest to me and the most faithful, not actually the dearest, tho' at one time he was that too ... My poor old Spencer.'[6]

In September 1914, she was back in the House of Commons for yet another Home Rule Bill that was automatically becoming law as the Great War threatened to engulf them all. Mary feared that Europe would bleed to death in the sacrifices that would be demanded, and indeed the greatest sacrifice was asked of them. Her nephew, Will Gladstone, the young squire of Hawarden, MP for Kilmarnock and a lieutenant in the Royal Welsh Fusiliers, was killed in action in April 1915. King George gave permission for his body to be brought home for burial at Hawarden.

In her seventies and fighting against crippling arthritis, Mary picked up her pen and turned to her memories. She contributed an article on her father's library to *The Nineteenth Century* but her greatest labour of love was a book on her mother, *Catherine Gladstone*, published in 1919. While her idea for this book was germinating, she lunched with Lord Rosebery and they talked about biographies and possible subjects. She suggested that 'it was not so much a question of greatness as of unusualness, distinctiveness' that were needed for a biography, qualities that she herself unknowingly possessed. In 1924 she wrote a book of essays on her father and Lord Acton and on others whom she deemed great enough to share the honours with these two, of whom she wrote, 'That which divided them was small indeed compared with that which united them.'

For the Christmas of 1927, Mary was back at Hawarden Castle, staying with Henry, who was now life tenant until the house and estate should pass to Stephen's eldest son. On New Years Day 1928, she had just gone to bed when she felt unwell. She called her maid, who brought her some brandy. Before the doctor arrived, she was dead. Her body lies beside her husband's, in Hawarden churchyard, among her family and friends, neighbours and villagers, where her spirit had always found peace.

Endnotes

1: Prime time (1879)

1 Lucy, H.W. (1908) *Memories of Eight Parliaments*.
2 Masterman, L. (ed.) (1930) *Mary Gladstone: Her Diaries and Letters*.

2: Glynnes, Gladstones and Lytteltons (1833–49)

1 Morley, J. (1903) *The Life of William Ewart Gladstone*, volume 1.
2 Glynne – Gladstone ms 32.
3 Foot, M. R. D. and Matthew, H. C. G. (eds) *Gladstone Diaries*, volume 3.
4 Battiscombe, G. (1956) *Mrs Gladstone*, p. 65.
5 *Ibid*, p. 62.

3: A visit to Scotland (1847–50)

1 Brooke, J. and Sorensen, M. (1971) *The Prime Minister's Papers: W. E. Gladstone 1: Autobiographica*, p. 53–5.
2 Morley, J. (1903) *The Life of William Ewart Gladstone*, volume 1.
3 Jenkins, R. (1995) *Gladstone*, p. 119.

4: 'Naples Mary' (1850)

1 Foot, M. R. D. and Matthew, H. C. G. (eds) *The Gladstone Diaries*, volume 4.

5: 'Half–witted' and 'wanting' (1851–9)

1 Glynne – Gladstone ms 759.
2 Glynne – Gladstone ms 614.
3 Woodham-Smith, C. (1982) *Florence Nightingale 1820–1910*, p. 203.
4 Glynne – Gladstone ms 993.
5 Glynne – Gladstone ms 747.
6 Drew, M. (1930) *Catherine Gladstone*.

6: 'Rigged, figged and launched into society' (1864–6)

1 Glynne – Gladstone ms 772.
2 Bassett, A. T. (ed.) (1936) *Letters from Gladstone to his Wife*, p. 101.
3 Gladstone, P. (1989) *Portrait of a Family*, p. 58.
4 Glynne – Gladstone ms 848.
5 Drew, M. (1930) *Catherine Gladstone*.
6 Masterman, L. (ed.) (1930) *Mary Gladstone: Her Diaries and Letters*.
7 Morley, J. (1903) *The Life of William Ewart Gladstone*, volume 2, p. 204.

7: Charities, country houses and Continental polish (1864–8)

1 Drew, M. (1930) *Catherine Gladstone*.
2 *Ibid.*
3 Morley, J. (1903) *The Life of William Ewart Gladstone*, volume 2, pp. 213–14.
4 Masterman, L. (ed.) (1930) *Mary Gladstone: Her Diaries and Letters*.
5 Glynne – Gladstone ms 848.
6 Masterman, L., *ibid.*

8: The passionate years (1868–75)

1 Glynne – Gladstone ms 948.
2 Jenkins, R. (1995) *Gladstone*, p. 295.

3 Glynne – Gladstone ms 948.
4 Magnus, P. (1963) *Gladstone*, p. 204.
5 Masterman, L. (ed.) (1930) *Mary Gladstone: Her Diaries and Letters.*
6 British Library ms 46222.
7 British Library ms 46222.
8 Egremont, M. (1980) *A Life of Arthur James Balfour.*
9 Masterman, L., *ibid.*

9: *Life without May (1875 – 6)*

1 Ponsonby, M. (1927) *Mary Ponsonby: A Memoir.*
2 British Library ms 46256.
3 Hagley Hall ms 35008.
4 British Library ms 46232.
5 British Library ms 46232.
6 Morley, J. (1903) *The Life of William Ewart Gladstone*, volume 1.
7 Drew, M. (1913) *Letters: Alfred Lyttelton to Mary Gladstone.*
8 Drew, M. (1924) *Acton, Gladstone and Others.*

10: *The Eastern Question and an Irish visit (1876 – 9)*

1 Magnus, P. (1963) *Gladstone*, p. 239.
2 Morley, J. (1903) *The Life of William Ewart Gladstone*, volume 2, pp. 550 – 1.
3 Glynne – Gladstone ms 869.
4 Sidgwick, E. (1930) *Mrs Henry Sidgwick.*
5 Morley, J., *ibid*, pp. 566 – 7.
6 Morley, J., *ibid*, p 566.
7 Gladstone, H. (1928) *After Thirty Years*, p. 265.
8 British Library ms 46258.
9 Masterman, L. (ed.) (1930) *Mary Gladstone: Her Diaries and Letters.*
10 Young, K. (1963) *Arthur James Balfour.*

11: *Mary as confidante and heroine (1879)*

1 Glynne – Gladstone ms 848.
2 Glynne – Gladstone ms 848.

3 Masterman, L. (ed.) (1930) *Mary Gladstone: Her Diaries and Letters*.
4 Paget, S. (ed.) (1921) *Memoir and Letters of Henry Scott Holland*.
5 British Library ms 46244.
6 Burne-Jones ms XXVI f. 130 no. 15.
8 British Library ms 46239.
7 Lago, M. (ed.) (1982) *Burne-Jones Talking: His Conversations 1895 – 1898*.

12: *Campaigning brings victory (1879 – 80)*

1 Masterman, L. (ed.) (1930) *Mary Gladstone: Her Diaries and Letters*.
2 British Library ms 46236.
3 British Library ms 46244.
4 British Library ms 46239.
5 Masterman, L., *ibid*.
6 Jenkins, R. (1995) *Gladstone*, p. 433.
7 Glynne – Gladstone ms 603.
8 Glynne – Gladstone ms 995.

13: *A room of her own (1880 – 1)*

1 Chadwick, O. (1976) *Acton and Gladstone*, p. 20.
2 *Ibid*, p. 16.
3 British Library ms 46236.
4 Glynne – Gladstone ms 603.
5 Ollard, S. L. (1919) *A Forty Years' Friendship*.
6 Morley, J. (1903) *The Life of William Ewart Gladstone*, volume 3, p. 54.
7 Masterman, L. (ed.) (1930) *Mary Gladstone: Her Diaries and Letters*.

14: *Irish matters dominate, with tragic consequences (1882 – 3)*

1 Ollard, S. L. (1919) *A Forty Years' Friendship*.
2 Glynne – Gladstone ms 848.
3 Lyttelton ms 33.

4 Hamilton, E. (1898) *Mr Gladstone: A Monograph.*
5 Masterman, L. (ed.) (1930) *Mary Gladstone: Her Diaries and Letters.*
6 Rosebery ms 10015.
7 Glynne – Gladstone ms 603.
8 Rosebery ms 10015.

15: *Cruises and country holidays (1882 – 3)*

1 British Library ms 46236.
2 Masterman, L. (ed.) (1930) *Mary Gladstone: Her Diaries and Letters.*
3 *Ibid.*
4 Drew, M. (1924) *Acton, Gladstone and Others.*
5 *Ibid.*
6 Gladstone, H. (1928) *After Thirty Years*
7 British Library ms 46244.

16: *The swings and roundabouts of politics (1884 – 5)*

1 Paget, S. (ed.) (1921) *Memoir and Letters of Henry Scott Holland.*
2 March-Phillipps, L. and Christian, B. (eds) (1917) *Some Hawarden Letters.*
3 Morley, J. (1903) *The Life of William Ewart Gladstone,* volume 3, pp. 88 and 151.
4 Masterman, L. (ed.) (1930) *Mary Gladstone: Her Diaries and Letters.*

17: *Private and public worlds collide (1885)*

1 Jenkins, R. (1995) *Gladstone,* p. 519.
2 Ollard, S. L. (1919) *A Forty Years' Friendship.*
3 Acton ms 8119.
4 Rosebery ms 10015.
5 Glynne – Gladstone ms 758.
6 Ollard, L., *ibid.*
7 Rosebery ms 10015.
8 Glynne – Gladstone ms 995.
9 Schlüter, A. (1922) *A Lady's Maid in Downing Street 1877 – 1890.*

18: *A new life for Mary, but the old life refuses to go away (1886 – 91)*

1 Magnus, P. (1963) *Gladstone*, p. 341.
2 *Ibid.*, p. 342.
3 Masterman, L. (ed.) (1930) *Mary Gladstone: Her Diaries and Letters.*
4 British Library ms 46270.
5 British Library ms 46262.
6 Morley, J. (1903) *The Life of William Ewart Gladstone*, volume 3.
7 Schlüter, A. (1922) *A Lady's Maid in Downing Street 1877 – 1890.*
8 Egremont, M. (1980) *A Life of Arthur James Balfour.*
9 Bonham-Carter, M. (ed.) (1985) *The Autobiography of Margot Asquith.*
10 *Ibid.*
11 Drew, M. (1930) *Acton, Gladstone and Others.*

19: *'As much Mr Gladstone's daughter as ever' (1890 – 3)*

1 Ollard, S. L. (1919) *A Forty Years' Friendship.*
2 *Ibid.*
3 Rosebery ms 10015.
4 Glynne – Gladstone ms 603.
5 Glynne – Gladstone ms 849.
6 March-Phillipps, L. and Christian, B. (eds) (1917) *Some Hawarden Letters.*
7 Burne-Jones ms XXVI.
8 Jenkins, R. (1995) *Gladstone*, p. 589.
9 Chadwick, O. (1976) *Acton and Gladstone.*

20: *A calling home (1893)*

1 Glynne – Gladstone ms 603.
2 Matthew, H. C. G. (ed.) (1994) *The Gladstone Diaries*, volume XIII.
3 Russell, G. W. E. (1911) *Harry Drew: A Memorial Sketch.*
4 Young, K. (1963) *Arthur James Balfour.*
5 Drew, M. (1924) *Acton, Gladstone and Others.*

6 Masterman, L. (ed.) (1930) *Mary Gladstone: Her Diaries and Letters.*
7 Drew, M., *ibid.*

Postscript (1898 – 1928)

1 Rosebery ms 10015.
2 Drew, M. (1930) *Catherine Gladstone.*
3 Russell, G.W. E. (1911) *Harry Drew: A Memorial Sketch.*
4 Glynne – Gladstone ms 949.
5 Masterman, L. (ed.) (1930) *Mary Gladstone: Her Diaries and Letters.*
6 *Ibid.*

Bibliography

Published letters and diaries

Bailey, J. C. (ed.) (1927) *The Diary of Lady Frederick Cavendish*, 2 volumes, John Murray, London.

Bassett, A. T. (ed.) (1936) *Letters from Gladstone to his Wife*, Methuen & Co., London.

Drew, M. (ed.) (1913) *Letters: Alfred Lyttelton to Mary Gladstone*, private publication.

Foot, M. R. D. and Matthew, H. C. G. (eds) *The Gladstone Diaries*, 14 volumes, OUP, Oxford.

March-Phillipps, L. and Christian, B. (eds) (1917) *Some Hawarden Letters 1878–1913*, Nisbet & Co., London.

Masterman, L. (ed.) (1930) *Mary Gladstone: Her Diaries and Letters*, Methuen & Co., London.

Ollard, S. L. (1919) *A Forty Years' Friendship: Letters from the late Henry Scott Holland to Mrs Drew*, Nisbet, London.

Paget, S. (ed.) (1921) *Memoir and Letters of Henry Scott Holland*, John Murray, London.

Schlüter, A. (1922) *A Lady's Maid in Downing Street 1877–1890*, T. Fisher Unwin, London.

Reference books

Battiscombe, G. (1956) *Mrs Gladstone*, Constable, London.

Bonham-Carter, M. (ed.) (1985) *The Autobiography of Margot Asquith*, Methuen, London.

Brooke, J. and Sorensen, M. (1971) *The Prime Minister's Papers: W. E. Gladstone 1: Autobiographica*, Her Majesty's Stationery Office, London.

Chadwick, O. (1976) *Acton and Gladstone*, Athlone Press, London.

Checkland, S. G. (1971) *The Gladstones: A Family Biography 1764–1851*, CUP, Cambridge.

Drew, M. (1924) *Acton, Gladstone and Others*, Macmillan, London.

Drew, M. (1930) *Catherine Gladstone*, Nisbet & Co., London.

Dugdale, E. (1930) *Arthur James Balfour: Chapters of Autobiography*, Cassell & Co, London.

Egremont, M. (1980) *Balfour: A Life of Arthur James Balfour*, Collins, London.

Gladstone, H. (1928) *After Thirty Years*, London.

Gladstone, P. (1989) *Portrait of a Family: The Gladstones 1839–1889*, private publication.

Hamilton, E. (1898) *Mr Gladstone: A Monograph*, John Murray, London.

Jalland, P. (1988) *Women, Marriage and Politics 1860–1914*, OUP, Oxford.

Jenkins, R. (1995) *Gladstone*, Macmillan, London.

Lago, M. (ed.) (1982) *Burne-Jones Talking: His Conversations 1895–1898*, John Murray, London.

Lucy, H.W. (1908) *Memories of Eight Parliaments*, Heinemann, London.

Lyttelton, G.W. (1904) *Glynnese Glossary*, John Murray, London.

Magnus, P. (1963) *Gladstone*, John Murray, London.

Matthew, H. C. G. (1988) *Gladstone 1809–1874*, OUP, Oxford.

Matthew, H. C. G. (1995) *Gladstone 1875–1898*, OUP, Oxford.

Morley, J. (1903) *The Life of William Ewart Gladstone*, 3 volumes, Macmillan & Co, London.

Ponsonby, M. (1927) *Mary Ponsonby: A Memoir*, John Murray, London.

Pratt, E. A. (1898) *Catherine Gladstone*, Sampson Low, Marston & Co, London.

Russell, G.W. E. (1911) *Harry Drew: A Memorial Sketch*, Henry Frowde, London.

Sidgwick, E. (1938) *Mrs Henry Sidgwick*, Sidgwick & Jackson, London.

Woodham-Smith, C. (1982) *Florence Nightingale 1820–1910*, Constable, London.

Young, G. M. (1960) *Portrait of an Age: Victorian England*, OUP, Oxford.

Young, K. (1963) *Arthur James Balfour*, Bell & Sons, London.

Main sources of unpublished manuscript collections

Acton mss, Cambridge University Library.

Edward Burne-Jones papers, Fitzwilliam Museum, Cambridge.

Glynne – Gladstone mss, St Deiniol's Library, Hawarden.

Lyttelton papers, Hagley Hall, Worcestershire.

Margaret Leicester-Warren diaries, Tabley House, Knutsford.

Mary Gladstone Drew mss and additional mss, British Library, London.

Rosebery mss, National Library of Scotland.

Index